Human Resource Experts Love this Book

"Jan Masaoka has great insight and a gift for accurately translating very complex ideas into a simple, compelling framework. The Nonprofit's Guide to Human Resources *will be a great help to you in building your organization's human capital."*

— **Pete Manzo, President and CEO, United Ways of California**

"Jan Masaoka has created the essential how-to that should be on the desk of every manager—and actually smart reading for any nonprofit employee."

— **John Pratt, Executive Director, Minnesota Council of Nonprofits**

With The Nonprofit's Guide to Human Resources *Jan Masaoka has created a much-needed, essential reference that both 'accidental HR managers' and professional HR staff will find invaluable. Designed for organizations with fewer than 100 staff, the comprehensive and attractively designed guide is written in clear, jargon-free language and is full of common-sense advice, real-life examples, useful tips and worksheets. No nonprofit should be without it.*

— **Jonathan Spack, Executive Director, Third Sector New England**

"For nonprofits who have made silly but costly personnel mistakes—and those who have not ... yet—this detailed but engrossing reference book provides soup to nuts about nonprofit human resource management, a much neglected topic. And true to form for Masaoka, it's chock full of real life and attention grabbing cautionary tales, and simple but powerful tips."

— **Ruth McCambridge, Editor in Chief, Nonprofit Quarterly (Boston)**

"Whether you are human resources director or volunteer coordinator, this book is an essential tool for anyone managing staff in a nonprofit setting."

— **Paul Kawata, President, National Minority AIDS Council (Washington DC)**

"Here, in one book, in the style those familiar with Jan Masaoka and Nolo Press will recognize and welcome, is practical, hands on advice, worksheets, case studies and examples. What comes through in addition to the knowledge Jan has is a deep respect for nonprofit staff and a genuine desire to make workplaces the most healthy places they can be."

— **Kim Klein, Klein & Roth Consulting, author of** *Fundraising for Social Change*

"Great nonprofits are driven by great talent. Getting great talent depends on attracting, choosing and supporting great people. The Nonprofit's Guide to Human Resources *offers a systematic method for recruiting and retaining the right talent to fuel a nonprofit to achieve its all-important mission."*

— **Nora Silver, Director, Center for Nonprofit and Public Leadership**

"Masaoka offers a comprehensive, yet stimulating guide to managing human resources that is immensely useful. This is a must-read for anyone engaged in nonprofit human resource management, from the 'accidental HR person' through the seasoned professional."

— **Shelly M. Schnupp, Associate Director, Helen Bader Institute for Nonprofit Management**

"This is a worthy HR desk manual for any nonprofit executive director. Thanks to Jan Masaoka and her superb team of advisors for creating a fabulous resource for categorizing, analyzing and solving issues relating to both employees and volunteers."

— **Cassandra M. Flipper, Executive Director, Bread & Roses**

NOLO Products & Services

Books & Software

Get in-depth information. Nolo publishes hundreds of great books and software programs for consumers and business owners. Order a copy—or download an ebook version instantly—at Nolo.com.

Legal Encyclopedia

Free at Nolo.com. Here are more than 1,400 free articles and answers to common questions about everyday legal issues including wills, bankruptcy, small business formation, divorce, patents, employment and much more.

Plain-English Legal Dictionary

Free at Nolo.com. Stumped by jargon? Look it up in America's most up-to-date source for definitions of legal terms.

Online Legal Documents

Create documents at your computer. Go to Nolo.com to make a will or living trust, form an LLC or corporation or obtain a trademark or provisional patent. For simpler matters, download one of our hundreds of high-quality legal forms, including bills of sale, promissory notes, nondisclosure agreements and many more.

Lawyer Directory

Find an attorney at Nolo.com. Nolo's consumer-friendly lawyer directory provides in-depth profiles of lawyers all over America. From fees and experience to legal philosophy, education and special expertise, you'll find all the information you need to pick the right lawyer. Every lawyer listed has pledged to work diligently and respectfully with clients.

Free Legal Updates

Keep up to date. Check for free updates at Nolo.com. Under "Products," find this book and click "Legal Updates." You can also sign up for our free e-newsletters at Nolo.com/newsletters.

1st edition

The Nonprofit's Guide to Human Resources

Managing Your Employees & Volunteers

Jan Masaoka

FIRST EDITION	OCTOBER 2011
Editor	DIANA FITZPATRICK
Cover Design	SUSAN PUTNEY
Book Design	TERRI HEARSH
Proofreading	ROBERT WELLS
Index	ELLEN SHERRON
Printing	BANG PRINTING

The nonprofit's guide to human resources : managing your employees and volunteers / by Jan Masaoka. — 1st ed.
   p. cm.
 Summary: "Provides the legal information for those in charge of human resources at small to medium 501(c)(3) organizations. It explains how to identify, face and resolve daily legal issues related to hiring, compensation, letting employees go, dealing with volunteers, and communicating with employees."—Provided by publisher.
 ISBN 978-1-4133-1375-8 (pbk.) — ISBN 978-1-4133-1376-5 (epub e-book)
 1. Nonprofit organizations—Employees—Legal status, laws, etc.—United States. 2. Nonprofit organizations—Personnel management—United States. I. Masaoka, Jan.
 KF3452.N65N665 2011
 658.3—dc23
                                    2011023257

Please note

We believe accurate, plain-English legal information should help you solve many of your own legal problems. But this text is not a substitute for personalized advice from a knowledgeable lawyer. If you want the help of a trained professional—and we'll always point out situations in which we think that's a good idea—consult an attorney licensed to practice in your state.

Acknowledgments

My thanks first to Diana Fitzpatrick, Marcia Stewart, Lisa Guerin, and Ilona Bray of Nolo for their interest, expert help, and partnership on this book.

My grateful thanks, too, to the book's advisers, whose time and thinking informs the material on every page.

Colleagues who have assisted in unique and valuable ways include Cissy Dendy, Mary Lester, Stephanie McAuliffe, and Lynora Williams. Consulting clients from my time at CompassPoint Nonprofit Services and since then gave me the opportunities to learn that which allowed me to write this book.

Indefinable but much appreciated help has come from Paul Rosenstiel, Kimi Rosenstiel, and Keiko Rosenstiel.

I have been a most imperfect supervisor and a perfectly irritating subordinate. To everyone who has ever reported to me or to whom I have reported: I hope it's a small comfort to you that my mistakes and your patience will, through this book, help others in their work.

With a salute to all the underappreciated people in the nonprofit sector with responsibilities in HR,

Jan Masaoka
San Francisco

Table of Contents

Your Companion to HR in Nonprofit Organizations 1

Differences in Nonprofit and For-Profit HR 3

The Long and Short of Employment Law 5

How This Book Is Organized 6

1 Who Will Join Your Team? Recruiting and Hiring Staff 7

Who Will Be Doing the Hire? 10

Hiring: A Five-Step Process 11

Step 1. Defining the Job and the Candidate Profile 11

Step 2. Recruiting a Strong Pool of Applicants 17

Step 3. Screening and Selection 23

Step 4. Making the Job Offer 41

Step 5. Bringing the New Hire on Board 46

2 Salaries and Benefits 53

What Is Compensation? 57

Laws You'll Need to Know 58

Setting Salary Ranges and Individual Salaries 62

Looking at the Big Picture: Overall Compensation Analysis 67

Incentive Pay in Nonprofits 72

Cost of Living Adjustments (COLA) 76

Classifying Your Employees: Who Gets Overtime or Benefits? 77

Minimum Wages and Exceptions 82

Rest Breaks and Travel Time 85

Benefits: Compensation Beyond Wages 86

Noneconomic Benefits 102

Administering Your Benefits Plan 106

3 Performance Reviews 107

Reasons for Performance Reviews 111

Special Considerations for Small Organizations 114

Types of Performance Reviews 115

Defining What's Expected of Employees 124

Keep Track of Employee Performance 125

Gathering the Building-Block Information 126

The Role of Judgment 128

Setting Up Your Review Process 130

A Step-by-Step Look at the Review Process 134

**4 Strengthening Performance:
Supervision and Team Leadership** 137

One-on-One Supervision 140

Dealing With Poor Performance 142

Legal Reminders for Supervisors 142

The Important Role of Team Leaders 144

Coaching and Mentoring 147

Staff Training and Education 150

Titles: More Than Just Words 159

Leadership Development 160

360-Degree Feedback 162

5 **Terminations and Layoffs** 167

Trying to Improve Employee Performance and Behavior 171

Before Firing—Steps to Take 174

Firing At-Will Employees 176

Termination for Cause 178

Firing "On the Spot" 179

Once You've Decided to Fire 179

Layoffs 184

Handling Exit Interviews and Forms 188

Avoiding Layoffs Through Furloughs 191

Temporary Layoffs 192

Postemployment Health Insurance 192

What Happens If an Ex-Employee Sues? 193

Who's Eligible for Unemployment Insurance 196

Providing References 198

6 **The HR of Volunteers** 199

Managing Volunteers 201

Defining Volunteer Jobs 205

Recruiting Volunteers 210

Screening Volunteers 216

Getting the Right Insurance Coverage for Volunteer Activities 219

Preparing for Your Volunteers' First Day 220

Creating Leadership Positions for Volunteers 221

Volunteerism Practices and Policies for Volunteer Board Members 223

Thanking Volunteers 224

Professional Development for Managers of Volunteers 226

7 **Bringing in Outside Help: Independent Contractors**............ 229

Employee or Contractor? 231

Benefits and Drawbacks to Hiring Independent Contractors 233

Criteria for Classification 236

Independent Contractor Questionnaire 240

Creating an Independent Contractor Agreement..................................... 243

Managing Independent Contractors 247

Paperwork for Independent Contractors 249

8 **The Board's Role in HR**... 251

The Board's Oversight of the Executive Director 253

The Board's Oversight of HR 256

Guidelines for the Board's Role in HR 257

9 **Unions and Nonprofits**.. 263

What Is a Union? 266

Laws Governing Unions... 266

Who the Union Represents... 267

How a Union Contract Is Created: Collective Bargaining 268

What's in a Union Contract... 269

How Union Drives Work... 270

HR Under a Union Contract 272

Employees Who Are Not Part of the Union... 273

Day-to-Day Union Representation:
   Business Agents and Shop Stewards 274

10 **Creating a Safe and Productive Workplace Environment**..... 277

Protecting Employees' Health and Safety... 280

The Workers' Compensation System.. 283

Ergonomics and Preventing Repetitive Strain Injury (RSI) 285

If Jobs Involve Driving 287

Employee Use of Cell Phones 289

Smoking in (or Near) the Workplace 290

Employee Abuse of Drugs or Alcohol 291

Preventing Harassment and Bullying 294

Workplace Violence 298

Shaping Your Organizational Culture 300

Policies for Email and Internet Usage 306

Workplace Romances 310

Dress and Grooming Codes 312

Off-Hours Conduct 314

Gaining Insights From Employee Climate Surveys 317

11 Organizing HR Functions 323

Staffing the HR Office 326

HR Attorneys and Consultants 330

Outsourcing HR Functions 331

Who Does HR Report To? 333

Providing Feedback to HR About HR Functions 334

Professional Development for HR Staff 335

Personnel Files 337

Employee Handbooks 341

HR's Role in Change Management 347

HR Audits 349

Index 353

Your Companion to HR in Nonprofit Organizations

Differences in Nonprofit and For-Profit HR 3

The Long and Short of Employment Law 5

How This Book Is Organized 6

F or nonprofit organizations, human resources—that is, people—
are at the heart of mission delivery. Nonprofit staff and volunteers
take care of our elderly, clean up our rivers, help kids learn
through sports, present plays and operas, organize marches for civil
rights, feed hungry families, help people confront their demons, settle
refugees, develop treatments for the sick, and in every way, bind our
communities together and bring about social change.

What Lies Behind the Changing Language for HR

The term Human Resources Management ("HRM" or "HR" for short) is
relatively new. The field used to be referred to simply as Personnel. Other
terms are becoming popular and jockeying for traction, including Talent
Management, Employee Relations, and Human Capital Management.
One dynamic behind the choice in terms is the perception of staff's role
in an organization. Under one view, staff is seen primarily as a commodity
or "resource," where the employer seeks to maximize its return on its
investment in this human capital. Alternatively, instead of being considered
a resource, employees may be seen as creative, complex, social beings. This
way of thinking implies the employer has a responsibility to these individuals
that extends beyond simply supporting their ability to perform their work.
Regardless of the term used, most organizations end up with some kind of
balance in terms of how they handle employees and employee relations.

In this book, we use "HR" because it is the most widely used and
understood term. A simple working definition for HR management might
be the management of people and performance in a structured way
toward organizational goals. Particularly in nonprofits, those goals are likely
to include organizational and HR goals that go beyond financial ends.

This book is for the many people in nonprofits who work with,
manage, and support these people. In other words, it's for people who
work in Human Resources, or "HR." Some organizations have an
HR Director, while in other organizations these responsibilities may
fall to the administrative manager, the finance director, the executive

director, or whoever seems willing and able to take them on. In fact, the "Accidental HR Person" is a remarkably common staff position and a key audience for this book. Senior staff and board members—who may not have direct responsibilities for HR—will also find this book helpful.

The HR material presented here provides guidance and answers for the formal and informal HR questions that arise every day. It also provides a framework and point of reference for nonprofits wanting to build or improve their compensation structure or performance review process or overall working environment. With all issues, we also address the legal context for the decisions you will be making every day.

Differences in Nonprofit and For-Profit HR

Managing people in a nonprofit context is quite different from managing people at a small business or large corporation. There are similarities— for instance, all employers must follow the same rules about minimum wage laws. But nonprofits will have additional questions related to stipend volunteers and interns. As another example, all employers must follow the same nondiscrimination laws when it comes to hiring people with disabilities. But in the nonprofit sector, an organization may have mission-related reasons to discriminate in favor of hiring people with disabilities. This book covers HR in all contexts but focuses on the type of issues most likely to arise in a nonprofit and how these issues can best be handled in these distinct workplace environments.

The technical differences between HR in a nonprofit and for-profit world are few, and this book touches on them when they arise. For example, in the section on payroll, we point out that while nonprofits are subject to state laws about state unemployment insurance (SUI), they are exempt from federal unemployment taxes (FUTA).

The larger differences in HR matters—such as compensation, hiring practices, and team management—are related to the particular characteristics of nonprofits. This book pays special attention to the aspects that characterize nonprofits and how they impact HR. Some of the important characteristics addressed include the following:

- volunteers make up a large part of the nonprofit workforce
- nonprofits are typically small employers, often with fewer than 50 or even 15 employees
- nonprofits are governed by boards of directors and the top executive is an employee, not the owner
- nonprofit staff are idealistic about how systems should work and bring that idealism to their own management systems, and
- most nonprofit employees have a commitment to the mission and work of their organization.

This Book Is for 501(c)(3) Nonprofits

There are more than 25 different kinds of nonprofits identified in the Internal Revenue Code. Only one of these is the kind of nonprofit we are referring to when we use the term "nonprofit": 501(c)(3) organizations. Only these organizations can receive donations that are tax deductible to the donor. While 501(c)(3) organizations range from the Sierra Club to the American Cancer Society to the NAACP, the classification also encompasses PTAs, all-volunteer community gardens, and medical research laboratories. Although universities, hospitals, and some other large 501(c)(3) institutions can benefit from this book, our emphasis is on the nonprofit with fewer than 100 staff, a segment that encompasses 96% of all 501(c)(3) organizations.

HR is essential and complicated work and requires great sensitivity and knowledge, particularly in the nonprofit sector. And yet too often this important work is overlooked. If you are a person with HR responsibilities in your nonprofit, keep the faith. Other staff may forget about HR until there's a problem, not realizing that it's good HR practices that have kept problems from arising. But when HR work is done well, all employees and volunteers benefit and as a result, so do the communities you serve. This book will help you make sure you have the tools and knowledge you need to provide the best HR in your working environment.

The Long and Short of Employment Law

HR practices are deeply influenced by the thousands of federal, state, and local laws related to employment. In addition, HR practices are informed by insurance requirements and the impact of both successful and unsuccessful lawsuits. In fact, sometimes a nonprofit manager trying to be a fair, effective supervisor will feel stuck between the hard rock of law on the one side and insurance on the other.

As a nonprofit, you will want to keep your HR practices on the right side of the law. Throughout this book, we explain the best ways to make sure your organization stays legal and minimizes its potential liabilities.

At the same time, we realize that not everything will end up getting done exactly by the book. In fact, despite the importance of legalities in human resource management, many situations will demand judgment based on the circumstances at a particular time.

> **EXAMPLE:** The staff at a mental health clinic was looking forward to an all-day retreat at a donated mountain chalet and had organized into car pools for the next day. The HR director read an article on employee driving and suddenly realized that the organization had never verified drivers' licenses or car insurance for the employees who would be driving (they did not usually drive for work). She went to the executive director and recommended that the staff retreat be postponed until the proper verification could be obtained. The executive director felt stuck. Should she cancel tomorrow's retreat?

In addition, some important aspects of managing people are not covered by the law, nor would we want them to be. For example, while there is abundant legal guidance on what can and can't be asked when interviewing a job applicant, nonprofit managers also need to know how to obtain a large and diverse pool of qualified applicants—something not covered by rules or laws (or most books on HR). Staff development and team leadership are examples of other areas of HR not regulated by law. In this book, we cover it all—both the legal and nonlegal aspects of HR.

Although you may have heard the phrase "people are our most important asset," your organization may not have all the tools for managing people well. This book is dedicated to helping you make the most of this crucial, complicated, altogether important asset: human resources.

How This Book Is Organized

This book is based on many years of hands-on HR experience in real-life nonprofit organizations by the author and the advisers. A few tips on the book's presentation:

- **Examples.** All the examples set off in boxes are based on true stories, but the individuals and organizations have been given fictitious names, and some minor details may have been changed.
- **Chapter advisers.** Each chapter has been informed and reviewed by an adviser, whose profile opens the relevant chapter. Advisors come from very small (two) to very large (200) staffs, from around the country, and from different fields. They represent a variety of positions, including HR director, CEO, HR consultant, and administrative director.
- **Myths.** Each chapter includes a commonly held myth about HR in nonprofits, and goes on to explain what's really true.
- **Reference book for HR staff and others.** Use this book as a reference for HR practices, but also to educate and strengthen the perspectives of supervisors, senior management, board members, and others. The book is not aimed at lawyers, but written instead for HR staff, the "Accidental HR Manager," and everyone who has a role in recruiting or managing staff, or in strengthening staff performance and organizational culture.

Get Updates and More Online

When there are important changes to the information in this book, we'll post updates online, on a page dedicated to this book: www.nolo.com/back-of-book/HRNON1.html. You'll find other useful information there, too, including author blogs, podcasts, and videos.

Who Will Join Your Team?
Recruiting and Hiring Staff

Who Will Be Doing the Hire?..10

Hiring: A Five-Step Process...11

Step 1. Defining the Job and the Candidate Profile 11

    The Job Description Worksheet...13

    The Short Version of the Job Description..16

Step 2. Recruiting a Strong Pool of Applicants 17

    Determine the Scope of Your Search...18

    Post the Position Internally 19

    Circulate the Announcement to Constituents..19

    Advertising Online and in Newspapers 20

    Working With a Search Consultant 21

Step 3. Screening and Selection 23

    Telephone Screenings..24

    The In-Person Interview 25

    Antidiscrimination Laws: What You Can and Can't Do 26

    After the Interview 30

    Testing for Skills 31

    Background Checks...33

    Reference Checks..36

    Internal Hires...39

    "Internships Are the New Interview" 40

Step 4. Making the Job Offer 41

    Letting Others Know They Weren't Hired 41

    First-Day Paperwork 42

    At-Will Employment..43

    Employment Contracts..45

Step 5. Bringing the New Hire on Board 46

    Integration Into the Organization 48

    Information About the Organization 49

    Orientation Sessions 50

    Probationary or Trial Periods..51

Meet Your Adviser

Meg Busse
Title: Vice President for Community and Communications
Organization: Internships.com
Location: Portland, Oregon

What she does: Meg is involved in all aspects of word-related things at Internships.com, heading up content, communications, and community. She also enjoys thinking about infrastructure and consequently served on the Young Nonprofit Professionals Network (YNPN) National Board for the past three years. Prior to Internships.com, Meg managed the Career Center at Idealist.org, a nonprofit site that connects nonprofits and people looking for jobs and volunteer opportunities.

What her organization does: Internships.com is an online internship marketplace for employers, educators, and students.

Best tip for HR manager, including the Accidental HR manager: Use your staff to help with hiring—recruiting should be on everybody's mind all the time. Make it easy for your staff to share information about job openings by sending them a short blurb about available positions that they can post to Facebook or Twitter. Be sure to include a link to the full posting.

HR lesson learned the hard way: It's easy to get bogged down in the weeds and the details. Set out some goals for the year so you don't spend the whole year filling out forms.

Song title with an HR message: Because of my Jersey roots, the song that comes to mind when thinking of HR is Bon Jovi's "I'll Be There for You." As all good HR folks are.

Attracting and recruiting the right people is not just an administrative task; it is essential and strategic work for any nonprofit. Your organization may have a great vision and goals, but without the right staff, that vision will not get very far. Besides, you will be investing time and attention with these new recruits, so you want to be confident that they're good fits for your organization. And, bringing people on in the right way can establish a professional, warm, and mission-oriented tone that will carry forward throughout the individual's employment at your organization.

In this chapter, we focus on the steps you can take to most effectively find, hire, and integrate paid staff into your organization. In addition to paid staff, your workforce may include volunteers and independent contractors. These are covered separately in other chapters of this book.

Who Will Be Doing the Hire?

In most cases, whichever manager will be responsible for supervising a new employee is also the one who will recruit and hire that employee. But others might be involved in the hiring process, as well. In a larger nonprofit, the Human Resources (HR) department may recruit and screen candidates for certain positions and then the manager will step in at the end to make the final choice. In many smaller or less-established nonprofits, there may not be an HR department at all, although typically someone is charged with responsibility for HR matters.

Whether you have a full-fledged HR department or a lone, "sole provider" HR person, HR should work with managers to ensure that a strong candidate is found, hired properly, and effectively brought into your organization.

> **EXAMPLE:** Program Director Jackie hired a new educator. In response to his question about vacation time, she said, "Everyone starts off with four weeks of Paid Time Off per year." Within the new hire's first two months on the job, he wanted to take a week off with pay. The HR director explained that the four weeks PTO was earned over

the course of the first year, and that new employees didn't begin with four weeks PTO already in the bank. Unintentionally, Jackie had miscommunicated about the benefit package, and the ensuing anger and resentment on both sides lasted for months. After this incident, Jackie made sure that she didn't discuss benefits with applicants or new hires; she referred these questions to HR.

Hiring: A Five-Step Process

In the remainder of this chapter, we break down the hiring process into five steps and explain how each of these steps works.

Step 1. Defining the job and the candidate profile

Step 2. Recruiting a strong pool of candidates

Step 3. Screening and selection

Step 4. Making the job offer

Step 5. Bringing the new hire on board.

Step 1. Defining the Job and the Candidate Profile

A first step will be to write a job description that defines the job to be done, the job requirements, and the desired skills and talents of the person you want to hire. The exercise of writing a job description can be valuable: It makes managers articulate the tasks and responsibilities for the position, and consequently understand what the job truly requires. In addition, a written job description helps ensure that there is agreement within your group or organization about what the job will entail and how it will fit into the organizational structure. (If, for example, the executive director thinks that your new development associate should be seeking corporate sponsorships while the development director is hoping to give the person a back-seat role designing a new donor database, some further discussion is in order.)

If, like most nonprofits, yours has an organizational chart that lays out who reports to whom within the organization, you'll also want to figure out in advance where the new hire will fit within the organizational chart.

The job description also plays a role in encouraging candidates to apply. Part of your goal is to attract as many qualified applicants as possible. Potential applicants will read the job description carefully. So you'll want to take advantage of this opportunity to talk about the job in a way that's both accurate and attractive to potential candidates, highlighting your organization as a financially stable and satisfying place to work.

When you describe what your organization does, make it sound as bold and exciting and important as it is. Your job candidates most likely include many people who care deeply about your area of work, regardless of the actual job they'll be doing. Some of them could likely earn more money elsewhere, but will choose to accept a lower salary out of commitment to the mission.

The job description will also provide a basis for developing interview questions and for assessing the merits of candidates. And after the hire, the job description will serve as a reference point for supervision, and as a tool in performance evaluation. In short, the job description has both a management and a marketing role to play.

But let's not forget the basics: As shown in the sample below, your job description should provide all the key information applicants will need: the title of the position, the location of the job, whether the job is full- or part-time, the salary and benefits, and how to apply for the position. It should also list key job functions, information about your organization, and any requirements or desired skills, experience, or background necessary for the job. While you will, as mentioned above, want to market the job and your organization to attract a wide pool of applicants, you don't want just anyone to respond. The description should also serve as a screen, so that candidates who lack crucial qualifications or don't like your mission will choose not to apply.

The hiring manager and HR manager should develop and review the description together to be sure that it is accurate and complete, meets legal requirements, and is in line with your organization's other job descriptions.

CAUTION

Don't run afoul of antidiscrimination laws. Before sending or posting a job description, read through it again with an eye toward legal risks. In particular:

- **List only those functions that the job truly requires.** If a food bank warehouse worker will be operating a forklift most of the time, the ability to lift and carry 50 pounds may not be an essential job function, and requiring it can result in screening out qualified female applicants and applicants with disabilities.
- **Use inclusive terms.** Instead of "busboy" use "dining room attendant"; instead of "youthful" say "enthusiastic" (if that's what you mean).
- **Don't overplay diversity characteristics.** Make sure you don't appear to be searching only for employees of a particular gender, age, or other protected characteristic. Don't say, "Preference given to minorities and women." You *can* say, "We are an equal opportunity employer, and we encourage applications from women and underrepresented populations."
- **Reconsider degree requirements.** If the position for which you are hiring really does require a degree or advanced degree, that's fine. But many don't— and requiring applicants to have a degree can screen out qualified people who (perhaps because of their economic background) do not have degrees.

The Job Description Worksheet

Here's a handy way to develop your job descriptions: Use a worksheet like the sample shown below. The worksheet provides a summary of the job and all the elements and relevant information in column format. We have added a notes column on the right to explain how to use the worksheet.

Worksheet and Sample Job Description

Development Associate Position: Family Support Network

Title: Development Associate

Classification and time: Full time, exempt

Reports to: Development Director

Job Description	Notes
Location San Diego, California	Especially if your organization has more than one location, or if the job is of a sort that is commonly done from the field, be sure to indicate where the job is physically located.
Key job functions • Maintain donor database, including recording and responding to donations • Maintain calendar for donor solicitations, follow-ups, grant proposal submissions, report due dates, and other fundraising-related deadlines. • Assist with grant proposals, correspondence, Web content • Assist with fundraising events	These are the "must do" components of the job. Be as specific as possible. For example, rather than saying, "Responsible for all fundraising events," say "Responsible for raising $400,000 through special events including annual luncheon, auction, and one new event to be developed."
Requirements • Exceptionally strong English written communication skills • Demonstrated ability to manage confidential information with integrity • Strong computer and Internet skills • Ability to work in a fast-paced environment • Commitment to the organization's goals and values	

Worksheet and Sample Job Description (cont'd)

Desired skills, experience, background • Experience with nonprofit fundraising and/or special events as a staff or volunteer • Familiarity with field of children and disabilities • Verbal and written skills in Spanish a plus	Some organizations may add a note related to constituency: "As an organization working with after-school programs in the East School District, we encourage applications from people living or working in the district area."
Salary Full time, exempt. $28,000–$35,000 depending on experience	You may choose to post a specific salary, post a range, or choose not to include a salary in the job description. If you don't post an amount, you may want to use the phrase, "Salary dependent on experience" or something similar.
Benefits Cafeteria health plan (that is, one from which the employee can select a variety of health benefits), 3 weeks paid time off annually, other.	If you have attractive benefits, by all means include them, briefly. Make sure your description is accurate.
Equal Opportunity statement Family Support Network is an Equal Opportunity Employer. We do not discriminate on the basis of age, race, ethnicity, faith, national origin, gender, sexual orientation, or disabilities.	Some organizations may add a statement like the following: As part of our commitment to a diverse workforce, we encourage applications from people of color.
About this organization This organization's mission is to support families of children with any kind of disabilities and special health care needs, ensuring that they have the knowledge, access, and assistance to make informed choices. We provide counseling, peer support, referrals, information, and other services, and we advocate for supportive services.	The opportunity to work on an important issue is a key drawing point for many nonprofit staff. Take advantage of the opportunity to explain your organization's work in a compelling way. Be careful to avoid off-putting jargon.
How to apply Email a cover letter and resume—with your full name in the subject line—to hr@familysupportnetwork.org. Position open until filled. No calls, please.	Include instructions and if applicable, a deadline. You can suggest questions that you would like answered in a cover letter, such as "Include a comment as to why this organization is of interest to you."

TIP
Talk internally with the workgroup before you post and hire.
Gather the people who will be working with the new hire, says adviser Meg Busse. "They can talk about what they need the new person to be doing, and what kinds of personal attributes they think would add to the team." Personal attributes might include a team-oriented outlook, sensitivity to the client population, or a calm presence. She adds, "You'll also surface conflicting desires and unrealistic expectations: better to discuss these before you hire than after."

CAUTION
Don't make the job requirements into a wish list. If you do, you may discourage some qualified applicants. For example, when hiring a program manager, if a Master's degree isn't required for the job, don't make it a requirement in the job description. Don't say you require five years of experience if you'd be open to meeting strong candidates with only four years of experience. Use the term "preferred" or "desired" when possible in discussing backgrounds.

The Short Version of the Job Description

You will probably want to have a shorter version of the job description that you can use for other purposes. For example, if you take out a Help Wanted ad or send it around to colleagues or others by email, you will want something short, concise, and in text form instead of the longer column worksheet format. You will need to provide the essentials— name of organization, title of position, short job description, basic skills or experience required, and information on salary and how to apply.

Here is an example of this type of job description for the same position as described above in the job description worksheet.

Short Version of a Job Description

Family Support Network, an innovative, community-based nonprofit helping families of children with all varieties of disabilities, is seeking a full-time Development Associate to join an exciting team. The job involves maintaining donor records and assisting other staff in developing grant proposals and holding fundraising events, including our annual "Celebrity Waiter" luncheon. This job is well suited for someone with excellent written communications skills and experience with fundraising who wants to build toward a development director or executive director job, and make a difference in the lives of children with disabilities and their families. Competitive salary and benefits. For complete job description see www.familysupportnetwork.org/jobs. To apply, send cover letter and resume to hr@familysupportnetwork.org.

 RESOURCE

For more information on job descriptions, see *The Job Description Handbook,* by Margie Mader-Clark (Nolo). In addition, Bridgestar has an article on nonprofit job descriptions along with several samples for top-level nonprofit positions at www.bridgestar.org; type "writing the job description" into the search box.

Step 2. Recruiting a Strong Pool of Applicants

Compared to how much time most managers spend on screening and interviewing potential candidates, relatively little time is typically spent on generating applicants into a qualified pool. However, investing more time in recruiting applicants can greatly improve the quality of the candidates you get. In the end, this is always a better investment of time than meticulously choosing the best candidate from a weak pool.

> **TIP**
> **Lead with your mission when recruiting.** Your mission not only serves to attract applicants, it can help them understand whether they are a good fit. For example, consider an accountant whose mother recently died of cancer. A brief and compelling statement about your organization's cancer-related work may go a long way toward attracting this person to your organization instead of somewhere else.

> **TIP**
> **Think about the organization's whole workforce as you recruit for a particular job.** Hiring is usually done in the context of finding a particular person for a particular job—such as a coach for your afterschool basketball program, or a biologist for your environmental advocacy team. But a vacancy doesn't stand on its own; it exists in the context of the whole staff. For example, a nonprofit may seek to have a workforce that reflects the racial and ethnic population it serves, or it may want to recruit from among its clients and former clients.

Determine the Scope of Your Search

At the beginning of each hire, the person or team making the hire will need to establish the scope of the search. You might decide to start your search by posting the position internally for a specified length of time (such as two weeks). If you do this, you may choose to hire an internal candidate without ever posting externally. You can also advertise both internally and externally from the beginning, making it clear that a hire will not occur before a certain date.

At the narrowest, some organizations look only among existing staff and volunteers or reach out to known connections using word-of-mouth publicity. For example, if you are hiring a neighborhood organizer and want someone who has a long history in the neighborhood, word-of-mouth might be the best approach. At the other end of the spectrum, if you are hiring an adoptions manager, you might want to reach out to adoption networks nationally.

A wider scope for a search doesn't necessarily mean that better candidates will be recruited, but it does open the doors for a wider array of candidates. For example, if you are hiring an accountant but only search through nonprofit networks, you won't know about for-profit accountants who are looking to change sectors.

Post the Position Internally

Even if you don't think there is an internal candidate for a job, it's good practice to post all vacancies internally. Doing so demonstrates a commitment to staff development that employees will appreciate. And sometimes an employee will surprise you with ambition and skills of which you were unaware.

In the announcement, include information about how to apply, and a reminder that such applications and inquiries will be kept confidential. You can assure your staff that no hiring decisions will be made during the first week that the position is posted. This ensures that internal candidates will be considered if they have applied within the first week.

Circulate the Announcement to Constituents

People who already know and like your organization are an important pool from which to recruit. Posting an announcement on your organization's website and Facebook page are ways to publicize the opening to volunteers, donors, and others. Placing an "Open Position" ad in your newsletter encourages readers to let others know of the opening.

Ask direct service staff to think about who among clients, students, audience members, and others might be encouraged to apply. Adviser Sarah Gort notes, "When I was at the housing clinic, 30% of our staff came from the client base. Case workers would recommend clients they thought were ready for an open position."

Encourage staff and board members to send the job announcement from their own email addresses to people they know, and post the opening on their Facebook pages. The subject/status line could read: "Great opening for Volunteer Coordinator at River Rescue Nonprofit," or "Job Fighting Big Pharmaceuticals." Especially when you are trying to recruit from a particular population, asking someone who has connections in the community to reach out with a personal note can produce great results. To involve your staff more actively in recruitment, offer a modest bonus (such as $100 or $500) for referrals that turn into hires. Adviser Meg Busse comments, "Yes! There are so many instances of employee referral programs being incredibly beneficial for nonprofits."

TIP

Help your staff and connections to help you. Adviser Meg Busse suggests: "Make it easy for staff and others to share the opening via Facebook, Twitter, and so forth. Send them an email with the posting blurb in the subject line, and include a link to the full posting."

Have the opening announced at nonprofit meetings in your area. One way to do this is to find out who in your organization attends professional association meetings and ask them to announce the opening in person. For instance, if you know the Association of Fundraising Professionals is holding a meeting, have someone attend and announce that you have a fundraising position open.

Reach out to other networks, such as the Young Nonprofit Professionals Network (YNPN) and the Latino Mental Health Network, and ask them to circulate or post the job announcement. For many organizations, recruiting through email networks—sometimes with phone follow-up—is the most successful approach to recruiting.

Advertising Online and in Newspapers

Posting jobs with online services and in local newspapers is a good way to extend your reach beyond the usual suspects. In particular, don't neglect the niche newspapers, such as the local neighborhood newsletter and the ethnic press (both print and online).

Online advertising typically works best with either local websites or nonprofit networks. Many communities have free and low-cost job sites for nonprofits.

The Internet makes it easy for jobseekers who want to move to look for job openings in a particular geographical area. For senior positions that can attract applicants to relocate, consider advertising on regional or statewide nonprofit sites, or on national online listing services such as Idealist (approximately $60 an ad), Craigslist's nonprofit job section ($0 to $75, depending on location), and Opportunity Knocks (approximately $100).

RESOURCE

Blue Avocado maintains a directory of nonprofit job sites. Go to www.blueavocado.org and type "nonprofit job sites" into the search box.

New America Media maintains a national ethnic media directory including print, online, radio, and television media; see www.newamericamedia.org.

EXAMPLE: T.J. Booker, President and CEO of the Capricorn Theater, comments that its HR Director plays an important role in ensuring a racially diverse workforce "reflecting the very diverse community here in northern Virginia." He explains: "We have very specific goals for attracting minority candidates; if there isn't at least one minority candidate in the final three, I am going to question it. We have a commitment to diversifying our work force; we want our workforce to look like the face of our community."

Working With a Search Consultant

For some high-level, difficult-to-recruit positions such as executive director, chief financial officer, or development director, you might consider hiring a professional search consultant. This might happen right at the start of a search or later if you've been unsuccessful trying to do it on your own. Search consultants are expensive; they typically charge a fee equal to one-third of the annual salary of the position being filled.

If you contract with a search consultant, be sure to choose someone with strong experience in nonprofit searches and a track record of developing capable and diverse candidates from a variety of backgrounds. Talk with their previous nonprofit clients and be sure you understand the process, requirements, and fees. There are many consultants to choose from, and a lot of them have mixed track records and results.

Once you opt to move forward with a search consultant, try not to second-guess your decision. In some cases, you may end up awarding the position to a local candidate who was already known to you. Nevertheless, having gone through a broad-based or national search can reassure you and your constituents that you have hired the best possible candidate for the job, even if it turns out to be someone on the inside. And it may make the position more attractive to potential candidates.

> EXAMPLE: A small historical, ethnic museum's board hired a search firm to conduct a national search for a new executive director. They ended up hiring a local candidate, Eddie, whom nearly half the board members already knew. Was the search consultant a worthwhile expense or a waste of money? Board members complained, "The firm didn't find him; we already knew him!" Eddie later let it be known that initially, he wasn't that interested in the position. But after the search consultant convinced him that the museum was looking to raise its profile and was conducting a national search, the job became more attractive to him. He saw that the board was interested in positioning the museum as a nationally recognized cultural institution. He wanted to be a part of helping to realize their ambitious vision.

MYTH

Lower Salaries Hurt Nonprofit Recruiting Efforts

Are you worried that it will be harder for your nonprofit to recruit staff because the salaries are lower than candidates might find in the for-profit sector?

Actually, says adviser Joanne Krueger, it is harder to recruit staff for nonprofits than for-profits, but not because of salary levels. "When you're hiring a manager for a manufacturer, there is a huge pool of candidates, and the size of the pool is largely determined by how much you pay," she says, drawing on her corporate background. "But in a nonprofit, you're limited to the pool of people who believe in your cause, which might be almost everybody but it might not. You have to be much more targeted in recruiting for a nonprofit, but once you find the people who believe in your work, salary will probably not be the deciding factor in whether they work for you or somewhere else."

Step 3. Screening and Selection

Hopefully, your job postings and outreach efforts have resulted in a number of inquiries and applications. Before you begin reviewing cover letters and resumes, however, you'll want to make sure you have your internal process in place. You need to identify the decision makers on the hire, the first-round interview group, the second-round interview group (if appropriate), and the time frame for making a decision. Once you know who is responsible for what, you can start to review the cover letters and applications and resumes you receive.

Here is an overview of a selection process that works well for most organizations:

Step 1. Select from five to 15 applicants for telephone screenings from the resumes and applications you receive.

Step 2. Select three to five applicants for in-person interviews based on the telephone screenings.

Step 3. Conduct in-person interviews, typically with the direct supervisor and an additional staff person.

Step 4. If appropriate, conduct second-round interviews, typically with the direct supervisor and one or two additional staff.

Step 5. Conduct reference and background checks for the top one or two candidates.

Step 6. Proceed with an offer letter to the top candidate.

> **TIP**
> **Acknowledge all applications and emails you receive.** You can do this with a simple email reply or postcard. If you don't plan on interviewing the applicant, you can simply thank them for their inquiry and say that you received many responses and have chosen to follow up with other candidates who appear better suited for the position. This reduces phone calls from people wondering if you received their resume, and it helps your organization maintain a reputation for professionalism and respect. And don't forget that some of these applicants may be future volunteers, staff, staff in partner organizations, or funders.

Telephone Screenings

Talking briefly on the telephone with applicants is an efficient, cost-effective way to do an initial screening. The objective in these 20- to 30-minute conversations is to determine which applicants you will ask to come in for interviews. It's also important to communicate a positive image of your organization during the telephone screening; you don't want to turn off a qualified applicant.

Ask about the experiences, skills, and interests that you've noticed in the cover letter or resume. For example: "Tell me a little more about your degree in Internet Marketing." If there is something you suspect may be a barrier, the screening call is a good time to ask about it. "Your resume shows a great deal of experience. I want to be sure you know that the salary range for this position is $40,000 to $50,000. Is that a range you are comfortable with?"

Listen for whether the person seems like a good fit with your organizational culture: "Can you tell me what about this job and about this organization interests you?" Finally, give the candidate an opportunity to ask questions, but keep the phone interview under 30 minutes.

The In-Person Interview

Applicant interviews are typically conducted by a team of two or three people, including the supervisor for the position being hired. For some senior positions, it may also be useful to include in the interview some employees who will be working under the new person. In that situation, be clear to the applicant and to the staff participating that the staff's role is to give input to the hiring team or person, not to make the ultimate decision about whom to hire.

Board members sometimes participate in the interview process, especially if the person being hired will be working with the board. For instance, the board treasurer might participate in interviewing candidates for the top finance job, or the board chair might interview finalists for development director and give feedback to the hiring committee or person. Make sure it's clear whether the board committee or board member has hiring authority or veto power or whether they are simply advising staff on the hire.

> **EXAMPLE:** Lisa was the new executive director of a family law nonprofit with seven staff members. One of her first tasks was to fill the vacant controller position (the top finance position). After two interviews with applicants, she realized her legal background wasn't much help in determining whether applicants knew accounting or not. The board treasurer—a nonprofit CFO herself—offered to sit in on the interviews, although the hire decision would be Lisa's. Because of her expertise, the treasurer was able not only to help Lisa screen

for technical expertise but also to ask important and useful questions about moving from for-profit accounting to nonprofit accounting.

In most cases you will want to have two or more interviews with the final candidate or candidates. For example, in the first round of interviews, two people might interview the candidate together, then one of them and the hiring manager would conduct second-round interviews.

While it's a good idea to have two or three people in the interview, having more than four can intimidate candidates and make the interviewers self-conscious. Have a brief discussion before the interviews to prepare everyone for their role. Decide who will lead off and who will close the interview; review the "What You Can and Can't Ask" chart below, and go over any questions you want to be sure to ask.

Antidiscrimination Laws: What You Can and Can't Do

Discrimination in hiring is not only illegal, it can result in an organization missing out on the best candidates for a job. Through the hiring process, you will need to be aware of antidiscrimination laws and how they apply in the context of recruiting and hiring.

Federal laws prohibit discrimination on the basis of race, color, national origin, sex (including pregnancy), religion, age (40 and older), disability, citizenship status, and genetic information. State and local laws may prohibit discrimination based on additional characteristics, such as sexual orientation, marital status, smoking, or weight. When hiring, the best practice is to avoid asking about characteristics that you cannot legally consider in making your decision—or closely related characteristics. For example, you cannot make decisions based on an applicant's national origin, so you shouldn't ask questions about the applicant's birthplace or "native" language. The chart below will help you stay on the right side of the line.

What You Can and Can't Ask: Lawful and Unlawful Preemployment Questions

Subject	Okay to ask	Do not ask
Name	Full name Have you worked for this organization or one of its affiliates under a different name? Is any additional information relative to a different name necessary to check work records? If yes, please explain.	Maiden name "Original" or prior name(s)
Address and duration of residence	How long have you been a resident of this state or city?	Do you rent or own?
Birthplace	No legal questions	Birthplace, or birthplaces, of parents, spouses, or other relatives Require submission of birth certificate or naturalization record
Age	Are you 18 years old or older? This question is permissible only for determining whether applicants are of legal age for employment.	How old are you? What is your date of birth? Are you in the same age bracket as the seniors we serve?
Religion or creed	None	Inquiry about religious affiliation or religious holidays observed
Race or color	None	
Photograph	None	
Height, weight	None	Unless there is a specific reason related to the job function, do not ask about height or weight.
Marital and parental status	Is your spouse or domestic partner employed by this organization?	Are you single? Married? Do you have any children? What is your spouse's name? Do you plan to have children?

What You Can and Can't Ask: Lawful and Unlawful Preemployment Questions (cont'd)		
Subject	Okay to ask	Do not ask
Gender	None	Require selection of title such as Mr., Miss, and so on.
Disability	These [provide list] are the essential functions of this job. How would you perform them?	Inquiries about an individual's physical or mental condition not directly related to the requirements of a specific job.
Citizenship	Are you legally authorized to work in the United States on a full-time basis?	Inquiries about citizenship naturalization status, whether parents or spouse are citizens, or a requirement that applicant produce naturalization papers.
National origin	What languages do you speak and write fluently?	How did you learn that language? Do not ask questions outside the federal I-9 requirements.
Education	List academic, vocational, and/or professional education, including schools attended and degrees earned, and professional certificates awarded.	

RESOURCE

Need additional guidance on discrimination in hiring? Check out the website of the Equal Employment Opportunity Commission, the federal agency that interprets and enforces the laws prohibiting discrimination, at www.eeoc.gov. You can find additional articles and guidance at Nolo's website, www.nolo.com; select "Employment Law," then "Human Resources."

In addition to asking what can be legally asked, you will want to ask questions about the candidate's skills and experience, and to see how well the individual is able to address questions and communicate thoughts. It's a good idea to have five or six questions to ask in each interview, although you'll need to tailor them to fit an applicant's particular experience and the job you're hiring for.

Here are some examples of general background questions you can ask to learn more about previous work experience and start a conversation:

- What were your key responsibilities on your last job?
- [*For support staff*] Working for several people can be stressful. How have you managed your work when getting assignments from multiple people?
- What experience have you had with volunteers? What are some things you've learned about how best to work with volunteers?
- [*For management position*] How many people reported to you directly? What are some ways you supervised them individually? As a group?
- [*For management position*] Have you ever fired someone? Looking back, how did you handle the situation? Is there something you might have done differently?

Most nonprofit jobs—regardless of level—require an ability to work with others in a team setting and to communicate well with that team and other coworkers, clients, donors, and others. Here are some sample questions you may want to use to probe for these skills:

- If we were to interview some of your coworkers from your last job, what would they describe as your strengths? Your weaknesses? What suggestions would they have about how best to work with you?
- Can you think of a time when you didn't work well with a supervisor? What was the outcome, and how would you have changed the outcome?
- We have a work group that is diverse in age and in racial backgrounds, and sometimes there are misunderstandings. Can you give an example of a time when you have misunderstood someone from a different background and how you handled it?

In many positions, employees will perform better and will be happier if they are in tune with the organization's larger goals and vision. Here are some sample questions that can help you understand an individual's sense of self and relationship to an organization and its work:

- Tell us something about the mission and work of the nonprofit where you worked.
- What is interesting to you about this position? About working at this organization?
- Have you done any volunteering recently? What are some of your volunteer experiences and why did you choose them?
- What are some things that your previous company/nonprofit could do to be more successful?

After the Interview

It's a good idea not to discuss each candidate with other interviewers right after the interview. Instead, keep your thoughts to yourself and wait until all the interviews are complete to discuss your assessments with the other interviewers. It is important to discuss the candidates in a way that allows for a free flow of reactions and ideas. You want to avoid "groupthink," in which everyone on the hiring committee begins to think as one, instead of offering creative, individualized input. Interviewers can each ask themselves:

- "Which of these candidates has the background most suited for the position?"
- "Which can contribute the most to the organizational culture and team approach of our organization?"
- "Who do I think are the top two candidates?"

Then organize the discussion in a way that will keep observations focused. As you discuss candidates, return to the job description. It's easy to abandon the job description you spent so much time on and focus on discussing which candidates seemed the most appealing. Instead, start by assessing each candidate, one by one, against the job description and profile.

For each candidate, ask: "How suited is this person for this job?" You still might choose someone who is not the "best suited for the job" because of other qualities, but you will be clearer about the strengths and weaknesses of the person you hire. The process will help you arrive at an assessment that can also help frame orientation and training activities for that person. After the first round of interviews, the group decides which applicants—if any—should be asked to come in for a second round of interviews.

Many executive directors are involved either during or right after a hire as part of ensuring a good fit and a good entrance into the organization. Adviser Terrence Jones, President and CEO of Wolf Trap Foundation for the Performing Arts, comments: "I interview the final two or three candidates for every job at Wolf Trap. It's important because I want everyone who comes to work here to understand what our organization believes in, our mission, and how we communicate that. We have 80 full-time staff plus part-timers and volunteers, and I want everyone to be part of the Wolf Trap experience."

Testing for Skills

Despite the obvious dangers of relying on the word of applicants as to their skills, testing is typically underutilized in nonprofits. Skills tests can not only improve the selection process by making sure the applicant has the skills he or she claims to have, they can also help a supervisor know which skills a new hire needs help with.

> **CAUTION**
>
> **Don't make assumptions.** It's easy to assume that someone has a particular skill because it was needed on the last job or because the person has a related degree. For instance, someone may have been the wellness program director at a large nonprofit, but don't assume that he or she knows about either wellness or program development. It's possible the person was fired from that job for poor performance, or that the program used "wellness" in a completely different way.

The word "test" may conjure up images of a formal exam in which the candidate is asked to fill in circles with a No. 2 pencil as if she or he is taking a high school standardized test or the SAT. But skills tests can encompass a variety of formats. You can test writing, presentation ability, spreadsheet expertise, accounting knowledge, cooking skills, and so forth. For example, if you are hiring an administrative assistant, you can ask your final applicants to compose and type a brief thank you letter to a donor for a donated set of chairs. You will get an idea of the person's writing skills as well as computer skills. If you are hiring a natural history instructor, ask each of the final candidates to give a ten-minute presentation on something in nature. These kinds of tests give you an opportunity to see a candidate in action.

> **EXAMPLE:** Melissa was delighted with Jon, the top candidate for the position of executive assistant. He seemed bright and well educated, and had gone to a well respected college. She was sure he would fly through the test which asked him to write a thank you letter to a volunteer. Instead, she was surprised at how many errors he made: he misspelled the volunteer's name, used incorrect grammar, and made promises to the volunteer about future activities. Melissa was so surprised she gave him a second writing test, which he also flunked. Melissa learned her lesson; she would not make assumptions again about skills.

There are some things to be careful about when you use testing:

- **Be consistent.** For example, if you have two finalists for a position, test both of the finalists, not just one.
- **Do not devise a test that is a thinly veiled attempt to get a candidate to do unpaid work for you.** For example, you should not ask a fundraising candidate to write a funding proposal, nor should you expect an applicant for a position in the communications department to develop a full-blown communications strategy paper.
- **It's best not to use personality/aptitude tests.** Personality/aptitude tests attempt to ascertain personality characteristics and attitudes, such as motivational bases, sociability, "ego-drive," and so on.

Because these tests (such as Meyers-Briggs or Caliper Profile) ask personal questions and make judgments based on assumptions about personality types, their reliability is questionable, especially in a multicultural setting. You could also be opening your organization to charges of discrimination.

EXAMPLE: The board members of one nonprofit were pleased that they had two strong candidates, Jason and Gilbert, for an executive director position. Both men seemed like they would be capable leaders for the group. Jason was from Israel; Gilbert was African American. There was one red flag: the personality test administered by the search consultant indicated that Gilbert had "unresolved anger" issues. In discussions, board members were alarmed by this and they began to veer toward Jason. But during their deliberations, one board member, a white woman, said, "You know, if I was a young black man in a society in which racism remains a challenging fact of life, I might be angry, too!" Her observation was well received by the other members of the board, and they ended up hiring Gilbert. They were rewarded with a strong, consensus-oriented leader. One of the participants in the hiring process reflected after working with Gilbert for some time that he was the "least angry person I know."

Background Checks

Background checks can be used to verify information that an applicant has provided. For example, you may want to check that someone you're hiring for a social worker position does in fact have the advanced social work degree that is listed on his or her resume. Many organizations conduct background checks on all candidates after the person has accepted the offer but before he or she is officially hired. The offer letter should state that the offer is subject to a background check.

You'll want to be reasonable and careful about information you obtain from a background check. Finding out something unexpected about a person should not rule that person out for a job unless it is likely to affect his or her ability to work.

A red flag for one organization may be a green flag for other. For example, having served time in prison or being in recovery may be a reason why an individual would be especially suited for a particular job.

If you conduct background checks, be sure to do so legally. You have a right and a responsibility to do some digging but applicants have privacy rights as well that should be respected. Here are some of the legal issues to be aware of.

Verification of educational degrees. Particularly in human services and in health care, certain procedures or responsibilities can be performed only by individuals with certain required degrees, licenses, or certificates. In most cases, schools and universities will not release information without the written consent of the (former) student.

Verification of work-related certificates and licenses. Most professional associations and licensing institutions will confirm this information with the written consent of the applicant. Examples include Certified Public Accountant (CPA), Certified Association Executive (CAE), and Substance Abuse Counselor Certificate.

Review of public information. "Googling" or searching for information about an applicant on the Internet can often produce interesting and useful data, but comes with risks. First, information on the Web is often inaccurate or incomplete. Consider the student who is reported in the press as part of a cheating ring, yet the newspaper never reports that this student was later cleared of all charges. In addition, you may find out something about an applicant that should not be used in the hiring process—perhaps that the applicant has children or made campaign contributions to a particular political candidate. If you do not hire the applicant and have a record of search results, you can be open to charges that you did so based on such information.

Criminal record checks. Most states now have laws requiring fingerprint checks for any staff person or volunteer who will have direct contact with children or other vulnerable populations such as the elderly or disabled. Criminal background checks are difficult and problematic to conduct well. Information is typically kept on a state-by-state basis, and there is great variation among states on the type of information kept and the reliability of the data. In addition, state laws vary on what can and can't be asked. Some states only allow you to ask about a person's convictions but not about their arrests. And some states permit criminal history checks only in connection with certain types of jobs, such as teachers or nurses. The United States Equal Opportunity Commission has stated that using arrest records as a basis for employment decisions may discriminate against African Americans, who are more likely to have been arrested without cause than others. Commercial services (such as Intellicorp and LexisNexis) that perform background checks are convenient for large organizations with many staff, but often imply a comprehensiveness or reliability that is unrealistic. Because of the state law variations, you should consult a lawyer before you institute pre-employment criminal record checks.

Driving records. If driving is required for a job, obtain the driving records (usually for a small fee) from the motor vehicles department of the state where the candidate lives or works—and if the candidate lives close to a state border, in the nearby state(s). You will need the consent of the applicant.

Drug and alcohol testing. Except for employers subject to federal transportation and national security regulations (the trucking, airline, and nuclear power industries, for example), drug and alcohol testing is governed by state law. In states that allow employers to test applicants, employers generally have to give applicants written notice that drug testing will be required as a condition of employment. Don't forget that drug tests are not infallible: they may be subject to false positives and laboratory errors. And if you opt to test only for illegal drugs, don't forget that this will not help you to identify someone with a serious and potentially harmful alcohol or prescription drug problem.

 RESOURCE

For more information on background checks, see *The Manager's Legal Handbook,* by Amy DelPo and Lisa Guerin (Nolo).

Reference Checks

Past performance is an important—but not perfect—indicator of how a candidate will perform a job in your organization. It's estimated that 20% to 44% of resumes "exaggerate or outright fabricate" employment history, so you will want to gather information from sources other than the applicant. However, there are many pitfalls in conducting reference checks. In some cases, past employers may be unwilling to or legally constrained from discussing an employee's performance. In other cases, you may have mixed references about one candidate but be unable to obtain any references for another candidate. How will you weigh this kind of unbalanced information? And finally, don't forget that an individual can often work well in one environment but not in another, or someone may have had a specific personality conflict with someone at a prior job.

Here are some guidelines for doing reference checks:
- Let final candidates know you would like to check references. Ask them to sign a written release.
- During the interview, ask what the reference might say about the candidate's performance. Not only might this give you some insight into the candidate's self assessment of strengths and weaknesses, it will give you something useful to raise in the reference check: "Jane told us that you appreciated her creative problem solving. Can you tell me more about that?"
- The new hire's immediate supervisor should be the one to make the phone calls about finalists. A reference check from a peer is more likely to elicit a candid response than a call from an assistant or someone in the HR department. If you are calling another nonprofit in a related field, take a moment to establish a sense of camaraderie, perhaps about shared involvement with particular projects or community events.
- Ask open-ended questions, such as "What was his title?" rather than "He was the COO, right?"
- Ask: "If I were to hire this person, what tips would you give me in how best to work with her?" This type of question often does

a better job of eliciting meaningful comments than the more common question about strengths and weaknesses.

- Listen carefully to the tone of voice as well as to the content of the response. Many people are reluctant to make negative comments, but they will often convey their feelings through suggestions, what is left unsaid, or the tone of their voices.

EXAMPLE: The state Society for the Humanities was impressed by the out-of-town candidate for development director. In particular, they noted the fundraising success of the arts organization he had worked for in another city. But there was something "off" about the references; they weren't from direct supervisors but from coworkers and foundation funders. When asked for additional references, the candidate revealed that there had been a "personality conflict" with the executive director. Other reference calls were met with pained silences and the faintest of praise. Reluctantly, the Society decided to hire someone else. Later they learned that their out-of-town candidate had been fired for poor performance and for diverting funds from unrestricted support to grants for his favorite projects.

If you are unable to reach a former employer by phone, you can always do a reference check by mail or email. That way you will at least have confirmed the prior employment history.

Occasionally, a candidate will include a letter or letters of recommendation with his or her resume. Don't forget that such letters are not done in confidence and therefore may not be candid assessments of the applicant's strengths and weaknesses. These recommendations may have limited usefulness.

Sample Reference Check Letter

Dear_____:

This letter requests background information about a former employee of your organization/company, _____.
He/She has applied for a staff position with our nonprofit and has given us permission to request this information. A copy of that permission is attached.

Please provide us with the following information concerning this former employee:

- dates of employment

- positions and titles held

- responsibilities

- salary and other compensation

- the reason(s) why this individual left your organization's staff; for example, terminated for cause, resigned, or laid off

- any other information that would be relevant to our hiring process.

You can respond by email _____, by fax _____, or by telephone _____.

If you have any questions or other comments, please call me at _____.

Thank you for your consideration. I will be telephoning you in a few days to follow up on this request.

Sincerely,

_____

[*Your name and title*] [*Name and website of your organization*]

Internal Hires

Hiring for a position by choosing someone who is already on staff or is a volunteer or intern has many advantages, including:

- you already have a good sense of the individual's capabilities and work style
- an internal hire will often become integrated into the position and the work group in a shorter period of time, and
- hiring internally is good for morale; it demonstrates that managers want to develop, keep, and promote staff, volunteers, and interns.

A disadvantage to internal hiring is that you lose the opportunity to bring in fresh blood and a different perspective from the outside. Every organization suffers to some degree from groupthink, and particularly at the senior level, there are distinct advantages to bringing in fresh eyes and different kinds of backgrounds.

There are other possible complications (not necessarily disadvantages) in hiring internally that will need your time and attention:

- Some individuals will need coaching as they establish a different relationship with their coworkers, such as becoming a supervisor to people who were previously peers or who have been with the organization longer.
- If a capable person is promoted into a position but cannot perform well there, it is unlikely that returning to the previous position will be possible or productive.
- The internal hire enters the job with baggage, both good and bad. Many staff will already have opinions about the person who has been hired internally, and, if there was more than one internal applicant, about the choice as well.
- You now have a different position that has become vacant, giving you the opportunity to hire someone new in that position (or promote someone else).

A common temptation is to hire a well-performing, well-liked staff person into an open position without a rigorous process. Remember to screen and interview for the skills and perspective needed for the open position, and not just look at how the applicant is performing in his or her current job. Use the employee's current supervisor as a reference in much the same way you would use an external reference.

> **EXAMPLE:** Kathleen hired Sarah straight from graduate school and liked the energy and knowledge that she brought to answering calls on the cancer information hotline. When a supervisory position opened up six months later, Kathleen decided to hire Sarah for the job. But although Sarah was well informed about cancer and cancer patients, she was ill-prepared for the transition to management, especially when it came to supervising women who were significantly older and longer-tenured than she was. It took months of coaching before Sarah could effectively lead her workgroup,

Hiring a volunteer onto staff is a different kind of internal hire. Many of the same advantages and concerns apply when hiring a volunteer as when hiring someone already on staff. Volunteers often bring familiarity with operations but may lack the fresh perspective that an outside hire might bring. If you hire a volunteer, set aside time to talk over the transition—including changed expectations and roles and so forth—with the individual as well as the staff.

"Internships Are the New Interview"

Adviser Meg Busse points out that many nonprofits successfully hire for new positions by intentionally creating short-term internships that act informally as "tryout" periods for new hires. In effect, she says, the internship becomes an extended training and interview period. If you choose to hire an intern after such a period, you will know his or her abilities and weaknesses well, and you will have given the person extensive training at an intern's rate of pay. One downside of this strategy: Some potential staff members may not be able to afford to do an internship. As a result, you may find yourself inadvertently limiting your organization's staff to people who can afford to do an internship with low or no pay.

Step 4. Making the Job Offer

Once you have chosen your candidate, you will want to call that person right away. You know the person is looking for a job so if you wait even a few days, he or she may accept an offer elsewhere.

When you call, first and foremost, be enthusiastic and let the candidate know how excited you are to be extending the offer. Reiterate the job title and, if you are not the direct supervisor, the name and title of the person the new hire will be reporting to. If you have already established the salary, include this in your call. If not, set up a time to finalize your salary negotiations by phone or in person. Then send an email or letter as follow up.

Here's a checklist of the things you want to cover in your offer phone call:
- how excited you are that the candidate will be joining your team
- title of the job or description of the position being offered
- name of the person to whom the new hire will report
- salary, benefits, and any pertinent working conditions (such as location or shift) or how these will be negotiated
- date by when you would like the applicant to respond, and whether the response should be by phone, email, or other form
- name of the person to whom the response should be given, and
- name of the person the candidate can call with questions about benefits. (This should be a person responsible for benefits administration or HR, not the supervisor.)

If the offer is accepted on the phone, establish the first day and time of work, and (if different) the day on which the person will come in to complete preemployment paperwork. Let your new hire know what documents, if any, to bring. (See "First Day Paperwork" below.)

Letting Others Know They Weren't Hired

After you have a signed offer letter, don't keep the other candidates hanging. It's both courteous and good business sense to telephone those who have been interviewed in person to let them know you have hired someone else, and to send a note via email to any other applicants who were not hired. Some of the applicants will be your organization's job applicants, volunteers, clients, patrons, or colleagues in the future.

Sample Rejection Letter

Dear Ms. _____

Thank you for your interest in the position at the West Side Arts Council. We're sorry to inform you that you have not been selected for the position, as we had many fine candidates. Good luck with your job search. Our mutual interest in arts education may cause our paths to cross in the future, and we look forward to that occasion.

Sincerely,

_____

First-Day Paperwork

On the first day of work, a new hire will need to complete employment forms for the government and some of your internal forms as well. Be sure the new employee's supervisor has set aside time for this paperwork to be completed, either by HR staff or by the supervisor.

- IRS Form W-4, *Withholding Allowance Certificate.* New employees use this form to tell your organization how much income tax to withhold from their paychecks. Go to www.irs.gov for information.
- USCIS Form I-9, *Employment Eligibility Verification.* The federal government requires employers to complete this form verifying that new hires are eligible to work in the United States. Employees will need to show documentation such as a United States passport, Permanent Resident Card ("Green Card"),

United States work permit, and/or other documents. See www.
uscis.gov for more information.

- Reporting on new hires. Federal law requires that information
on new hires must be sent to a state agency, which uses it to find
parents who owe child support. For information on your state's
requirements, go to www.acf.hhs.gov and select "Employer Info"
under the "Working with ACF" tab.

The new hire will also need to complete some internal organizational
materials, which might include:

- an offer letter or employment contract
- an employee information form, including cell phone number and
emergency contact information
- an acknowledgment of receipt of the Employee Handbook
- benefits paperwork, such as insurance enrollment forms
- an acknowledgement and signatures, where appropriate, of
receipt of organizational policies, such as conflict of interest
policy/form, email policy, and confidentiality policy, and
- an acknowledgment of having received any organizational
property, such as keys, badges, laptop computer, cell phone, and
so on.

Create a checklist that is specific to your organization to help you
make sure that no steps are accidentally overlooked.

At-Will Employment

Most nonprofits will want to establish an "at-will" policy for their
employees, meaning that the employer can terminate an employee "for
good cause, bad cause, or no cause at all," and the employee is equally
free to quit or leave at any time. In many states, employees are presumed
to be hired at will, unless there is an employment contract with different
terms or the organization is in collective bargaining with a union. In
all states except Montana, nonprofits can institute an at-will policy.
(In Montana, employees who have completed an initial "probationary
period" cannot be fired without cause).

At-will policies have two key advantages. They provide:

- a strong defense against wrongful termination lawsuits, and
- the latitude to dismiss employees for inappropriate behavior or underperformance without requiring an onerous documentation effort.

Even if you have an at-will policy, it's important to ensure that other policies or verbal statements of managers don't inadvertently imply that there is an employment contract in place. For instance, if a manager assures new hires: "As long as you do your job, you won't get fired," an employee fired for misconduct can claim that a promise was made that superseded the at-will status.

Keep at-will employer rights in place by following these steps:

- Make sure employment or personnel handbooks state that employment is at will, and explain what that means.
- Have employees sign an at-will agreement as part of the hiring process. A signed agreement makes the point that the employee has agreed to at-will employment as a condition of being hired.
- Train managers—and periodically retrain them—not to make statements that can be construed as altering the at-will employment agreement.

EXAMPLE: Mitch was hired as an IT specialist to provide desktop computer support to 20 employees under an at-will employment agreement. Although Mitch did the technical parts of his job well, he managed to rub just about everyone the wrong way. When he was terminated as a "sour apple," he sought an attorney to help him sue for wrongful termination because he had not been subject to disciplinary action or given a warning. The attorney advised Mitch that because he had signed an at-will employment agreement and there weren't any grounds for claiming his at-will status had changed, his employer had the right to terminate his employment at any time and for any reason. Mitch backed off from suing.

Employment Contracts

Although relatively rare, some organizations use employment contracts for senior employees, in particular the executive director or development director. A key feature of employment contracts is that they specify a length of time for the contract and severance agreements if either party decides to end the employment before the contract period ends. For example, a CEO's three-year contract may specify that if the board chooses to end the employment relationship before the three years are over, the nonprofit will pay 50% of the departing CEO's salary and benefit expenses for the remainder of the contract period.

Although commissions and bonuses are rare in nonprofits, some fundraising staff are hired with employment contracts as a way of spelling out specific procedures and benchmarks for these variable types of compensation. (See Chapter 2 for more information on bonuses and incentive pay in nonprofits.)

Proponents of employment contracts see contracts as a way of putting the employee and employer on more equal footing. Setting up penalty expenses, for example, will cause an employer to pause before terminating an employee prior to the end of the contract. Skeptics of employment contracts believe that the terms of employment can be set out within the job description and the offer letter, and that employment contracts can serve to keep underperforming executives on the job for longer than serves the organization.

Most nonprofits don't use employment contracts. Those that do typically use them only for one or two of the top positions. If you have a prospective employee who wants to have a contract, you'll need to weigh the pros and cons, including any messages that a contract for a top staffer might inadvertently send to others on staff.

Step 5. Bringing the New Hire on Board

After all the time and effort invested in finding the right candidate, it's easy to give relatively scant attention to helping the new employee become integrated and effective as soon as possible. In a nonprofit, new employees are not just "new hires"; they are members of a team working toward a common mission. It is important not only to do the paperwork correctly, but also to enlist them in the service of your organization's goals.

And remember that integrating the new person is not just for the benefit of the "newbie," but also for everyone who will be working or interacting with this person.

Employees often find themselves overwhelmed with new information on their first week on the job. At the same time, paradoxically, they may feel like they don't know what they're supposed to be doing. A good start will not only accelerate the employee's productivity, but will set an important tone for the future.

On the first day and over the first few weeks, try to provide a balance of these three components:

- integration into the organization and the workgroup
- providing information about the organization, programs, and processes, and
- getting the new hire started on accomplishing tasks.

CAUTION

Probationary periods can confuse at-will status. Some organizations have probationary periods in their personnel policies for new employees. This can be risky because it may imply to the employee that once the probationary period has passed, the employee's status has changed from one who can be fired for any reason to one who can be fired only for cause.

Checklist for Orienting a New Staff Member

Preemployment

☐ Signed and returned offer letter

☐ Phone call confirming date and time of first day; name of supervisor to meet

First day

☐ Welcome by supervisor

☐ First-day paperwork

☐ Workspace and computer set-up

☐ One-on-one orientation with supervisor and/or workgroup members

☐ Lunch with supervisor and/or coworker

☐ First assignment (examples: send and receive email; obtain information from intranet; complete a departmental process)

First week

☐ Exposure to program work and clients/patrons/constituents

☐ First-month objectives set

☐ Brief interviews with other staff with whom new employee will be working

☐ Review job description; ongoing feedback and coaching

☐ Introduction to the executive director

First month

☐ Completion of first assignments

☐ Attend meetings/observe work processes to meet key people and learn about department, organization, field

☐ 30-day performance review

☐ If appropriate, three-month job objectives

☐ Discuss future training

☐ Order business cards

☐ Formal new employee orientation, if available

Integration Into the Organization

A simple but neglected way to help new hires feel like they belong is to be welcoming to them. Supervisors (rather than HR) should meet their new hires on the first day and begin by welcoming them, showing them where they will be situated, and introducing them to those with whom they will be working. Simple steps that make new staff feel welcome and accelerate their integration into the organization include letting other staff know when a new person will be starting (and the new person's email address), what the new hire's job responsibilities will be, and to whom the new person will report. Let others know you are positive and excited about the new staff person. For senior staff, include information on the person's previous work.

Make sure the new employee's desk or work area is clean and includes a "welcome wagon" of supplies such as pens, notepads, granola bars, an organizational T-shirt, or other materials. If the employee will be using a computer, have the computer and email accounts set up ahead of time.

Introduce the new staff person to the head of the department and the executive director and schedule a time later for the new hire to meet the organization's leadership. Have coworkers take turns having lunch with the new employee for the first week. Assign a "buddy" for the first month: a peer—perhaps from a different department—who can help with integration into the informal culture and procedures of the organization. Make sure the buddy knows the responsibilities of this assignment and asks periodically: "What information would help you feel situated here?"

If the new hire will not be working directly with clients or patrons, find a way in the first week to expose him or her to the organization's programmatic work. A new webmaster at a nonprofit theater should be taken to see one of the plays or an audition. A new receptionist should sit in on an hour of the diabetes classes or be taken on a walking tour of the surrounding low-income neighborhood.

TIP

Make sure new hires understand your computer system and programs. Some new employees will find it easier to get up and running on your software and network than others. Don't assume that everyone is proficient in Outlook, Yahoo IMs, intranets, or other technology used in your organization. Schedule a time for someone in your technology department to sit with the new person. The technology staffer should walk through the systems and identify areas that are challenging to the newcomer, for which further training might be necessary.

Information About the Organization

New employees have much to learn—about their jobs, the organization, their new coworkers, and the organization's work. Try not to communicate all this through a long lecture and a 300-page employee manual. Instead, talk and walk your new hire through the ins and outs of your organization. Make sure the new hire has everything needed to understand how to get around and fit in appropriately, including:

- keys, badges, security cards, or other access tools
- information on building safety highlights, such as emergency exits
- parking and public transportation information
- training on how timesheets or time logs are kept and submitted
- information about where to ask questions on HR, computer systems, and organizational policies
- an organization chart: "Where Do I Fit?" and
- computer access codes and an email account set-up.

If you have a formal orientation session, go over organizational policies briefly. New employees are inevitably on a bit of information overload. Rather than a lecture, give new employees copies of policies that they can use as references, including:

- computer, email, intranet, and Internet policies and protocols
- conflict of interest and confidentiality policies

- codes of ethics, values statements, diversity policies, and
- whistleblower protection and procedures.

The employees at a nonprofit typically have chosen to work there not just because they need a job, but because they see themselves as contributing to something greater than themselves. Don't give them an inaccurate and negative first impression by failing to discuss mission and programs. You should give the new employee materials to read over time, especially documents that the newcomer would not have uncovered while doing research to prepare for the job interview. Here are some materials to share:

- organization brochures and newsletter
- annual report
- list of organizational websites, Facebook pages, and blogs
- newspaper articles about the organization or an award given to one of the staff or volunteers
- materials that showcase the organization's mission or work: perhaps a transcript from a good speech given by the CEO about the crisis in world hunger, or a journal article by a staff scientist on the importance of wetlands, and
- an abbreviated version of the strategic plan.

Orientation Sessions

If you have only one or a few new employees, consider walking through these steps on a one-to-one or small group basis. However, if your organization has several new employees starting in the same month, a half-day New Staff Orientation session can be an effective way to combine information and team integration. This session should aim to develop a positive impression of the organization and group camaraderie as well as to impart information. Do not include topics that are different for different positions, such as completing time sheets or managing confidential client information. That will be different for various positions and individuals.

Here's an overview of a typical orientation session:

Welcome. Begin with a welcome by the person leading the session, such as Human Resources Director, COO, Deputy Director, or another manager.

Self-introductions. Everyone present should introduce themselves. Ask for preferred name (perhaps Tom rather than Thomas), position, how long at the organization so far, something they want to learn during the session, and perhaps an interesting personal tidbit.

Organizational overview. Mission and vision, programs, fundraising/revenue activities, organizational chart, and Q&A.

Remarks by executive director with an emphasis on organizational goals and values, followed by questions and answers.

Benefits briefing by an HR manager, including choices, forms, deadlines, and how to get more information. Be sure to have a handout that includes key dates and requirements.

Walking tour of facilities/offices, including emergency exits and access procedures.

Lunch with invited other staff.

Probationary or Trial Periods

Some organizations hire new employees with a trial period—a probationary period—for 30 days, 90 days, or a similar length of time. During this period, the employee can be terminated without cause or warning. Once the employee has passed probation, there is an assumption that the employee is now working on a permanent basis—and cannot be fired without good cause.

Some nonprofits like trial periods because it may seem easier to fire an employee immediately when it is clear the person is not suitable for a job. However, a big risk with probationary periods is that they can undo at-will employment if the employee believes that completing the probation period gives the employee job security. After all, a probationary period creates an expectation that things will change once that period ends. They create an unstated implication—some say an implicit contract—that an employee whose probation is over is protected from being fired without warning or cause. As a result, it may be more difficult to fire the employee after the probationary period. (See "At-Will Employment," above, for more, and Chapter 5 on firing and terminations.)

Unless your employee manual specifies a probationary period, new employees are permanent from the first day of work. There is no "automatic" or legally required employment probation. A better idea: Create an at-will relationship and do not specify a trial or probationary period. If an employee is not working out—at any point—let that person go. ●

Salaries and Benefits

What Is Compensation?	57
Laws You'll Need to Know	58
Fair Labor Standards Act (FLSA)	58
Antidiscrimination Laws	58
Government Contracts	59
State and Local Laws	59
Legal Limits on Nonprofit Compensation for Top Executives	60
Setting Salary Ranges and Individual Salaries	62
Establishing Salary Ranges	63
Establishing Individual Salaries	66
Annual Salary Adjustments	66
Looking at the Big Picture: Overall Compensation Analysis	67
Analyzing Salary Ranges and Salaries	68
Benchmarking Your Salaries	69
Don't Forget Internal Equity	72
Incentive Pay in Nonprofits	73
Salary Increases	73
Bonuses for Individuals	73
Commissions for Fundraising	75
Cost of Living Adjustments (COLA)	77
Classifying Your Employees: Who Gets Overtime or Benefits?	77
Exempt or Nonexempt? The Rules for Classifying Employees	79
Calculating Overtime Pay	81
Employees or Independent Contractors?	81

Minimum Wages and Exceptions..82

Federal and State Minimum Wages...82

Living Wage Laws...82

Exceptions to Minimum Wage Laws...83

Rest Breaks and Travel Time...85

Rest Breaks 85

Travel 85

Benefits: Compensation Beyond Wages...86

Payroll Taxes 88

Health Insurance 91

Employee Assistance Programs...93

Cafeteria Plans 94

Dental Benefits..95

Vision Care 95

Health Savings Accounts (HSAs) 95

Life Insurance 96

Sick Pay or Paid Time Off (PTO).. 96

Retirement Benefits...98

Education and Training Benefits.. 100

Total Cost of Benefits: The Hidden Paycheck.................................. 101

Noneconomic Benefits 102

Flex Time 102

Alternative Work Weeks.. 103

Telecommuting or Teleworking... 103

Comp Time 104

Job Sharing.. 105

Discounts and Perks.. 105

Administering Your Benefits Plan 106

Meet Your Adviser

Daphne Logan, BA, SPHR
Title: Senior VP of Human Resources
Organization: Feeding America
Location: Chicago, Illinois

What she does: "I am responsible for the people strategy of Feeding America and all that encompasses: identifying talent, retaining talent, making talent successful, making sure that our people strategy and our organizational business strategy are aligned." Daphne manages a staff of 12 with responsibilities for HR as well as organizational knowledge and learning, and the Feeding America University.

What her organization does: Our mission is to feed America's hungry through a nationwide network of 200 member food banks, and engage our country in the fight to end hunger. Feeding America brings two billion pounds of food and grocery products each year to its mission.

Best tip for HR managers including the Accidental HR manager: Three tips: (a) It's okay to say you don't know; (b) Don't set a precedent if you don't have to; (c) Keep your policy manual to what you need to have in it, rather than everything you might want in it. You don't want the whole kitchen. Get it reviewed by an attorney.

HR lesson you learned the hard way: Presuming that we knew what staff wanted without asking them enough questions. Whether it's a policy or a type of health care provision, you have to engage the staff in being part of the solution. As an advocate for staff, you have to make sure you've found out what changes they want.

Song title that speaks to you about HR: I love to dance so I'd have to say, "Keep on Dancing."

I n some cases, the posted salary for a job opening is the first thing a jobseeker notices, with responses ranging from "Wow!" to "Hmm." Surprisingly, however, the compensation package—that is, the salary plus benefits—is rarely an applicant's deciding factor when it comes time to decide whether or not to take a job. Nevertheless, compensation is important, and anyone looking for a job is likely to view the salary and benefits you offer as an indicator of how your organization is faring financially, and how well it values its staff. And of course, compensation is important in retaining employees and keeping them satisfied with their jobs.

For many nonprofits, compensation represents 75% or more of the annual budget, another reason why compensation must be viewed as an organizational financial and strategic matter, not just a decision to be made about an individual.

In many organizations, figuring out how to set salaries and benefits can be fraught with issues—from sticking to any budgets in grant proposals to dealing with compensation set years ago and now out of line with current salaries. It's easy to get tied up in knots when trying to figure out what to pay people. But with a thorough understanding of what's involved and an analysis of your organization's strategies, values, and overall budget, the process will make it easier to manage.

This chapter will help you weigh the tangibles and intangibles that come into play when making decisions about how to compensate nonprofit staff members. It begins with an overview of the laws nonprofits need to know when determining salaries and benefits. Then we look at how to establish salary ranges for various positions and how to make sure the salaries you pay fit into your overall organization structure. We also examine benefits and nonfinancial compensation, such as compensatory time and flextime.

Because executive director compensation is uniquely established by the board of directors, we discuss it separately in Chapter 8.

What Is Compensation?

Salary is the key element of compensation and is often what people think of when they hear the term "compensation." However, there is more to compensation than just salary or wages. For HR purposes, compensation includes:

- base salary or wages
- pay increases
- bonuses and commissions, if any
- benefits, such as vacation, health insurance, and retirement, and
- nonfinancial benefits, such as flexible hours.

All of these taken together can be described as total compensation, and it is this bundle—not just salary—that individual staff consider and that organizational policymakers will take into account in their deliberations.

Nonprofits typically have multiple objectives when it comes to compensation. Sometimes these goals may even conflict with each other. Your compensation goals might include:

- staying within the organization's overall budget
- attracting the best talent
- retaining and motivating the best employees, and
- maintaining the desired degree of compensation equity across the staff.

You will need to address these competing objectives and come up with a strategic balance. This typically requires involvement of top management and perhaps the board.

TIP

There's no preestablished formula for setting salaries and compensation. Keep in mind this thought from Daphne Logan, Senior VP for Human Resources at Feeding America: "Compensation isn't science and it isn't an art. It's about looking at the science, and then making an artful judgment."

Laws You'll Need to Know

A wide variety of laws—federal, state, and local—govern the employer-employee relationship, including salaries and compensation. This is a complicated area and this book provides only an overview of some of the key laws and basic principles. For more information, see *The Manager's Legal Handbook*, by Amy DelPo and Lisa Guerin (Nolo). You can also refer to the U.S. Department of Labor's website at www.dol.gov and your state department of labor or department of employment's website for employment laws and information.

CAUTION
Do you have employees working abroad? Make sure you comply with foreign labor laws. Nonprofits with employees working in other countries often find it easier to find a partnering organization in the foreign country and to add employees to the foreign entity's payroll. That way, the other entity is responsible for complying with the local labor and tax laws and you simply reimburse it for compensation and related expenses.

Fair Labor Standards Act (FLSA)

First enacted in 1938, the Fair Labor Standards Act ("FLSA") is still the primary federal law governing wages and hours. The FLSA sets the federal minimum wage, establishes rules for overtime pay, and requires employers to keep records on the hours and pay of their employees. The FLSA doesn't apply to certain categories of workers—notably, independent contractors. Later in this chapter, we go over these exceptions in more detail.

Antidiscrimination Laws

There are several federal laws—some written as amendments to FLSA—that prohibit various types of discrimination in hiring, promotions, and compensation. These laws are overseen and enforced by the Equal

Employment Opportunity Commission (EEOC) and include the following:

- **Equal Pay Act of 1963.** Prohibits unequal payments or benefits for men and women doing "substantially" the same job. There are some exceptions, such as for seniority and productivity.
- **Civil Rights Act of 1964.** Prohibits wage discrimination on the basis of race, sex, color, religion, or national origin.
- **Age Discrimination in Employment Act of 1967.** Bans discrimination based on age against those 40 years old or older.
- **Americans with Disabilities Act (ADA) of 1990.** Prohibits discrimination against qualified workers with disabilities.

Government Contracts

Federal laws regulate wages and hours for employees who are paid as part of a federal contract or subcontract. Some state and local governments also have rules that apply to any entity that contracts with them. So, if your nonprofit has a contract with—or grant from—a governmental agency or entity, there may be additional federal, state, or local employment laws that you need to comply with. For example, under the federal Walsh-Healy Public Contracts Act, different minimum wage and overtime rules apply to employees paid on a government contract involving $10,000 or more. Other laws apply in other situations—for example, some municipalities require nonprofit employers with city government contracts to provide employees with certain benefits.

If you receive a grant from, or enter into a contract with, a governmental agency, you will be assigned a contract officer. This person can help you figure out whether any special employment rules come with the government contract or grant.

State and Local Laws

Some cities and localities have their own laws governing employment issues. Often these laws mirror federal or state antidiscrimination and equal pay laws, but in some cases, local laws go further than federal or state law. For example, some cities and counties have antidiscrimination rules prohibiting discrimination based on sexual orientation or marital status—categories not protected by federal law. Or, a city might have a living wage ordinance that requires employers to pay more than the federal or state minimum wage. Local laws sometimes apply to smaller employers or in other situations where federal and state law would not apply. To find out about local laws in your area, check with your contract officer if you have a government contract or city government officials, such as the city attorney's office.

Legal Limits on Nonprofit Compensation for Top Executives

At the top executive level, nonprofits are subject to greater scrutiny over compensation than for-profit businesses. Federal law prohibits nonprofits from awarding "excessive compensation" to top management employees. Nonprofits are required to pay "reasonable compensation," which is defined as "an amount as would ordinarily be paid for like services by like enterprises under like circumstances." If a nonprofit is found to have entered into an excess benefit transaction with an employee who is in a "position to exercise substantial influence" over the affairs of the nonprofit, both the nonprofit and the individual can be subject to harsh taxes and penalties. In short, the law's intent is to keep your top managers from awarding unreasonably high compensation to themselves.

In recent years, there have been a few highly publicized cases of nonprofits that have paid enormous salaries to their executive directors. In one Texas case, the president of a nonprofit foundation paid himself a salary of $975,000—while the foundation itself gave away a mere $1 million a year. Unfortunately, a few cases like this have created exaggerated fears in nonprofits about excess compensation charges, even when they are paying reasonable and modest salaries to their senior management.

It's not difficult to make sure that the salaries of your top executives are "reasonable." First, do a small salary survey and compare the salaries of your senior staff or most highly paid employees to salaries of people in comparable positions. One place to get such data is Guidestar.org, a nonprofit website that posts copies of Form 990s and Form 990-EZs.

These are mandatory annual financial reports filed by nonprofits, and they contain compensation information for each organization's most highly paid people. Look in the 990 Part VII, titled "Compensation of Officers, Directors, Trustees, Key Employees, Highest Compensated Employees, and Independent Contractors." You can also find local, state, and national nonprofit compensation studies from a variety of nonprofit and for-profit companies, such as Opportunity Knocks and Abbott Langer.

The board of directors should review and approve the compensation for your executive director and any other employees hired directly by the board (such as the artistic director in an arts organization). If the executive director or any relative of the executive director is on the board, exclude that person from the discussion and the vote on the executive director's salary. If you are concerned about salary levels for other senior staff, have those reviewed and approved by the board as well. Be sure to keep records of the comparability data relied on by the board.

> **EXAMPLE:** Starbound Girls Academy, a nonprofit elementary school, found an exciting candidate they wanted to hire as their new head of school. The candidate wanted the Academy to match her corporate salary of $120,000, which was $40,000 more than the departing head's salary. Some board members worried that the $120,000 salary would trigger excess compensation problems. The board checked the salaries of other school heads in the area and public school principals and found that the comparable salaries were approximately $115,000. For budget-related reasons, they decided they didn't want to match her $120,000 salary, but they were not worried about excess compensation rules after their comparative salary review.

If you don't feel comfortable relying on your own comparability research, you can hire independent executive compensation consultants or an attorney to do a more extensive analysis for you. Your local regional grantmaker association or United Way should have information on compensation consultants or law firms that perform such work for nonprofit clients. Compensation consultants almost always determine that the proposed salary is reasonable. Because of this, depending on your point of view, they either perform a valuable service or provide cover for inappropriate compensation.

CAUTION

Check your state law for rules on nonprofit executive compensation. A few states require nonprofits over a certain size to have compensation for their chief executive officer and chief financial officer approved by the board. Some of these laws were passed in the wake of the Sarbanes-Oxley Act, which was created to promote greater accountability and protection for investors in the for-profit world. For instance, California's Nonprofit Integrity Act requires board approval of CEO and CFO compensation for nonprofits with $2 million or more in nongovernmental revenue. Check with your state's charity office; links to all 50 state charity offices can be found at www.nasconet.org/agencies.

RESOURCE

Want to know more about excess benefits and compensation? You can read the full IRS language on excess compensation in the instructions for IRS Form 990 (available on the IRS website at www.irs.gov). For more information on the topic in general, see *Every Nonprofit's Tax Guide*, by Stephen Fishman (Nolo). Also see Chapter 8 for more on executive director compensation.

Setting Salary Ranges and Individual Salaries

You should establish a salary range for every position in your organization. For example, a legal services nonprofit might have a $65,000 to $140,000 salary range for attorneys and a $35,000 to $42,000 salary range for administrative support staff. You then set individual salaries within these ranges, depending on experience, responsibility, and so on. You'll want to set salary ranges and individual salaries that will help you:

- attract top talent to your organization
- retain and motivate the best employees, and
- establish internal equity within your nonprofit.

Establishing Salary Ranges

Salary ranges help managers keep salaries within the boundaries of what the organization can afford and appropriate relative to other positions in the organization. They also help grantwriting staff propose appropriate salaries in grant proposals and guide managers who need to keep salaries consistent with the organization's overall budget, strategies, and priorities. Yet many nonprofits don't get around to establishing salary ranges until a position is vacant and they need a range as part of the hiring process.

Whether you are creating a range for the first time or adjusting ranges across the board, you should address each of the following items:

Factors in Establishing a Salary Range

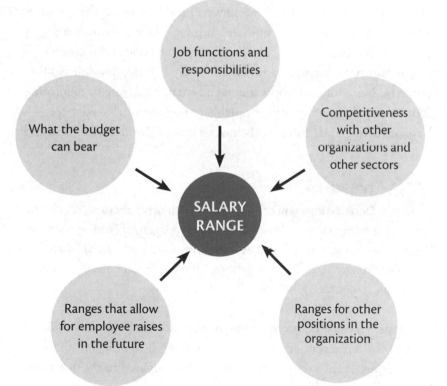

Job functions and responsibilities. When establishing the salary for a particular job, start by listing and analyzing the key functions of the job, based on the job description. This helps establish where the job fits within your organizational pay structure. It also provides a reference point for looking at compensation for comparable positions in other nonprofits, government, or businesses. For example, look at the salary range for an elder abuse victim advocate and compare that to the salary range for an elder abuse victim case manager. Do the salary ranges appropriately reflect the differing levels of responsibility?

Competitiveness. Although compensation is just one aspect of the job as you compete for talent with other nonprofits, companies, and government, it's a crucial one. Ideally, you will want to establish salaries in line with or above what comparable jobs pay in other nonprofits, and perhaps in for-profit companies or government if that's where your staff is most likely to come from. Find comparable salaries through local and national surveys. Or, as discussed above, check Guidestar, the nonprofit information website at www.guidestar.org for salary information on top paid staff. You can also call your local nonprofit association, United Way, or community foundation to find other salary information sources for your area. Nonprofit networks such as affordable housing or mentoring often make salary information available to their members. Also see, "Benchmarking Your Salaries," below for more information on this topic.

TIP

Don't assume you can't compete with other sectors. "It helps to have people from all sectors," says adviser Daphne Logan of Feeding America. "We have been able to recruit people from other food banks, from other nonprofits, from technology, from finance, from food sourcers, and commercial food supply chains."

Ranges for other positions within the organization. "Internal equity" refers to the fairness of one job's salary compared to others in the organization. Is the salary range reasonable compared to those for both higher and lower-paid positions?

Ranges that leave room for raises. Salary ranges should be broad enough to allow for raises as individuals improve in their jobs. For example, a range for a particular position of $24,000–$32,000 allows a new hire at the bottom of the range to see that there is opportunity to earn more while still at the same job.

MYTH #1

Nonprofits Don't Pay Well

One the biggest myths about nonprofits and salaries is that nonprofits pay almost nothing, and certainly far below what other sectors pay.

Actually, nonprofits frequently pay more than the for-profit sector for administrative support staff and lower-level positions. And although the data is sparse, it appears that nonprofit wages for top staff are comparable to small businesses of the same size if the owner's equity or debt isn't taken into account. In terms of benefits, a nonprofit with fewer than 20 employees is five times more likely than small businesses of the same size to offer health benefits.

MYTH #2

Nonprofit CEO Salaries Are Exorbitant

Ironically, another widely held belief is that nonprofits pay exorbitant salaries, way above what people make in for-profit companies.

Exorbitant salaries are so rare that when they are discovered—typically at salaries of around $1 million—they often make the news. In fact, the average CEO salary for large nonprofits with $50 million or more in assets is approximately $300,000, about half the salary of an average law firm partner.

Establishing Individual Salaries

When it's time for managers to determine salaries for individual positions, the task will be made considerably easier by the ranges you've already set. Many of the objectives discussed above for setting salary ranges will be relevant, namely job functions and responsibilities, the organization's ability to attract and retain good candidates, a comparison to other salaries in the organization, and the amount the budget can bear. In addition, whether negotiating a salary with a new hire or considering a raise for a current employee, a manager will also have to consider the circumstances of an individual candidate or employee. For example, if you have a salary range of $40,000 to $65,000, you might discuss a salary in the lower end of $40,000 to $50,000 with a relatively inexperienced candidate.

In some instances, a salary may be based on what was established in a government contract or grant. For instance, the county department on aging might have set salaries for cooks at senior meal sites at $21 per hour. When salaries are determined by outside funders, you can find yourself with a salary monkey wrench in your system, with a particular group of people being paid significantly more than other staff in comparable positions. If you can't afford to raise all salaries to where the funded positions fit in, find ways to discuss the differences with staff.

With current staff, don't make the mistake of using a salary raise as a reward for past performance. This might be tempting, but salaries should be established for future performance, not as payment for past work well done. Of course, the best indicator of what an employee will do in the future is what they have done up until now. But salaries are about what an employee will do, not what they have done.

Annual Salary Adjustments

Most nonprofits hold annual performance review discussions toward the end of the fiscal year to coincide with the development of the budget for the coming year. If your organization's fiscal year ends on December 31, the sequence of budget and salary adjustments might look something like this:

October 1: Review preliminary budget to figure out whether overall salary expense for current employees can be increased by a certain percentage for the next fiscal year.

October 1: Hold training session for supervisors on conducting performance reviews and salary discussions.

October 5: Issue performance review forms and guidelines to all staff.

October 6-25: All performance reviews conducted.

October 27: Supervisors submit recommendations on raises or other employee changes (such as changes in hours).

November 5: HR staff and senior management review supervisor recommendations for alignment with salary ranges, fairness across departments, and total expenses for upcoming year. Make changes as appropriate.

November 6-15: Supervisors go back to staff with salary changes. In each case, both the supervisor and employee sign an acknowledgment of the performance review and salary for following year.

November 10: Board approves budget for coming year.

November 15-30: Executive director reviews and signs all performance reviews and salary change forms.

January 1: New salaries go into effect.

Looking at the Big Picture: Overall Compensation Analysis

As discussed earlier, it's worth having your organization's managers devote some attention to how each new hire's salary fits into your larger compensation picture. The thinking process itself will help engage top managers in issues of internal equity and whether salaries are adequately benchmarked against the market. This analysis also provides a foundation of data for developing a compensation strategy.

Analyzing Salary Ranges and Salaries

Let's look at a simplified example of how an environmental research organization might break down its salary categories:

Senior executive. Members of the management team and department heads. Salary range $55,000 to $110,000.

Senior scientist. Principal investigators who bring in and direct major research projects. Salary range $60,000 to $135,000.

Project manager. Manages a smaller-scale scientific project or administrative area of responsibility, or has substantial responsibilities under a senior scientist or senior executive. Salary range $40,000 to $60,000.

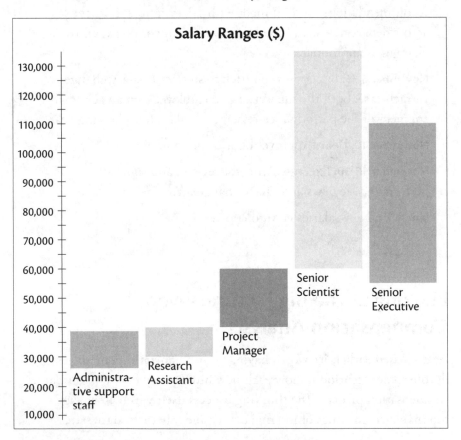

Research assistants. Salary range $30,000 to 40,000.

Administrative staff. Support staff. Salary range $26,000 to $39,000.

This organization shows wide ranges for senior scientists, especially compared with the ranges for administrative support staff. This sensibly reflects a wide potential range of skill and experience level for the position, as well as the size of the projects that might be brought in and managed by the person.

For each range you establish (particularly with wide ranges), you should identify the assumptions and variations that would underlie paying at the high, low, or middle end of the salary range.

Benchmarking Your Salaries

To begin a benchmarking process, choose a few positions in your organization that you can compare to those within other organizations of your type and size. In an environmental research firm, these might be the executive director position, a senior research biologist, a research assistant, and the office manager. Then find environmental organizations with similar revenue and compare their salaries to yours. For some positions, such as the senior scientist, it may also be useful to benchmark that salary against similar positions in state and local governments. You also want to take into account your geographic location in choosing what organizations to use as benchmarks. Try to identify areas with similar costs of living (or at least take cost of living into account when making your comparison). Don't expect salaries in Des Moines to match those in New York City, even if staff in both places does similar work.

Below is the same chart as the one above, with the median salaries for the benchmark position shown with the "B".

Charting like this allows you to analyze your organization's competitiveness in attracting new recruits. This chart shows that the organization is highly competitive for the senior executive, project or department manager, and support staff positions, but less competitive for the senior scientists and for research assistant positions. There could be many reasons for these discrepancies, including the level of scientific work required of the senior scientists or the type of research expected of

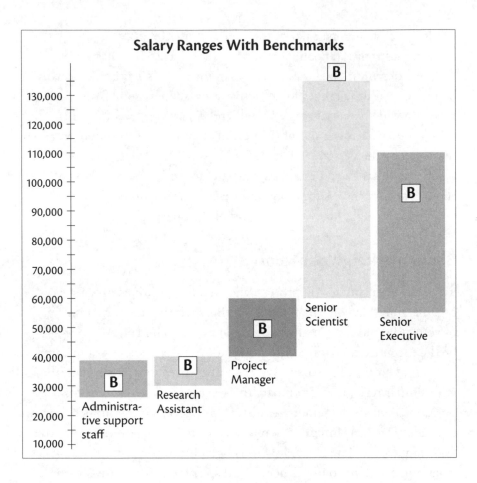

research assistants. But it may also be that this organization has simply fallen behind on salaries. Doing a chart like this allows you to get a snapshot of where you are; and then you can dig in and do the analysis you need based on your initial findings.

You can also chart the salaries of employees in your organization, as shown in the following chart. The benchmark salary information has been removed from this chart; these are just the salary ranges for positions and the actual salaries paid in each category.

In this example, there are two people who are paid above salary range: one research assistant and one administrative support staff. If you spot some oddities like this on your own chart, you'll want to take a

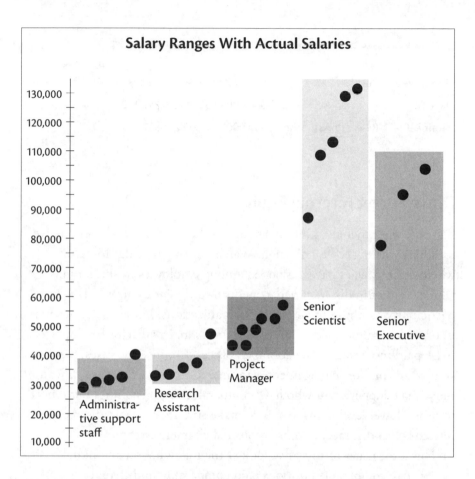

closer look at the particulars. For example, were these salaries approved by management, and if so, on what basis? In the example, the salaries for administrative support staff are bumping up toward the top of the range. Again, you would want to find out why. Is it because the people in those jobs have a lot of tenure? You'd probably want to think about whether that range needs to be raised or whether you need to let some support staff know that they are reaching the top of the range so that they have realistic expectations about their future salary growth.

Management team members will appreciate salary data presented this way rather than in a more typical salary schedule. Supervisors also will appreciate knowing where a given employee fits in the range for a given position. You can prepare individual salary information as follows:

Current Salary Positions Within Ranges				
Employee	Position	Salary Range	Salary	Position Within Range
Jack D.	Research Assistant	$30,000 - $50,000	$41,000	55%
Bonnie C.	Research Assistant	$30,000 - $50,000	$51,000	102%

Don't Forget Internal Equity

You will want to look at internal equity—the fairness of salaries relative to others within the organization. Watch out in particular for cases where discrepancies have developed among employees in similar jobs who are either in different departments in different locations. This is particularly common in larger-sized organizations. For example, it's not unusual for staff located at an organization's main office or headquarters to be paid more than those at branch offices. Or, in some cases, support staff who work for management team members may be paid significantly more than support staff who have comparable responsibilities but report to other, lower-level managers. Also make sure there are no discrepancies related to gender, race, or other protected characteristics.

To check for issues in this area, look at the following on an annual basis:

- Are comparable positions paid comparably in different departments?
- Are comparable positions paid comparably in different locations?
- Are women and men in comparable positions paid comparably?
- Are people with different race and national backgrounds in comparable positions paid comparably?
- Are support staff who report to management team members paid comparably to support staff who have similar levels of responsibility but report to supervisors who are not on the management team?

Incentive Pay in Nonprofits

In the for-profit world, a business that has a very profitable year can decide to share those profits with employees by paying bonuses at year end. In the nonprofit world, profits cannot be distributed to employees. All of the profits—"surpluses" in nonprofit language—must be kept by the nonprofit to use in furtherance of the organization's mission.

This doesn't mean that employees can't benefit from the nonprofit's financial success or from exceptional individual performance. Among the possibilities are salary increases, bonuses that meet certain narrow criteria, and commissions for fundraisers.

Salary Increases

The most common way for nonprofits to recognize strong performance or to reflect a better financial picture is to raise salaries for the upcoming year. Of course, this means that an employee must stay through the next year to reap those rewards. And such raises will make it harder to lower salaries later, if the source of the surplus (such as a one-year corporate grant) dries up.

Bonuses for Individuals

Under certain specified conditions, nonprofits can give bonuses to employees. To pass muster, any bonuses must be clearly spelled out in advance against objective (rather than subjective) benchmarks and established in dollar amounts rather than as a percentage of surplus or revenue. Your bonus criteria should include mission-related factors (such as number of people served) in addition to financial performance considerations (such as net income for the year). Here are some examples of bonus criteria that nonprofits have come up with, and our critique:

- "The development director will be eligible for a bonus at the end of the fiscal year based on performance."

  Not permissible. No objective benchmarks or criteria to measure performance.

- "If the organization finishes the fiscal year with a $50,000 or more surplus, the executive director will be awarded a bonus of 12% of the surplus."

  Not permissible. Bonus can't be based on a percentage of surplus.

- "If unrestricted cash gifts received from individuals are $350,000 or more during the fiscal year, the organization has a surplus of $100,000 or more for the year on an accrued basis (but prior to payment of the following), and goals for numbers of new major donors engaged are met, then the development director will be awarded a payment of $45,000 upon completion of the audit for the year."

  Permissible. Bonus based on objective benchmarks and stated as a dollar amount.

In addition, modest "spot bonuses—which are more like gifts—are permissible. For example, if an office manager has worked especially hard and well through an office relocation, or a social worker has solicited a substantial corporate grant outside of job duties, it might be appropriate to give each a $100 gift certificate in recognition.

If you decide to offer incentive pay, consider it carefully and make sure it falls within the permissible guidelines. Have your management team and board of directors review and approve any bonuses you give.

> EXAMPLE: The Emerald City Food Bank has more than 100 employees, and recently started an incentive pay program for all employees. If the food bank meets its targets for food and for funds, the incentive program is activated. Incentives are likely to amount to 1% to 5% of an employee's salary. Senior managers have had incentive pay for several years, with specific metrics and awards determined ahead of time. Bonuses are established as dollar amounts, but can reach up to 25% of a senior manager's salary. In addition, the senior management team can give awards of $5,000 to a group that has made an extraordinary contribution during the previous quarter. "An incentive pay plan takes constant monitoring and tweaking," commented the director of HR.

Commissions for Fundraising

Few nonprofits pay "straight commissions," that is, commissions to individuals based on sales only, without any salary. However, in a few nonprofit jobs—such as telephone fundraising or street canvassing—it's not uncommon to find wages combined with a commission. For example, an animal rescue nonprofit might pay a canvasser hired to seek donations $10 per hour, with a commission of $50 for every three donations obtained. Some nonprofits (and others) pay commissions for gathering signatures on petitions and initiatives, such as $1 per signature.

Commissions can be a risky business for employers. For one thing, minimum wage laws still apply to these employees, regardless of how much they earn in salary and how much in commission. So, regardless of how employees are paid, their total pay per hour must be at least equal to the applicable minimum wage—federal, state, or local. Also, although the commissions are intended to motivate employees, they can also tempt employees to be overbearing, make untrue claims to prospects, or falsify records. A better choice may be to pay a higher salary without any commission or recruit true volunteers who can then use the compelling pitch, "I'm a volunteer."

Some nonprofits contract with firms to conduct street canvassing, telephone fundraising, and other appeals on behalf of the nonprofit or its cause. Although doing so has certain advantages—for one thing, it can shield your nonprofit from the legalities of how that firm manages its employees—you should still make sure the employment practices of any firm you contract with are in line with your organization's values.

CAUTION

Laws are changing on "pay-per-signature." Some nonprofits (and for-profits) employ people to gather legal signatures on ballot propositions, recall efforts, petitions to legislators, and other documents where legally verifiable signatures are part of the political process. A few states have banned "pay per signature" compensation, and in at least one state such a ban has been passed but was then declared unconstitutional. Ballotpedia.org maintains current information; type "pay-per-signature" in the search box.

Commissions Are Controversial

Some in the nonprofit world don't think either staff or independent contractor fundraisers should ever be paid commissions. The Association of Fundraising Professionals (AFP) states in its Code of Ethics: "Members shall not accept compensation or enter into a contract that is based on a percentage of contributions; nor shall members accept finder's fees or contingent fees." Why this guideline? Because someone hired to fundraise might be tempted to sway a donor away from a pledge of $5 million over five years to an immediate $2 million cash gift because the fundraiser would receive a higher commission for the lower cash gift. As a result, commissions have gotten a bad rap in nonprofit circles, even though this type of situation would probably not arise outside the largest nonprofits, such as universities, hospitals, or foundations.

There are instances when commissions can make sense, such as with door-to-door fundraisers or if an organization wants to attract and keep a highly successful fundraiser but doesn't want to pay that person a salary that would dwarf other salaries in the organization.

Because of these complex issues, a good practice is to have any commission arrangements for employees or independent contractors discussed by your upper management and even approved by the board of directors, if appropriate.

CAUTION

Funders and constituents may not like having their funds used to pay commissions. Most government contracts and many foundation grants do not allow money paid by them to be used for a bonus, commission, or finding fee for the writing or solicitation of the contract or grant. Donors and volunteers also may frown on bonuses or commissions for fundraising—or even on the discovery that the person calling them isn't actually a part of the organization's internal staff—even if all the legalities are in place.

Cost of Living Adjustments (COLA)

The term COLA actually has two meanings. In some national and international nonprofits, a cost of living adjustment or allowance is for employees who live in areas with high costs of living. For example, an Idaho-based nonprofit that opens an office in New York City may adjust its New York salaries upward to compensate for the higher cost of living in New York. However, in the nonprofit sector, COLA more commonly means an across-the-board increase in pay due to inflation. In some contexts, notably Social Security benefits and wages under certain government contracts, salaries are raised by the amount that the Consumer Price Index has gone up. For example, if inflation was 3% over the past year, employees might expect to receive 3% increases.

COLAs were popular in the 1970s when inflation was high, but their use has declined sharply since then. One reason is that no one is willing to accept a pay decrease when the cost of living goes down. Other problematic issues with COLAs are that they benefit higher-paid staff more than lower-paid staff and make it more difficult to give raises based on merit or performance. Despite myths to the contrary, COLAs are neither common nor required in nonprofits.

Classifying Your Employees: Who Gets Overtime or Benefits?

How many hours do you expect your staff to work each day or week? Before coming to any conclusions, you'll first need to understand the distinction between exempt and nonexempt employees. Employees classified as exempt are not entitled to overtime pursuant to the Fair Labor Standards Act (FLSA) and related laws, while those classified as nonexempt are. Nonexempt employees must be paid 1½ times their regular pay for time worked over 40 hours per week. So, a nonexempt employee who earns $10 per hour is entitled to $15 per hour for each hour worked over 40 hours in a week. In some states, overtime is calculated on a daily basis and includes any time worked over eight hours in one day. Exempt employees are not subject to these rules.

The law in this area is difficult to navigate because there is no simple rule for deciding whether to classify an employee as exempt or nonexempt. However, it is important that you handle this HR function correctly, because the penalties for misclassification are severe. According to the Nonprofits Insurance Alliance Group, a national nonprofit insurer, two of the three most common liability problems for nonprofits are related to classification—namely, misclassification of exempt and nonexempt employees and misclassification of employees versus contractors.

TIP

Volunteers and independent contractors do not need to be classified. Neither of these groups of workers—volunteers and independent contractors—are considered employees, so they don't have to be classified and are not subject to FLSA overtime rules.

MYTH

If Someone Agrees to Exempt Status, It's Okay to Classify Them as Exempt

Some nonprofit managers want to classify a position as exempt because the person goes to meetings at night or works extra hours and they don't want to pay overtime. Or they might think the employee wants the status of being exempt.

There's a widespread misconception that if an employee agrees to be exempt, it's legal to classify them as exempt.

A person with new HR responsibilities can't assume that just because someone's been classified one way for years, that it's okay. And jobs change over time. Call an HR consultant or attorney if you have a question in your mind about classification; better to do it right than face a lawsuit.

Nonprofits often fail to pay adequate attention to classification. One reason is that a "we're a team" spirit can make people reluctant to divide the staff into "professional" and "nonprofessional" workers. And proper classification isn't easy; rather than a single factor driving classification, you'll need to look at a number of factors and make a judgment based on all the pertinent information. Be sure that someone in the organization takes the time to learn the rules, pays attention to classification, and revisits decisions periodically.

Exempt or Nonexempt? The Rules for Classifying Employees

An employee's classification will usually depend upon the type of work the person does and how the person is paid. Exempt employees are generally professional, executive, or administrative staff who are paid salaries. They are expected to accomplish their work to a professional standard as opposed to working a certain number of hours. A nonexempt employee, on the other hand, is usually paid an hourly wage. And, employees who make less than $455 per week ($23,660 per year) are always nonexempt.

In practice, these rules can get confusing. For example, an executive director who earns $22,000 (below the threshold) is nonexempt and must be paid overtime, even though the position is salaried and considered "professional." On the other hand, not all employees who are paid $455 or more per week ($23,660 per year) are exempt. To qualify as exempt, the employee must perform a certain type of work—generally, work that requires an advanced degree, is managerial or supervisory in nature, or requires the employee to make relatively high-level business decisions.

Here are the basic requirements for the administrative, executive, and professional exemptions:

- An administrative employee must perform office or other nonmanual work that is directly related to the management or business operations of the organization or its beneficiaries, and must exercise discretion and independent judgment regarding significant issues.

- An executive employee's primary duty must be managing the employer's enterprise or a recognized department of that enterprise; the employee must regularly supervise at least two full-time employees (or the equivalent) and must have the authority to hire and fire or have significant input into hiring and firing decisions.
- A professional employee's primary duty must either be performing work that requires advanced knowledge in the field of science or learning, of a type that is usually attained through an advanced course of study; or performing work that requires invention, imagination, originality, or talent in a recognized creative or artistic field.

Exempt or Nonexempt Employee Status

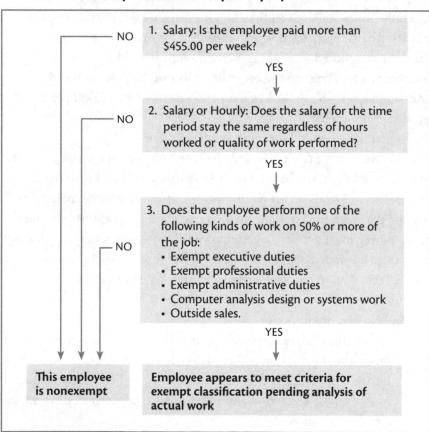

EXAMPLE: A 25-staff nonprofit classified the office manager as exempt because the work was viewed as "professional." In the same organization, an administrative assistant was classified as nonexempt. The two often worked late together on projects where the administrative assistant earned overtime because of her nonexempt status but the manager did not. Although the office manager had a higher salary and was considered a higher-level employee, the administrative assistant was earning more with overtime. The office manager asked for a classification review and her position was reclassified to nonexempt because it was found that while her job included some work that would have deemed "professional" under the regulations, this type of work was not her primary duty.

Calculating Overtime Pay

You must pay your nonexempt employees overtime at the rate of time and one-half for any time over 40 hours per week. For example, if you have a nonexempt employee who is paid at least $22 per hour and works 43 hours in a week, you will have to pay that worker for the extra three hours at $33 per hour. If you have a different workweek than 40 hours (such as 37.5 hours), overtime still starts with the 41st hour. See "Classifying Your Employees: Who Gets Overtime or Benefits?" above, for more on nonexempt employees and overtime rules.

Consider establishing a policy that requires written approval, in advance, for overtime work. Too often, nonprofits discover after the fact that their nonexempt staff has been routinely putting in a couple of extra hours a week and getting paid at overtime rates when their supervisors weren't even aware of it.

Employees or Independent Contractors?

Another key classification issue is making sure that anyone you hire is properly classified as either an employee or independent contractor. In a nutshell, employees are on payroll, are eligible for benefits including unemployment benefits, and must be managed in line with federal, state, and local labor laws. In contrast, independent contractors—including consultants—are people with separate businesses with which your nonprofit contracts. Independent contractors are not on payroll, are not eligible for benefits, and are not subject to most employment laws. That makes it very tempting for employers of all kinds to classify people as independent contractors. But beware: If you are paying people as independent contractors whom a government agency later determines should have been classified as employees, your nonprofit can be subject to severe fines and penalties.

See Chapter 7 for more on independent contractors.

Minimum Wages and Exceptions

Although many nonprofits pay everyone well over minimum wage, it's important to understand minimum wage laws and make sure you comply with them. There are also some important exceptions you should be aware of that are relevant to nonprofit work.

Federal and State Minimum Wages

The minimum wage is established by the federal government, and applies to both hourly and salaried employees. States can also establish minimum wage guidelines that are higher than the federal standard. About one third of the states have minimum wages above the federal rate. The Department of Labor (www.dol.gov) maintains a list of current minimum wage rates in all states. If an employee is paid a salary by the week or month, the total pay divided by the total hours must be the minimum wage or higher.

Living Wage Laws

Some states and local governments have established living wage ordinances that may be applicable to all employers, certain types of employers, or, in some cases, just to those employers with government contracts. Living wage rates are calculated city by city, take a variety of living costs into account, and typically range from $3 to $7 above the federal minimum wage. Check with other nonprofits and city officials to see whether such laws have been enacted in your area.

Exceptions to Minimum Wage Laws

There are some exceptions to minimum wage laws.

Younger workers. In most states, you can pay employees 20 years old or younger at a lower rate for the first 90 days of their employment. These laws were designed to allow employers to create low-paying summer jobs for students, and often make it possible for nonprofits to hire young constituents or other young people for summer projects. Be sure to check your state and local laws before paying a younger worker at a rate below the minimum wage.

Employees with disabilities. Under federal law, you can pay employees with disabilities at less than minimum wage under certain circumstances, such as in sheltered workshops operated to employ people with disabilities. In most instances, an employer must obtain a waiver of minimum wages at both federal and state levels before paying disabled workers below minimum wage. Unless you have a large number of workers with disabilities whom you want to pay below minimum wage, it makes sense to simply pay minimum wage or higher.

Stipended volunteers. Minimum wage laws do not apply to government-sponsored stipended positions, such as AmeriCorps VISTAs and people serving as foster grandparents through the Corporation for National and Community Service. For more on paying stipends to volunteers, see Chapter 6.

Interns. The term "intern" is widely used and widely misunderstood, particularly as it relates to minimum wage laws. You can pay an intern below minimum wage—such as a stipend of $2,000 for a summer's work—provided all six of the following criteria are met:

- your organization derives no immediate advantage from the intern's activities

- the intern does not displace a regular employee, but instead works under the close observation of an employee
- the intern receives training similar to what would be given in a vocational or academic institution
- the training is for the benefit of the intern (not your organization)
- the intern is not entitled to or promised a job as a result of the internship, and
- the nonprofit and the intern understand that the intern is not entitled to wages for time spent in training.

Although regulations on interns are flouted widely in both the nonprofit and for-profit sectors, pay attention to the rules. If you want to pay someone a small amount of money for a temporary job, it is often better to classify that person as a volunteer who can receive some funds for travel and "enabling" expenses (such as parking passes that enable them to volunteer), rather than as a stipended intern. See Chapter 6 for more information on volunteers.

> **EXAMPLE:** For several years, ArtKids used interns who each worked 20 hours per week over the summer to help with two annual summer projects: a street fair for families and a fundraising luncheon. The interns were college students who did a lot of the logistics: telephoning, mailing, set-up, and staffing for the events. The interns were each paid $1,000 for the summer's work. One intern applied for unemployment after the summer and a state auditor checked up on ArtKids' internship program. The auditor determined that because ArtKids benefitted from the interns' work, the interns were in fact employees who should have been paid at least minimum wage. ArtKids ended up having to pay a fine of $4,000 and owed back pay to the interns for the difference between the stipend and minimum wage.

Staff in residence. Many states allow employees who receive housing and meals as part of their compensation to be paid less than minimum wage. For example, employees who live full time at residences such as halfway houses, homes for children with disabilities, wilderness camps, or assisted living facilities can be paid less than the minimum wage. Talk to similar nonprofits in your area to find out how they calculate room and board and hours worked; your auditor can also help you determine fair rates.

Rest Breaks and Travel Time

Though the rules are sometimes a bit complicated, you will need to take the time to establish clear policies on how often employees can take breaks and how they will be compensated for the time they spend on the road. These policies should be captured in your employee manual and should be well understood by all employees. Otherwise, staff members may push themselves to the point of burnout, or develop resentments over what they see as disparities in the way that break-time and travel rules are applied.

Rest Breaks

You are not required under federal law to provide time off during the workday, although many states have such laws. For instance, some states require employers to give workers a ten-minute paid break for every four hours they work or an unpaid meal break of 30 minutes or more for every four or five hours worked. Even if rest breaks are not mandated by law, providing them regularly and consistently to employees whose job doesn't allow them to get up or move around—such as the front desk in a medical clinic—is a humane and sound practice. Check with your state Department of Labor for relevant regulations. The federal Department of Labor website has links to state and regional Department of Labor offices at www.dol.gov/dol/location.htm. Nolo's website has good information as well (go to www.nolo.com; enter "rest breaks" in the search box).

Travel

You don't need to pay employees for time or expenses related to their regular commute between home and work. However, if a nonexempt employee travels as part of the job, and the time required for that travel extends beyond the time the employee would normally spend at work, you must pay the employee for that time. For example, if a nonexempt employee is required to attend an all-day seminar that adds an extra hour of traveling to his or her normal commute, then you must pay the employee for the additional hour of travel time. There are other special rules that apply to nonexempt employees who are required to travel to another location for work. How these rules apply depends on whether the travel involves an overnight stay. For more information about these rules, see *The Manager's Legal Handbook*, by Amy DelPo and Lisa Guerin (Nolo).

TIP
Develop policies for overseas travel if you send employees abroad.
Nonprofits that do international work often have staff who take long overseas flights and then work long days while they are away. To identify appropriate rules for overseas travel, consult other organizations with employees that have similar employee travel issues. Make sure your employee manual specifies the rules about overtime pay for such trips.

Benefits: Compensation Beyond Wages

A benefit is any type of compensation that is not part of the employee's salary, such as:

- health benefits, such as health insurance, dental, or vision benefits
- retirement benefits, such as contributions to a 401(k) savings plan
- other economic benefits, such as life insurance, long-term disability, or EAPs, and
- noneconomic benefits, such as flexible time.

In addition, employers contribute to payroll taxes, including Social Security and Medicare taxes.

Employers are not required to provide any benefits other than mandatory payroll tax benefits. In fact, only 62% of companies with between three and 199 employees provide health benefits at all and many require employees to cover at least part of the cost.

> **CAUTION**
>
> **Doing meaningful work should not be portrayed as a benefit.** For many nonprofit staffers, the chance to work in a cause and organization they believe in, and to do meaningful work in their professional lives, are crucial reasons why they have taken their jobs. In addition, nonprofit staff members typically want to work in teams, to participate in establishing goals, and to be appreciated by their supervisors and their peers. But these attributes of nonprofit work are not benefits in the same way that health insurance or flextime is a benefit. Instead, working for a worthy cause is more similar to working in a desirable city or in a building near a park: It's a feature that can help recruit staff, but not a substitute for reasonable pay.

For most nonprofits, benefits are a substantial expense, often adding 20% to 35% of total payroll expense to the budget. But attractive benefits are crucial to recruiting and keeping staff, and benefits help staff stay healthy and able to do their best work. In fact, many nonprofits offer better benefits than their for-profit counterparts, in keeping with their social conscience and perhaps in recognition that their salaries are on the low side. Benefits are designed to:

- help employees stay healthy, both physically and emotionally
- assist employees and their families with finances due to death, disability, illness, retirement, or other inability to work
- provide peace of mind to employees who may be worried about catastrophic illness, injury, or other concerns, and
- help employees manage personal responsibilities, such as staying home with a sick child or taking an elderly parent to the dentist.

Managing employee benefits takes time, knowledge, and an approach that is both professional and sympathetic. Networking through your local Society for Human Resource Management (SHRM) or nonprofit association is often the best way to get information. You can find out what nearby nonprofits are offering, with which companies they are contracting, and how to manage the questions and concerns that will arise in any workplace over benefits.

Another resource is HealthCare.gov, a site managed by the U.S. Department of Health and Human Services, where you can find lists of government, nonprofit, and commercial health insurance providers in your area (go to http://finder.healthcare.gov).

If you are adding benefits for the first time or considering additions to an existing benefits package, conduct a survey of your current staff to learn what their priority needs are, which benefits they would be most likely to use, and how much they would be willing to pay. For instance, you may learn that more employees want flex time than you had anticipated, or that more employees want dental insurance than want vision care, but that they won't pay for it unless 80% or more of the cost is paid by the nonprofit.

Payroll Taxes

Managing payroll—including payroll deductions—is complex and time-consuming, and must be done right. As a result, many nonprofits contract with payroll services that manage the paperwork, issue paychecks, pass along withheld taxes to the government, and issue W-2s at the end of the year. Even though a payroll service takes away much of the work and worry, you'll still need to understand the fundamentals of payroll taxes and deductions in order to monitor the service's work.

The term "payroll taxes" refers to two very different types of withholdings from employee paychecks. One part is the withholding of federal and state income taxes that are owed by the employee to the government and which the nonprofit sends on the employee's behalf of. The other comprises taxes the employer must pay from its own pocket.

Social Security: FICA (Federal Insurance Contributions Act). The government requires employers to withhold 6.2% of gross pay from the employee's paycheck and remit it to the government; this amount is nicknamed FICA-EE. (For 2011 only, employee contributions were reduced to 4.2%; check with www.nolo.com to learn whether this provision is extended.) In addition, you must match this amount equally with an employer contribution, nicknamed FICA-ER. (The employer contribution remained at 6.2% for 2011 even though the employee contribution for that year only was reduced to 4.2%.) When an employee's gross pay reaches $106,800 for the year (2011), then both you and the employee can stop making these FICA payments. (The annual ceiling changes each year.)

Medicare tax. You are required to withhold 1.45% of the employee's wages and pay a matching amount. There is no ceiling on this tax.

Federal unemployment tax (FUTA) exemption. Nonprofits that are 501(c)(3) organizations are exempt from paying FUTA. Be sure your payroll service knows this.

State unemployment taxes. These state taxes ("SUTA") are paid only by the employer and go into state funds that provide unemployment benefits. States set their own unemployment tax rates, which many states then adjust for each employer based on the employer's history of unemployment claims.

State disability insurance (SDI). Disability insurance provides partial replacement of wages for workers who cannot work due to an injury or illness that is not job related or is for pregnancy or childbirth. The benefits vary from state to state, but typically employees receive approximately 50% of their wages for anywhere between six months to a year. Five states (California, Hawaii, New Jersey, New York, and, Rhode Island) have mandatory state disability programs, although each has some exemptions. Rates vary state by state. In California, the rate is 1.1% of gross wages up to $90,669 (2010). Note: in some states SDI is paid by the employer, while in others it is paid by the employee.

Workers' compensation insurance. "Workers' comp" pays for medical care and partial replacement of wages for employees who become ill or are injured in the course of their job. Workers' compensation is administered on a state-by-state basis and the rates and state laws vary greatly, including, for example, at what point—usually based on number of employees—the insurance becomes mandatory. In many states, nonprofits can choose to purchase workers' compensation insurance through their commercial insurance carrier rather than through the state. In some states, all employers must participate in a state-affiliated insurance pool while in other states employers can self-insure. The administration of workers' compensation claims is covered more in Chapter 11.

RESOURCE

Payroll regulations and rates change frequently. Stay up to date in this area with the following resources:

- IRS Publication 15, *Employer's Tax Guide*, Circular E, available at the IRS website at www.irs.gov
- www.servicelocator.org/OWSLinks.asp (map of states with links to state unemployment offices).

Sample Payroll Tax Worksheet

Here is how you would figure the payroll taxes for an employee with a salary of $24,000 per year where payroll is paid semimonthly. The employee's gross pay for this period is $1,000, and this is the first week of the year.

Employee-paid taxes:	
Employee federal income taxes withheld	$80.00
Employee state income taxes withheld	$24.00
FICA-EE withheld	$62.00
Medicare tax withheld	$14.50
State disability insurance (SDI)	0*
Total	$182.50 withheld
Employer-paid payroll expenses:	
FICA-ER	$62.00
Medicare tax	$14.50
State unemployment insurance tax	0
State workers compensation insurance	0
Total	$76.50

*Assumes a state that does not require SDI.

> (!) **CAUTION**
> **Check for other state payroll taxes.** Some states and cities have
> additional payroll taxes that you may owe. Be sure to work with your local
> government officials or a reputable payroll company to determine what your
> payroll tax liability is.

Health Insurance

While not required by law, health benefits are greatly prized by employees
and are at the same time an increasingly difficult cost burden on
employers, including nonprofits. Nevertheless, it appears that nonprofits
have done relatively well in this area. A recent study found that nonprofits
with fewer than ten employees were nearly five times more likely to
provide health benefits than for-profit companies of the same size.

As the 2010 federal health care reform legislation is implemented—
with most employer provisions slated to become effective in 2014—the
types of health care offerings available will change, as will the rules
for if and when health care must be provided to employees. More than
ever, you'll need to stay involved with local nonprofit associations and
networks of human resource professionals to see what state and local
options are available.

If you choose to provide health benefits, you'll need to decide
which plans to offer and what part of the costs your nonprofit will pay
compared to how much employees will pay. A "bare bones" health
benefit plan might only pay for major medical health insurance for
employees, which covers them only for catastrophic injury or illness,
typically with a high deductible. A step up from that would be to offer
membership in an HMO (Health Maintenance Organization) that
restricts members to using the HMO's doctors and hospitals but ideally
offers health-promotion benefits such as smoking-cessation classes or
support groups. A more flexible program might allow employees to
choose between a major medical plan, two HMO choices, and a PPO
(Preferred Provider Organization), where employees are restricted to

using medical providers who have contracted with that PPO. With HMOs and PPOs, employees can utilize medical care outside those systems, but typically will have to pay a large part of the expense.

In each of these situations, you can choose to pay a percentage or all of the costs. You could offer a health plan and require employees to pay 100% of the costs or you could pay 100% of the health insurance costs for your employees. Many nonprofits adopt a compromise where the nonprofit pays the full HMO costs for an inexpensive HMO plan, and employees who want better plans must make up the difference in price.

Some of the factors to consider include:

- how much of the cost (if any) you want to pay for your employees
- whether you want to pay for all, none, or a percentage of coverage for dependents or family members of employees
- the amount of deductibles and co-payments for your employees, and
- whether you want to offer prescription benefits and, if so, what you will provide.

Nonprofits vary widely in the health benefits they provide. Some small nonprofits provide very generous health benefits, while others offer none; the same is true of large nonprofits. Some nonprofits, such as disabilities or cancer-related organizations that employ a higher-than-typical percentage of employees with significant medical needs, may find it simultaneously more expensive and more crucial to provide health benefits.

TIP

Consider individual health plans. If you have only one or two employees and they are in good health, it might be simpler to have your employees choose and enroll in their own individual health plans. Then the nonprofit can pay the premium, or a percentage of the premium.

Employee Assistance Programs

Many nonprofits offer Employee Assistance Programs ("EAPs") in conjunction with health insurance. EAPs help employees (and often their family members) with personal issues. Any information about services provided is kept strictly confidential from the employer. Under most programs, the services are free for the employee and include mental health counseling, alcoholism counseling, referrals to caregiver resources, legal assistance (such as tenant counseling), personal finance counseling, and so forth. EAPs usually cost the employer approximately $4 per month per employee, often a worthwhile investment in reducing absenteeism, supporting employee mental health, and demonstrating that your nonprofit is supportive of staff.

If you decide to offer an EAP program, make sure that your staff knows about it; these services are often underused. Send out occasional reminders and mention that any information about services provided is confidential. Sometimes staff will be reluctant to use EAP services; try to find opportunities to show that even senior staff or others take advantage of the program.

EAPs Provide Social Worker–Type Benefits

An EAP is an inexpensive and great benefit for many nonprofits. Nonprofit managers often have social-worker-like desires to help out; for example with an employee with an alcohol problem or someone dealing with a domestic violence situation. Instead of providing this kind of help directly—which confuses the employer relationship—they can refer someone to the EAP.

If you have an EAP, you can also make mandatory EAP referrals. For example, if an employee confesses that the reason her performance is suffering is because she has been drinking too much, you can require her to use an EAP referral as a condition of the job. Pay her for the time, and the EAP will just document the fact that she used the referral, not what it was for or what occurred there.

> ! CAUTION
>
> **EAP providers are not well regulated.** Be sure to work with a provider with a strong track record and good reputation. Check with your health insurer to see if it can recommend an EAP provider.

Cafeteria Plans

Flexible benefits plans, also known as cafeteria plans, are often preferred by employees but can be complicated for employers to set up and administer. In this type of plan, you establish a dollar amount for your employees that they can then "spend" in a "benefits cafeteria" that includes health insurance, child care payments, funds for acupuncture, and so forth. For example, if your nonprofit decides to give employees $300 per month to spend on benefits, one employee may use that money to pay for membership in an HMO, while another, who is covered through a spouse's plan, might use the money for chiropractic and vision care.

One disadvantage of cafeteria plans is that you have to provide this coverage for all your employees. With other plans, there are usually a few employees who will not participate because they are covered through a spouse's or parent's plan, receive health care from the Veterans Administration, or for some other reason. However, cafeteria plans must provide all employees with benefits, so it may cost your nonprofit more.

On the other hand, cafeteria plans allow an employer to control the amount it will spend on benefits, because there is a dollar cap on what you promise employees. If a benefit is expressed in nondollar terms—such as, "We provide full health insurance"—that cost may increase dramatically from year to year and your nonprofit remains obligated to pay it. In, in a cafeteria plan, by contrast, you might describe the benefit in absolute dollar amounts—such as, "We pay $300 per employee per month"—or at a specified level, such as, "We pay an amount equal to 100% of the monthly payment for the lowest-cost HMO."

Many employees view cafeteria plans as being fairer than other systems. For instance, a veteran who receives free care at a Veteran's Administration hospital does not benefit from employer-paid health insurance. With a cafeteria plan, the veteran can use the dollars for other benefits.

Dental Benefits

Dental insurance is another benefit highly desired by many employees. Usually dental insurance costs approximately $500 per employee per year and the employer typically pays all or a part of the cost. Just as there are HMOs, PPOs, and other options in health insurance, there are dental HMOs, dental PPOs, and other options available.

Vision Care

Vision care is often available as a relatively inexpensive addition to health insurance. It pays for eye exams, eyeglasses, contact lenses, and other vision-related devices. If an employee survey reveals a strong desire for vision care, ask your health insurance providers how much the addition will cost—it's usually not terribly expensive.

Health Savings Accounts (HSAs)

Health Savings Accounts are similar to personal savings accounts, but the money can be used only for health care. Employees benefit from HSAs because they can put pretax funds into their HSAs. If, for example, an employee decides to put $3,000 into an HSA, he or she will not pay Social Security or Medicare taxes on the $3,000. Employees can establish HSAs through banks, credit unions, and other institutions; an employer-sponsored plan is not the only way to have an HSA. HSAs require more advance planning and record keeping than some people can manage; unless this benefit is strongly desired by many employees, consider encouraging those who want HSAs to set them up on their own.

Life Insurance

Group life insurance is typically inexpensive and pays the family either a flat sum or a multiple of salary (such as two years' salary) upon the death of an employee. When an employee dies, it is a comfort to the family to have the funds, and other employees are also relieved that the family is receiving some help. Life insurance is often available for less than $200 per year per employee for payouts of $50,000. Allow employees to contribute toward higher coverage if they wish.

TIP

Read the "fine print" on any life insurance policy. In some cases, a nonprofit will terminate an employee due to prolonged illness, and when that individual dies several months later, life insurance isn't available because the individual is no longer an employee. Be sure you understand the insurance company's requirements so that your paperwork will support the insurance payout at the time a former employee dies even if the person is no longer working.

Sick Pay or Paid Time Off (PTO)

Although tracking time off is typically managed in the finance/payroll department, the person in charge of HR needs to understand the choices and make recommendations to management about how to structure time off. Traditionally, paid time off has been a combination of sick pay and vacation pay, such as five paid sick days and ten paid vacation days per year. An important distinction is that when an employee leaves an organization, any remaining vacation days earned may have to be paid out in cash in most states, while unused sick days need not be paid out.

Increasingly, employers—including nonprofits—combine sick and vacation days into what's called Paid Time Off (PTO). This would mean, following the above example, giving employees 15 days of PTO per year to use as they wish. Some employees appreciate the ability to "mix and match" vacation and illness days, and not to have to pretend to be ill in order to use a sick day. (That's why you'll sometimes hear the term "mental health day.") A modest disadvantage to the nonprofit may be that PTO is legally treated as paid vacation, so in states that require employers to pay out unused vacation time, employers will have to pay all unused PTO. Regardless of which system you use, you should put a cap in place for how much paid leave can accumulate, lest you find yourself having to pay out hundreds of hours in unused vacation or PTO. Once an employee reaches the cap, the employee can't accrue any more vacation time until some is used. However, most states prohibit employers from taking away vacation time employees have previously earned by, for example, zeroing out an employee's balance at the end of the year (called a "use-it-or-lose-it" policy).

And because time off is valued by most employees, many nonprofits increase paid leave for longer-tenured staff.

Sample Paid Leave Policy

A paid leave policy might look something like the example below. However, limits on days that can be carried forward are not legal in some states so check the rules in your state before adopting a policy.

- Fifteen days Paid Time Off per year
- No more than five days can be carried over to a subsequent year.
- Employees with five or more years of continuous employment will receive 20 days PTO per year, with a maximum carryover of eight days per year.
- Employees with nine or more years of continuous employment will receive 25 days PTO per year with a maximum carryover of 10 days per year.

Retirement Benefits

Retirement plans provide funds to older people once they are no longer working. Particularly for senior-level positions, retirement plans have been shown to be powerful components in recruiting and retaining employees. Many over-50 jobseekers even express a stronger desire for retirement benefits than for comparable dollars in salary. And given that many nonprofit employees work at many places over the course of their careers, they tend to want retirement benefits that will move with them when they change jobs.

Offering retirement benefits sends a message that nonprofit work is real work, not just casual employment for housewives or students. Retirement benefits also make a statement about your nonprofit's confidence in its own future and its support for career-length nonprofit employment.

Only a very tiny percentage of nonprofit employers have traditional "defined benefit" retirement plans. These are plans that pay, for instance, 60% of salary each year to employees who have left after 30 years of work. Such plans have never been prevalent in any but the largest and oldest nonprofits and they are in steep decline in the for-profit sector.

Instead, what you're more likely to find in nonprofits today are plans where both employers and employees contribute to retirement savings. For employees, these plans offer a way to save money for later, defer taxes, and, if the nonprofit also contributes funds, enjoy additional compensation.

Nonprofits can use 403(b) plans, 401(k) plans, and 457 plans. In all instances, employees can use payroll deduction to move some of their wages into the retirement plan and thus not pay income taxes on those sums until they are withdrawn, presumably after retirement when their income tax rate will be lower. In addition, nonprofits can contribute to individual retirement accounts ("IRAs").

Benefit Plans and the Changing Perceptions of Nonprofit Work

Up until 1958, nonprofits could not establish retirement programs because charity jobs were not seen as career jobs where employees would need benefits. As nonprofit work came to be viewed as more legitimate, Congress allowed for the creation of 403(b) retirement savings plans, which could be established only by nonprofit 501(c)(3) organizations, public schools, self-employed clergy, and a few others.

Two important restrictions on 403(b) plans were that employers could not make contributions to the plans (only employees could), and funds could be invested only in annuity products offered by insurance companies. In 1974, it became permissible to invest 403(b) funds in mutual funds as well. While nonprofits can now offer either 403(b) or 401(k) plans (or both), many nonprofit managers are not aware that nonprofits can now use 401(k) plans. These gradual changes that make retirement planning more similar for nonprofits and for-profits reflect a growing respect for nonprofit work and a recognition that nonprofit employees, teachers, and clergy are breadwinners who should earn "real" wages and benefits.

In some cases, the nonprofit will choose not to make any employer contribution and establish a plan simply so employees can take advantage of it. Or, a nonprofit may contribute a percentage—such as 3% of salary—into the plan. In order to encourage employees to save, some nonprofits match contributions that employees make into their accounts.

Nonprofits can change the amount of employer contributions that will be made into retirement plans, perhaps giving 5% of salary but lowering that to 2% in a difficult economic setting. Employee handbooks should explicitly state that employer contributions may change, if that's your policy.

Before starting a retirement plan for the first time, survey employees about their willingness and desire to participate in such a plan, and how much they might want to contribute. Lower-paid employees are less likely to make their own contributions to their plans, and more likely to withdraw all deferred compensation within a year of leaving the nonprofit. Work with a broker to identify the best plan for employees—and one that has manageable paperwork and administrative costs. Retirement savings programs demand a significant amount of time from HR and finance staff.

(!) **CAUTION**
Nonprofit organizations themselves typically can't use retirement plan tax advantages. Many retirement programs for employers are structured to give tax benefits to the employer, and not all brokers or companies understand that such tax benefits are rarely useful to nonprofit organizations. Be sure to work with a broker that has experience with nonprofits of different sizes.

Education and Training Benefits

Helping employees continue their educations often strengthens their current performance and their future job prospects. Think about education benefits that may be particularly appreciated and in line with your organizational mission, such as:

- paying tuition and books for low-income clients hired into staff positions who attend community college classes at night, or
- paying partial tuition for managers with three or more years of outstanding performance for graduate work in related fields, such as a Master's in Social Work program or Arts Administration.

Increasingly, employees see training opportunities as ways to augment their skills, increase their responsibilities on the job, and to enhance their marketability for jobs in the future. While in the past, training was seen predominantly as a benefit to the employer, today's staff—especially younger staff—value training as a benefit to themselves.

Total Cost of Benefits: The Hidden Paycheck

Understanding the total cost of employee benefits is useful for two reasons. First, when employees understand the "hidden paycheck" they receive in the form of benefits, they often appreciate their total compensation more fully. Second, the cost of benefits as a percentage of payroll is useful when budgeting for grant proposals and contract bids.

If the average salary in an organization is $45,000, the benefits can be costed as follows:

Annual Cost of Benefits per Employee Based on Average Salary of $45,000		
Benefit	**Notes**	**Average Cost per Employee**
Health insurance	Total expense divided by number of employees	$3,500
Dental insurance	Same	$350
Life insurance	Same	$175
Holidays	11 per year	$1,904
Paid time off	15 days (3 weeks). 20 days after 5 years of service	$2,596
Contribution to 401(k)	@ 4%	$1,800
Workers' compensation insurance	Compensation if injured on the job	$400
Employer-paid unemployment insurance	Compensation if laid off	$55
State disability insurance	Compensation if unable to work due to disability or illness	$45
Employer-paid contribution to Social Security and Medicare	Retirement and Medicare benefits	$3,443
Total cost per employee		**$14,268**
Benefit costs as percentage of salary		**32%**

Noneconomic Benefits

The terms "noneconomic" and "nonfinancial" benefits refer to aspects of working conditions that do not represent additional costs for the employing nonprofit. For example, noneconomic benefits might include providing working conditions and flexibility that allow nonprofit staff to maintain a more balanced work-life equation. And uniquely, nonprofits often have noneconomic benefits related to their missions, such as allowing staff to bring their dogs to work at an animal rescue organization, or passing out free tickets to employees and volunteers at a nonprofit film festival.

Flex Time

Flexible time generally refers to an employee's opportunity to shift the workday: to work, for instance, from 11 a.m. to 7 p.m. instead of 9 a.m. to 5 p.m. For many employees, flex time allows them to manage their children's care, avoid the worst commute times, or simply suit their personal schedules. Of course, flex time isn't appropriate for every position—it won't do you much good if your receptionist, for example, works from 12 to 8. Establish a policy about flex time, which covers important issues, such as when requests require approval in advance and which hours can or can't be accommodated (for example, prohibiting working from midnight to 8 a.m.). Also clarify which positions are and are not amenable to flex time.

> **EXAMPLE:** Laura, who had been a reliable employee for several years, was increasingly late to work on her job as custodian in a home for children with disabilities. Her supervisor was worried the cause was medical. It turned out that Laura's elderly mother had moved in with her and Laura couldn't leave for work until the home hospice worker arrived—often late. By changing Laura's hours so that she could start later and have a shorter lunch break, Laura's schedule became more consistent and she was less stressed, and grateful for the flexibility.

A popular variation on flex time is compressed time, where an employee works four ten-hour days per week (although this could be a problem for nonexempt employees in states that calculate overtime on a daily basis rather than weekly basis).

Alternative Work Weeks

Nonprofits often want to establish a workweek that is different from the default workweek of Monday through Friday. Common examples:

- 10-4 workweek or four-day workweek, where employees work ten hours per day for four days each week
- 9/80 work schedule, where in a two-week period, the employee works eight nine-hour days, one eight-hour day, and has one day off
- Alternative calendar days, where the workweek is established at, say, Thursday through Wednesday, with working hours Thursday through Tuesday, often appropriate for congregational staff.

If you want to establish alternative work weeks, you'll need to create schedules, eligibility criteria, processes, and forms. Work with an HR consultant or attorney to make sure you have everything in place.

Telecommuting or Teleworking

For some nonprofit positions, telecommuting is a necessity of the job, as would be the case with a community organizer or researcher who works far from the organization's office. When working from home (or a coffee shop or other offsite location) is required and is for the benefit of the nonprofit, the organization should also plan to provide a laptop, cell phone, and other technology and furniture that supports working remotely.

If employees request telecommuting privileges for their personal benefit, they typically ask to work from home one or two days per week. In such instances, the employees usually provide their own equipment and sign an agreement related to their responsibilities for their home offices.

In general, work-related injuries that occur at home are covered by employers' workers' compensation insurance as long as the employee can prove that the injuries happened as a result of his or her work. That means that, for example, if an employee trips over a power cord in a home office, the fall could be considered an on-the-job injury, although the insurance company may dispute the claim. However, if you have employees who work at home, check with your insurance carrier about whether you have this coverage. In addition, state regulations on telecommuting and home offices vary and are changing all the time, so be sure to check with your state OSHA office about any regulations that apply to you.

For more information about telecommuting and a sample agreement for employees, see www.blueavocado.org and type "telecommuting" into the search box.

Comp Time

Compensatory time—"comp time"—is the practice of giving employees time off instead of overtime. For example, if an administrative assistant works eight hours on a Saturday to help with a board retreat, she might be given Monday off.

In general, comp time is not legal. Federal law safeguards against nonexempt employees being cheated out of overtime pay. If you have an employee who works an extra eight hours during a pay period, the employee should be paid time-and-a-half for those hours. What you can do instead is to give that person 12 hours off within the pay period. That way the pay will remain the same for the pay period, and you will have "compensated" him or her at time-and-a-half (12 hours off for eight hours extra work).

For exempt staff, comp time doesn't exist legally, but does exist as a common, informal practice within the nonprofit sector. For example, if a full-time, exempt employee works Saturday and Sunday at a conference, it might be understood that Monday and Tuesday can be taken off. Be sure that such "adjustments" take place within the pay period.

EXAMPLE: At Wilderness Peaks, the departing executive director demanded that 413 days of paid comp time—more than a year's salary—be paid to him as comp time. The Employee Handbook did in fact allow for uncapped comp time for exempt employees, and required that it be paid upon the employee's departure. The director had worked over 40 hours during many weeks, if 24 hours per day were counted on the many escorted hiking/camping trips he took on the job. When an attorney advised the board that they would probably lose in court, the board succeeded in settling out-of-court for two-thirds of the amount.

Job Sharing

Job sharing—splitting one full-time job between two people—is a way to allow valuable employees to stay on the job without having to work full time. Nonexempt jobs are usually not conducive to job-sharing; it makes more sense simply to have, for instance, two part-time paratransit drivers rather than have two drivers share one job. Professional and management positions can be shared successfully, but the two people involved must have great interaction and trust in each other and understand that each will probably work more than half time. In some cases, married couples share an executive director position. The nonprofit must decide whether it will pay health insurance for both or pay on a prorated basis, and develop a process for if and when one of the job-sharers leaves.

Discounts and Perks

Some nonprofits are able to provide their staff (and sometimes volunteers) with various perks at no cost to the nonprofit, such as discounted tickets to Disney World or a nearby aquarium, group membership rate at a gym, and so forth. Adviser Daphne Logan points out that staff often appreciates and values these kinds of perks, and that HR staff needs to remind staff periodically about what's available.

Administering Your Benefits Plan

Administering benefits requires strategic work—such as determining which benefits to offer and which companies to choose as providers. It also includes very detailed, specific work, such as helping an employee understand how to make the best use of disability pay. Too often this work is handed to the finance department or the operations manager without appreciation for the expertise, time, and sensitivity needed. Every nonprofit needs to identify a person in charge of benefits administration, and to give that person the time, budget, and authority necessary to be effective.

Here are some specific tips on how to make this work:

Help employees choose the right benefits. Give everyone enough time and information to understand and choose among the benefits that your organization offers. Ask companies you use to make presentations to staff. Offer presentations in Spanish, Chinese, or any other languages spoken among your employees.

Help people use their benefits. Hold lunchtime education sessions or issue occasional "benefits newsletters" that explain a little-used benefit, or that explain the confidentiality in EAPs. Consider allowing employees to go to two medical appointments and one dentist appointment per year without having to use paid time off. (You'll reap the benefits of them taking preventive measures instead of waiting until they "have to" visit the doctor or dentist.)

Survey staff occasionally. Find out what benefits they most appreciate, and which make them scratch their heads. If you are thinking about changing benefits, ask employees to tell you which are the most important ones to them, and how much they would be willing to pay if the cost were borne jointly by the nonprofit and the employee.

Look for unique opportunities to give small benefits. Employees appreciate benefits that demonstrate thoughtfulness, even when there may not enough funding for raises or more expensive benefits. For instance, if employees do a great deal of driving—perhaps conducting home visits in a rural area—consider offering a modest allowance toward audio books as a benefit. Issue an iPod to everyone in nighttime janitorial who works at your home for children with disabilities, or the choice of a magazine subscription for ESL teachers.

Performance Reviews

Reasons for Performance Reviews..111

Special Considerations for Small Organizations...114

Types of Performance Reviews...115

    Checklist Reviews...117

    Narrative Essays 121

Defining What's Expected of Employees 124

Keep Track of Employee Performance.. 125

Gathering the Building-Block Information 126

    Personnel Records... 126

    External "Customer" Feedback... 127

    Internal Feedback 127

The Role of Judgment 128

Setting Up Your Review Process 130

    Legal Issues in Performance Reviews.. 131

    When to Conduct Reviews... 132

    Reviews and the Budget 133

    Performance Review Forms.. 134

A Step-by-Step Look at the Review Process.. 134

Meet Your Adviser

Ashwin Jayaram, MILR
Title: HR Consultant
Organization: Nonprofit HR Solutions
Location: Washington, DC

What he does: Ashwin provides HR consulting services to nonprofits, taking care of every employee issue from compensation to benefits to performance management to employee relations to talent management. He also designs and analyzes employee engagement/satisfaction surveys, and develops performance management systems for clients. Ashwin's background includes HR work at Dell, Intel, and other Fortune 500 companies.

What his company does: The company provides HR consulting, staffing services, executive search, direct HR staff placements, conferences, and research, exclusively focused on nonprofit organizations.

Best tip for HR managers including the Accidental HR manager: There are a lot of free resources online and offline; go there and educate yourself! First understand how it "can" be done and then tailor it to work for your organization.

HR lesson learned the hard way: You need to first understand the organization's mission/business, and strategy; don't do HR for HR, do HR for the organization. You have to design systems that fit in with the strategy, mission, and culture and help managers see that HR contributes to supporting the organization's mission and philosophy.

Song title that speaks to you about HR: "I'm too busy to listen to music!"

Meet Your Adviser

Lisa Brown Morton
Title: President and CEO
Company: Nonprofit HR Solutions
Location: Washington, DC

What she does: Lisa runs the company she founded, a rapidly growing HR consulting firm to the nonprofit sector. Lisa is also the former Vice President of HR with LeadingAge (formerly known as AAHSA) and Director of HR and Administration with the American Symphony Orchestra League.

What her company does: The company provides HR consulting, staffing services, direct HR staff placements, executive search, and education and information, exclusively focused on nonprofit organizations.

Best tip for HR managers including the Accidental HR manager: Know what you don't know. Don't pretend to navigate the waters without the help you need. Seek out HR related training from those who know the field. Getting people-management right is the difference between an organization maximizing its human capital—its staff— and simply surviving. And make sure you get help from right people; for example, don't use a general lawyer for HR concerns; use an employment lawyer.

An HR lesson you learned the hard way: You can never be an expert in all areas of HR. For example, my strength isn't in retirement planning design. But I know to get help when that's the issue. It costs too much to make a mistake.

A song title that speaks to you about HR: Aretha Franklin's "R-E-S-P-E-C-T!"

P erformance reviews are rarely on anyone's list of favorite activities. Supervisors often view them as unpleasant year-end chores that beg for procrastination—many months' or years' worth of procrastination, in some cases. Employees tend to dread them as well.

Yet, when handled well—as we'll show you how to do in this chapter—performance reviews are a key part of creating positive employee relations, managing staff performance, creating functional work teams, and ultimately achieving your nonprofit's goals. If you skip over the reviews, you're removing a key piece from the larger puzzle of performance management that includes goal planning, coaching, training, team development, and discipline. And you're shortchanging the employee, who may not realize which areas of the job are going well and which could use more attention. Finally, the way that performance reviews are done is a crucial way in which an organization's values, standards, and commitment to mission are communicated to employees. Don't miss this opportunity to instill the organization's sense of purpose in both supervisors and employees.

Appraisal, Review, Assessment, Evaluation—Is There a Difference?

The terms appraisal, review, assessment, and evaluation are often used interchangeably. Nevertheless, the field has moved away from terms that imply that the review is about the person as opposed to the person's work. So, "performance evaluation" is preferred over "employee evaluation" as a way to signal that the process is about the work that the employee performs rather than the person. We use all these terms but have a mild preference for "review" because it conveys a message that it's part of an ongoing process as opposed to just one annual discussion. Regardless of the term you use, be consistent in your internal documents.

Performance reviews usually are seen as the end of an employee's year. Ideally, however, they should be thought of as the beginning of the employee's year. The review signifies the start of the next phase of training and staff development for the employee and a jumping-off point—an opportunity to make a fresh start or build on previous accomplishments.

Reasons for Performance Reviews

If performance reviews are not taken seriously in your organization, begin the process of shifting the culture by asking the management team to make a commitment to demonstrating and insisting on a strong process. Once you have secured that commitment, you'll need to actively promote the idea throughout the staff that reviews are beneficial for everyone involved—the employee, the reviewer, management, the organization as a whole, and its beneficiaries. You can have the performance review system presented at a staff meeting and all staff should be given training on it. In particular, supervisors will need training and coaching on each aspect of the process.

To lead the organization in changing its perspective on performance reviews, it helps to identify the goals that the different parties involved want to achieve from the process.

For the employee whose performance is being reviewed, a review can:
- provide a regular platform for ironing out minor difficulties with a supervisor
- clarify how the supervisor views the employee's performance and career potential
- provide an opportunity for self-reflection and thought about career and community goals
- result in a clear basis for measuring performance in the forthcoming period, and
- result in an agreed-upon plan for developing skills and responsibilities.

For the supervisor conducting the review, the review can:

- provide a platform for ironing out minor difficulties and for performance coaching
- support consistent goal-setting and reviews for those being supervised
- provide a legally defensible basis for personnel decisions, including merit pay increases, promotions, disciplinary actions, and terminations, and
- provide an opportunity to create skills development plans for all employees—and to encourage career advancement ambitions for high-performing employees.

Performance reviews can also be beneficial for staff and the organization's beneficiaries and partners. First, having consistent, fair appraisals demonstrates that your organization values communication and feedback. In addition, insisting on thorough and professional performance reviews helps improve your supervisors' ability to manage performance within their areas or departments. Management can use the reviews to look for any issues or areas of concern in the overall organization. Looking at appraisals from a particular work team or across the whole organization can reveal areas of weakness that need to be addressed.

Reviews also provide a regular opportunity to explicitly communicate the organization's values and mission to employees. For example, if a nonprofit's mission includes helping empower people with developmental disabilities, but one employee is perpetually late in returning client phone calls, then it would be important to emphasize during the employee's review that such behavior undercuts that mission by damaging the clients' progress and sending a disempowering message.

Finally, insisting on structured appraisals that are well documented and fair will be important later should you decide you want to fire an employee. Even a series of positive reviews may be helpful with an underperforming employee. By reacquainting you with the good work the employee has done in the past, those reviews may help you find ways to address the problem, or to narrow the employee's work to what you know he or she can do well.

Once you have gained a broad perspective on the value proposition of performance reviews, you will have an easier time persuading others in your organization to make the time and effort to engage more wholeheartedly in making the performance review a useful—even rewarding—part of the work experience. You will be better equipped to help employees see that the performance review can help them elevate their standing in their current position or advance to a new one. You can persuade busy supervisors that performance reviews can actually make their jobs easier over the course of the year. Importantly, you can change mindsets throughout the organization when everyone begins to see how the process—and thus each employee—connects to the wider goals of the organization.

> **EXAMPLE:** The Black Network for Foster Families takes pride in its performance evaluation systems. One reason: The group was conceived as an academy for developing African American leaders who will become future leaders at other organizations, and performance reviews are a key part of that staff development process. The coalition's leaders know that to achieve their mission of improving the lives of African American children without functioning parents, the Network must not only build itself as an organization, but also change and improve the responsiveness of many other organizations and institutions concerned with adoption and foster care. Thus, working hard to provide constructive feedback to coalition staff is an essential component of bettering the lives of African American children.
>
> "We're proud when our staff goes on to be development directors, program directors, and executive directors at other organizations," says board chair Mattie Lyons. "Our organization is contributing to the community in larger ways beyond our own work."

Special Considerations for Small Organizations

In organizations with a small staff—fewer than ten people total— everyone may drag their feet about conducting formal performance reviews. With such a small group and little formal hierarchy, there may be a feeling that everybody knows what everyone else is doing so there's no need for a review process. Managers may view staff as team members rather than as subordinates and may not feel comfortable reviewing their work. Last but not least, roles are often fluid in a small organization, making it seem even more challenging to review a job that has changed several times over the course of the year.

In these situations, performance reviews can actually be even more beneficial and important. For someone whose role has evolved over time, the review can provide an opportunity to articulate what the person's job has become and where it is going. This can be reassuring for the employee and useful for the manager who needs to define roles and assign responsibilities for particular areas. Going over the job description as part of the performance review also provides the opportunity to discuss what is being done well, what needs to improve, and what is being neglected.

⚠ CAUTION

Skipping performance reviews can seriously harm small organizations. The negative impact of an unsatisfactory employee is felt even more keenly in a small nonprofit, and insisting on structured reviews can help with terminating that employee at a later point. And, a high-performing individual in a small organization may not be acknowledged for good work if a performance review process is not in place that facilitates a formal revisiting of job description or title.

Types of Performance Reviews

There are many choices about what types of reviews to conduct, though nearly all performance appraisal systems share the following four components:

- measuring performance against established standards or goals
- inviting the employee's self-assessment or response to the review
- assessing or evaluating the employee's performance based on data collected, and
- establishing goals or courses of action for the next period.

Within this general framework, there are several ways you can format your reviews on paper. Discussed below are the three most commonly used review systems in the nonprofit sector—checklists, narrative essays, and a combination of the two. Some organizations use a fourth evaluation method called the 360-degree evaluation. Based on the idea of a person in the center of a circle (which has 360 degrees), 360-degree evaluations solicit and incorporate input from internal sources such as co-workers and subordinates, and external sources such as clients, funders, and collaborative partners. We believe that these processes are problematic in performance reviews, although they can be effective in strengthening performance. (See Chapter 4, Strengthening Performance, for more on 360-degree evaluations.)

You will want to develop a format and procedure that suits your organization's structure, activities, staff capacity, and culture. As you develop the forms for the review, make sure the set-up is consistent from department to department. Don't forget to include a signature section at the end of the form, since employees and supervisors must sign the completed form before it is added to the employee's personnel file. Also, you should spell out the extent to which the review is confidential (and train supervisors that performance appraisal findings are not to be shared with the employee's peers).

Online Systems Can Help Track Reviews

The HR department needs to keep on top of whether supervisors have done their employees' performance reviews properly and on time. One way to make the process easier is to use an online system. Online management performance or appraisal system software tracks which reviews have been completed, sends reminders to supervisors who have not completed their write-ups, and often stores the reviews online where they may be accessed from multiple locations. These systems facilitate paperwork centralization, which is particularly useful if your organization has more than one location or if more than one person needs access to a review. And, if employees are frequently out of the office, they can write and submit documents from anywhere. As adviser Ashwin Jayaram notes, "Even with as few as 15 employees, HR paperwork can be unwieldy. With an online system, it's easy for a manager to look back through previous reviews, for HR to see that reviews are getting completed on time, and to keep the process moving along established timelines."

These systems also make it easy for the ED or HR person to see at a glance which supervisors have completed their reviews or not. Another feature is the ability to compare evaluations if you use all the same types of reviews. For instance, you may see that one supervisor gave an average of four (out of five) to his staff while another supervisor gave an average of two to her staff. When you make this comparison, you can ask, "Is one supervisor too easy a grader or does the other supervisor have unrealistic performance expectations, or are they both making appropriate assessments?"

If you decide to purchase an online system, look for flexibility in creating different review types for different employees. The system you purchase should allow remote access by having all the data online rather than on the computer system at your office. You will need this so that staff can work on their reports while on the road and so that when an employee and supervisor work at different job sites, they can access the same documents.

Such a system can be found for as little as $500 to $1,500 per year. If you have a small group, say, 15 employees, a low-end system will cost about $800 per year. Then, if you add another 15 employees, it might to go up to something like $1,100 per year.

Checklist Reviews

For some types of jobs, checklist reviews—in which the supervisor rates different aspects of the employees' performance—are the way to go. They are the easiest for supervisors to complete. Also, some employees, especially those with modest English reading and writing skills, can use the checklists more effectively than a review that requires a lot of writing. Checklists tend to be straightforward, no-frills documents, written in plain language that is easy to understand.

At the same time, checklists can't convey warmth, appreciation, or nuance the way that a narrative can. Many organizations that use checklists encourage or require written comments as well.

Below are excerpted samples of three types of checklists that evaluate employee performance in different ways.

Checklist 1: Checklist Based on Rating Performance Standard (Unsatisfactory to Outstanding)

Checklist Based on Rating Performance Standard						
	Unsatisfactory	Nearing satisfactory	Satisfactory	Above satisfactory	Outstanding	Examples and Notes
Attendance						
Promptness						
Professional appearance						
In-person visitor hospitality						
Productivity—volume of work completed						
Relationships with coworkers						

This checklist rates employee performance on a scale that compares it to an implicitly understood "satisfactory" standard. When you create the work categories you are rating, make sure they focus on employees' actual work performance. You don't want to measure employees' abilities or traits—such as "really smart," or "lousy at math"—but instead want to show how they've done their job, regardless or in spite of those abilities or traits.

In certain circumstances, it may be worth the investment of time to develop detailed performance standards to clarify otherwise vague terms like "outstanding" or "satisfactory." For example, instead of "Professional appearance," use "Neat professional appearance when meeting with clients." If you are seeking to raise the quality of work and level of professionalism in a particular group, having the employees draft performance standards for their own areas can create a more effective review system. For example, only the legal assistants involved in helping immigrants obtain family visas might think to add "Number of applications rejected by U.S. government due to error" as a performance criterion.

Checklist 2: Agreeing or Disagreeing With Statements About Positive Behavior

Agreeing or Disagreeing With Statements About Positive Behavior					
	Disagree strongly	Disagree	Agree	Agree strongly	Examples and Notes
Employee is welcoming to in-person visitors					
Employee handles requests from other staff promptly and courteously					
Employee shows initiative in problem solving					

This checklist makes positive statements about behaviors, and supervisors note their agreement or disagreement with each statement. An advantage is that a statement such as "Employee is welcoming to in-person visitors" communicates more than "Satisfactory" for in-person visitor hospitality. Be careful not to make the statements too narrow so that, for instance, a receptionist who has been welcoming but keeps forgetting to have visitors sign in gets an inappropriately positive review.

Checklist 3: Measuring Performance Against Goals

Measuring Performance Against Goals						
	Strongly disagree	Disagree	Agree	Agree strongly	Examples and Notes	Objectives for next year
Caseload: Quality: Met basic standards for managing caseload of 70 to 80 concurrent clients						
Enrollments: Successfully enrolled 50 or more clients in housing						
Research: Led study team on Shallow Rent Subsidies and completed report on time and at a high level of quality						

This last form is a variation on what is known as Management-by-Objective ("MBO"), an approach that requires measurable objectives to be established for each aspect of an employee's work. MBO has declined in use across all sectors, in part because of its emphasis on quantitative goals. Particularly in a nonprofit organization, too much emphasis on meeting numerical goals can inadvertently work against the mission. For example, a case manager wanting to meet caseload number goals might close cases too quickly before the clients' needs have been fully met, or a department head might accept less-than-satisfactory volunteers into a program to meet recruitment goals.

This push-pull between quantity and quality is particularly important and particularly difficult to manage in nonprofit organizations. On one hand, the organization—and thereby the staff—needs to meet certain numerical targets, such as number of concerts produced or numbers of patients served. At the same time, quality in such work cannot be measured and standardized the same way as in manufacturing. This tension can't be "solved," but is rather something to discuss and manage in an evolving, ongoing way.

Below is an example that takes the qualitative, difficult-to-measure objective of "Maintains knowledge of developments in the field," and states specific criteria for evaluating performance. In some very large organizations such as hospitals, there may be these types of highly developed systems of review for many or all positions. Some fields have developed complete sets of standards for commonly held positions, such as case managers in HIV services. For most nonprofits, this type of detailed deconstruction of each performance objective is unnecessary.

Job Knowledge Standards for Social Worker Position

Outstanding. Published article(s) in peer-reviewed publications. Invited to present at professional conferences. Effective at transferring knowledge and inspiring interest in field development among coworkers.

Above satisfactory. Maintains active knowledge of developments in field through reading, conferences, professional development activities. Seeks out learning opportunities. Engages other staff in discussing developments and concepts.

Somewhat satisfactory. Reads intermittently in the field, is somewhat conversant in research, new developments, and approaches.

Conditional. Does not read actively or learn about developments in the field. Shows reluctance or resistance to learning opportunities when presented.

Unsatisfactory. Is not adequately up to date with thinking in the field as it develops. Has resisted or avoided learning opportunities when presented. Is consistently disdainful of research or conceptual developments in the field.

Narrative Essays

Most organizations use narratives as one part of performance reviews, but some organizations rely on them exclusively. In this type of review, you will typically be asking both your employees and supervisors to write several paragraphs in response to a set of questions. They will need to reflect on accomplishments and shortcomings, think hard about what points are the most important to raise, and then write it all up. As a result, narrative-based reviews are strong in terms of useful feedback to the employee, but are time-consuming, are intimidating for people with modest writing skills, and make it difficult to compare employee performance among several employees.

A simplified narrative performance review might work as follows. Both the employee and supervisor complete a form that has the same five to ten narrative questions. The employee and the supervisor sit down together, and at the beginning of the meeting, exchange their two versions. After reviewing them, the two discuss the employee's performance, based on the narrative. After the meeting, the supervisor develops a final product. The final version may or may not take into account the employee's written narrative and verbal response to the supervisor's narrative. The employee can request that his or her initial completed form be placed in the personnel file along with the final form written by the supervisor.

This process encourages employees to reflect on their own performances as they write their versions, and to have their first versions included in their personnel files if they wish. But it still maintains the authority of the supervisor in writing the official review.

Most supervisors and employees need training in the "how-tos" of narrative reviews. Overly brief or generic statements fail to provide meaningful feedback. Detailed statements with specific examples will go a long way toward a useful narrative review.

Narrative Essay—Sample Form

1. **What are the employee's three or four key areas of responsibility, and how do you assess performance overall in each area?**

   Matt's key responsibility is providing quality recreational activities for seniors in the senior center, and utilizing staff, paid contractors, and volunteers. His performance overall has been above average. Now that he has been in this position for a little more than a year, he has the basics of scheduling and coordination down. He can now turn his attention more toward creativity and quality in programming.

2. **Are there any accomplishments or areas of exceptional performance that should be noted?**

   Matt gets along very well with other senior center staff and is viewed as helpful by them. He pays attention to making sure that recreational programming does not disrupt other center activities. He is professional and courteous with volunteers.

3. **Are there areas of performance needing improvement or additional attention?**

   Matt began the position enthusiastically but to date has done little more than continue the programming that was already in place. He tends to see himself as a scheduler rather than a programmer. For example, we have wanted to expand quality live music performance events, coming out of the workshop on life enhancement research last year. However, Matt has not brought in new performers. In addition, to reflect our clients' cultures, Matt has been asked to increase the multiculturalism of recreational programming, but almost all programming still tends to be mainstream. Matt needs to pay more attention to knowledge in the field and apply that knowledge creatively to program development.

4. **Are there any contributions or impact (positive and negative) outside the employee's areas of responsibility that should be noted?**

   Matt's girlfriend works at the Forum Corporation nearby and he brought her and several of her coworkers to the Annual Work Day. This showed a commitment to the organization and all of its activities, not just the senior recreational program.

Narrative Essay—Sample Form (cont'd)

5. **List specific expectations and goals for the upcoming period, and what kind of support (such as training or coaching) will be part of reaching the goals.**

    Matt will pay more attention to developing fresh, quality, multicultural programming, including live music performance, with a goal of one or more quality music performances per month. He will continue learning about senior programming through reading and attending workshops. He will integrate volunteers in the senior recreation program into the donor database.

6. **Professional development plan**

    Matt will visit at least two other senior centers this year, including at least one located in a community of color, and interview the recreational program directors there. He will attend at least four workshops or seminars. He will continue one-to-one meetings with me twice a month. He will make a presentation to staff within three months on the philosophy, goals, and assistance needed in his program.

7. **Additional employee comments (optional)**

A narrative approach is more specific and may be more helpful to an employee than a checklist. Narratives can express nuances that don't emerge from a checklist format. On the other hand, a narrative is time-consuming for supervisors to write and some people may not have the English writing skills (or writing skills in a shared language) to do them easily or well.

One common choice is to include a brief narrative component with a checklist. For instance, you could use a checklist and then include any or all of the following sections for brief narrative comments:

- Notable incidents (positive and negative) during the review period
- Three key strengths to continue and build on

- Three areas for necessary improvement
- Three objectives in skills and career development
- Overall assessment of performance by supervisor.

Differences in approaches among supervisors are more likely to show up in narrative sections of a review. One supervisor might see appraisals as effective only when they focus on the positive and take an encouraging tone. Another supervisor might see appraisals as a time to focus on areas needing improvement and therefore not include much or anything about an employee's achievements. These differences can be minimized somewhat through supervisor training and by providing supervisors with samples of narratives. These steps can help the supervisory staff come closer to a happy medium. Even so, personal differences in the way narratives are developed are inevitable, and your organization should maintain enough flexibility to acknowledge and accept them.

Defining What's Expected of Employees

To accurately evaluate an employee's performance, you and the employee need some way to measure that performance. Ideally, for each employee, you will need to come up with performance objectives: job requirements and performance goals.

The performance review forms discussed above include ways to define job performance. For example, the performance goal for one employee might be to successfully enroll 50 or more clients in housing. If you have more than one employee in the same job, you can use the same objectives for all of them, although you may adapt or add to the objectives for employees.

> **EXAMPLE:** Baoba Health Care employs Javier, Bruce, and Ingrid as *promotoras*—outreach staff who work in communities to raise awareness of health, educational, and environmental issues. The three work in different neighborhoods. Sergio, the supervisor, evaluates all three using the same base set of objectives, but has an additional

objective for Ingrid. In the neighborhood where she works, residents are trying to advocate for health and environmental improvements. Therefore, Sergio also reviews Ingrid's performance in building coalitions among and between the groups in her neighborhood.

Make sure objectives are achievable and directly related to the employee's job. If other managers supervise some employees who hold the same position, work together to come up with the objectives that all of you will use.

Once you have defined the requirements and goals for each position and worker, write them down and discuss them with the people who report to you. This will let employees know what you expect and what they will have to achieve during the year to receive a positive review. The discussion may also help you refine the goals or include aspects that did not occur to you at first.

Keep Track of Employee Performance

Throughout the year, track the performance of each employee. One way to do this is to keep a performance log for each person, either on your computer or on paper. Note memorable incidents or projects involving that person, whether good or bad. For example, you might note that an employee was absent without calling in, worked overtime to complete an important project, or participated well on a staff volunteer development committee. Encourage employees to do the same, as it will be helpful when they do their self-assessments.

If an employee does an especially wonderful job on a project or really goes sour, give immediate feedback. Orally or in writing, let the employee know that you noticed and appreciate the extra effort—or that you are concerned about the employee's performance. If you choose to give this kind of feedback orally, make a written note of the conversation.

Gathering the Building-Block Information

When preparing to give a performance review for an employee, the supervisor should begin by gathering information that already exists. Working with the HR department, the supervisor should pull together the employee's personnel file, any feedback on the employee's work from clients, vendors, organizational partners, or others who've come into contact with the employee, and also, information from people within the organization who work with or depend upon the employee in some way. These are the building blocks of a performance appraisal: bits of information that the supervisor will weigh, along with his or her own assessment, to make a fair and honest appraisal.

Personnel Records

The easiest place to start when gathering information for a performance review is an employee's personnel file and any records that have been kept for the employee over the year. If you are the person with HR responsibilities, make sure that supervisors know what to look for and where to find the information. Usually, for starters, the person conducting the review should check for the following related to the employee:

- job description
- memos or correspondence from the employee's personnel file
- attendance records
- timesheets
- client feedback forms, audience appreciation forms, and any other forms that mention or relate to the employee being reviewed
- relevant program statistics, such as enrollments, theater attendance, or press hits
- team performance information for teams the employee was part of
- comments from coworkers, managers in other departments, or board members about the employee

- financially related information (such as hours billed or season tickets sold) or other information that might reflect work performed by the employee, and
- accident records or any other risk management incident involving the employee.

Too often, supervisors neglect to look at data from throughout the year, and simply reflect on what they remember. Collecting data helps supervisors think about the whole year of performance and consider all aspects of the job, not just those that are the most on the supervisor's mind. Supervisors can use notes they've taken while looking over the records or make copies of certain documents to share with the employee.

External "Customer" Feedback

For many nonprofit employees who work directly with clients or the public, there are likely to be systems in place that capture hard performance-related data, like the number of clients served by the employee who went on to enroll in community college, or the number of client families the employee met with. There may also be documents in the file that have been placed there over the year, perhaps a thank-you note from a recipient of home-delivered meals, the workshop evaluations from the last quarter, or an email that a donor sent to the executive director praising the development staff. This feedback and data from external "customers" is important information that supervisors should probably review on an ongoing basis and certainly in connection with a performance review.

Internal Feedback

Just as feedback from external customers is an important source of data for managers, feedback from internal customers is critical as well. Internal customers are people within the organization who depend on others in the organization to get their work done. For example, the head of the accounting department may have numerous internal customers who rely on financial information from the accounting department, including department heads, the executive director, and the board of directors. In a nonprofit dance company, the head of the facilities department has both external clients—attendees at performances who will complain if the chairs or plumbing don't work—and internal customers—the stage crew and dancers who might suffer if the heating system fails in the dressing rooms. If you are supervising the head of the accounting department, for example, you might want to check in briefly with some of that person's internal customers to see how satisfied they are with the performance of the accounting department in general and the department head in particular. If you supervise the head of facilities for a dance company, you might have a very brief survey of dancers and crew for feedback on safety, responsiveness to requests, and so forth.

In addition, supervisors should speak informally with some of the staff who work directly with the employee. They may be in a different department, but have worked with the employee on a committee or work project. Other supervisors may have interactions and joint responsibilities with an employee.

In organizations where a good deal of work is done by project teams, an effective practice is to identify the three most important projects an employee has worked on that year, and to have the team leaders write a brief summary of the employee's responsibilities and performance on that team.

The Role of Judgment

Performance appraisals are not scientific measurements such as measuring wind velocity. They require human judgment. Having a structured review process in place that includes checklists, narrative essays, a combination of both, or a 360-degree evaluation can help maximize focus on performance rather than personality traits. The goal is to avoid having the reviewer's judgment affected by non-performance-related attributes such as likeability, loyalty to a supervisor, or possession of a mission-related characteristic (like being a parent of a child with cancer in a children's cancer organization). These attributes should not be assessed and valued as part of the of performance review.

MYTH

Performance Reviews Are Totally Objective

Performance in nonprofit organizations is often a challenge to measure. Work such as teaching preschool, changing nutritional behaviors among patients, or acting in theater productions doesn't lend itself well to quantitative checklists.

And even for jobs (such as data entry) where performance may be easier to measure by objective standards, a high quantitative score can occasionally mask significant shortcomings in an employee's performance and a low quantitative score can sometimes fail to accurately convey what is actually strong performance. Why? Because everyone goes about their work differently—just as people have different ways of learning and different ways of communicating. And, of course, supervisors are humans, not Geiger counters that detect radioactivity. Because nonprofit work is complex, and because people are complicated, performance reviews can't be expected to be objective.

Remind both employees and supervisors that the primary goal in performance reviews is to be fair to both the employee and the organization, and to strengthen employee performance in service of the organization's mission.

Nonetheless, while data and numbers are crucial components of performance appraisals, supervisors will need to use their judgment skills. In addition to any building-block information gathered, the supervisor should consider his or her own observations and overall impression of how the employee is doing. Is the data in alignment with the supervisor's own impressions? Is most of the information positive, negative, or highly mixed? Where does the employee seem to do well and where is improvement needed? Are there patterns in performance that can help the employee improve overall?

In addition, judgment is required when interpreting data. For example, there may be one scathing letter in the file about a client interaction, yet hundreds of clients served without any complaint.

Encourage supervisors to draw upon the building-block information that is more representative, rather than becoming too preoccupied with the one piece of information that, while emphatic, is significantly out of line with everything else. Otherwise, the performance appraisal risks losing fairness and, consequently, credibility.

You may need to help supervisors understand the role of judgment in performance appraisals—finding a balance between a bureaucratic over-emphasis on numbers and data on the one hand and relying too much on personal impressions and non-performance-related attributes on the other. The goal is to improve—not avoid—judgment.

> **EXAMPLE:** Johannes is a van driver for the Golden Age Senior Center. He's a warm and likable young man who gets along with his coworkers, including David, his supervisor. He often brings home-baked treats to the center and he's known for checking in with David to see if he needs any extra help. The seniors who ride with him enjoy his company and look forward to seeing him. Therefore, Johannes earns an "outstanding" in the category "treats clients with courtesy and respect." However, that does not change the fact that Johannes often reports to work late and then gets behind on his route. Accordingly, David, no matter how much he likes Johannes, must check "needs improvement" in the "punctuality" and "performs duties as assigned" categories.

Setting Up Your Review Process

Sometimes managers are reluctant to carry out performance reviews because they are unclear on how to go about them, or perhaps the process is too complicated and daunting. In such cases, the system needs to be overhauled or at least refreshed, and staff members need training.

TIP

Revisit your performance review systems. Even if you're with an organization where performance reviews are done well and staff members are familiar with the process, adviser Ashwin Jayaram notes: "There's a tendency in nonprofits to assume it is okay to keep doing things the way they've been done up until now. Often, performance reviews have been done the same way for years, and nobody is really even happy with the system. Take the initiative and reinvent your system."

Performance Appraisal Checklist

❑ Keep performance goals within the scope of the job description. If an employee's job has changed during the year, use the performance review process to update the job description for the upcoming year.

❑ Encourage supervisors to keep logs or notes on performance throughout the year. Require entries on significant incidents and verbal reprimands or warnings. Encourage monthly entries.

❑ Encourage employees to respond in writing to the performance appraisal.

❑ Have employees sign completed performance appraisals to document their receipt of the document.

❑ Train supervisors in how to conduct performance appraisals legally and fairly.

❑ Review all evaluations performed by each supervisor to see if biases are revealed or inappropriate remarks included.

❑ Maintain confidentiality of performance reviews.

Legal Issues in Performance Reviews

Any system you create should incorporate certain basic legal considerations, and everyone involved with evaluating employees should be aware of these. Here are some key legal "dos" and "don'ts" for performance reviews:

- Keep at-will status intact by not making promises, including promises of continued employment. Avoid statements such as, "You'll always have a job here," or "Your work deserves a raise at the end of the year." Making such promises can nullify the employee's at-will status, and can be seen as a contractual promise that must be kept.

- Avoid attributing problem behaviors to demographic characteristics, thereby leaving yourself open to charges of discrimination. For example, don't say, "I know it's harder for older people to pick up computer skills, but you need to improve accuracy when using the timesheet program." Simply say, "You need to improve accuracy when using the timesheet program."

- Document all problems so that if a decision is made to terminate an employee for cause, the performance reviews will support that decision. If an employee has been having performance problems but verbal discussions have resulted in improvement, don't be tempted just to leave out the problems, as they may return. Document both the problem and the fact that the employee has improved (or not) after supervisory counseling.

When to Conduct Reviews

In some organizations, reviews for all employees are completed at the same time each year, while other organizations conduct them on the employee's hire anniversary.

"An advantage to anniversary reviews is that a manager is not loaded down with several reviews to accomplish during the same few weeks," says adviser Lisa Morton. "In such a situation, it's easy to give short shrift to the review process, and even for managers to dread the review period."

On the other hand, when all reviews are conducted at the same time of year, it's easier to connect individual performance with group or work team performance, team performance planning, and organization-wide goal setting. Despite the advantages of anniversary reviews, most nonprofits conduct all reviews in the same month each year.

A related question is whether to conduct performance reviews at the same time as salary reviews and changes. On one hand, employees are frustrated if they receive highly positive assessments and then don't see salary changes for many months. At the same time, if increases come immediately following performance reviews, some employees will see the review process as a place to argue for a raise rather than as a learning opportunity. If you conduct all performance reviews at the same time, ideally they should come before you establish salaries for the upcoming year, although individual salaries will need to be reviewed in the context of all proposed salaries before finalization. As a result, there may be only a month or two between reviews and new salary levels.

Reviews and the Budget

A common nonprofit dilemma is whether to conduct performance reviews in conjunction with the budget process or outside the budget process. Because most nonprofits tie performance reviews to pay increases, it makes sense to do reviews during the first part of the budget process. The initial budget projections will give managers a sense of whether raises will be possible with the new fiscal year and if so, what the organization-wide average will need to be.

Be careful not to inadvertently communicate false expectations to staff. For example, the budget may include an overall increase for total salaries of 3%. This doesn't mean that every employee will get a 3% raise. In fact, some salaries may be raised higher than that, and some may not be raised at all. Or, the increase may factor in salary expense for new staff positions and there will be no increases at all. Let staff know that the budget is a guide for total salary expense across the organization, not a guide for individual raises.

Performance Review Forms

Your organization probably has more than one department or working team, each with its own supervisor to carry out reviews. Even so, it's wise to use a standard form for the basic information about employees and the performance review—the core information that applies to all employees. Then, however, you might want to add a different "Part Two" for different employee categories. Just make sure the various forms are aligned in philosophy and you don't end up with too many different approaches. In a paratransit agency, for example, it would make sense to have different "Part Twos" for van drivers and fundraisers because of the different type of work they perform.

> TIP
> **The executive director's performance review is handled differently.** Because the executive director—or in the case of arts organizations, the managing director as well—reports to the board of directors, there is likely to be a completely different process by which the board reviews executive performance. See Chapter 8 for more on this topic.

A Step-by-Step Look at the Review Process

Now that we've described the many facets of the review process, let's take a look at how the performance review unfolds, from early planning through employee interview to final updating of the personnel files and oversight by senior supervisors.

As you've seen, a successful performance appraisal depends on careful preparation throughout the organization. The process should not feel endless, nor should it feel rushed. Here are eleven steps that will guide you through the process.

Step 1. HR department trains the supervisors. About a month before the performance review period, set up a meeting with everyone in your organization who will be conducting performance reviews. At the meeting, go over the review process, including any changes to the process from the prior year. Remind veterans of certain points and give people time to share experiences and tips. This is a good time to talk about goals.

Step 2. Supervisors gather data and reflect on employees' work. In the week or so before reviews start, managers should gather relevant data, including attendance records or time sheets, client logs, volunteer statistics, and any documents (such as commendation letters from clients or disciplinary memos) that have been placed in the employee's personnel file. For employees such as program managers who are responsible for a program, you'll want to see financial and programmatic data related to their program. Speak with team leaders whose teams have included the employee. In addition, supervisors should take some time to think back on their own observations and any anecdotal feedback they heard from others about the employee.

Step 3. Supervisor drafts the written review. If your organization uses a checklist, have the supervisors complete the checklist in draft form. For narrative reviews, supervisors should write up a report that draws on performance data, their own observations, and comments from others.

Step 4. Concurrently with Step 3, employees complete self-assessment forms. This involves filling out the checklist or the narrative form. Especially for professional-level staff, taking the time to reflect on their own performance is an important step.

Step 5. Have HR or another manager review the supervisor's draft report. Before an employee sees a performance review, have an HR person, the executive director, or another manager review the supervisor's draft report. The second set of eyes can help spot legal problems or unclear statements and suggest improvements. And people writing reviews will take more care if they know the review will be seen by their own manager as well as by the employee.

Step 6. Supervisor and employee meet face-to-face. Performance reviews should always be discussed in person, not on the phone or via email. The supervisor should set up a meeting and plan to go through the written report with the employee.

Step 7. Supervisor revises documents, if needed. After the meeting, the supervisor may want to make revisions to the report. The employee may have pointed out something the supervisor forgot, or may have persuaded the supervisor to revise something in the document.

Step 8. HR person reviews revised documents. The executive director or someone with an HR perspective should review all performance reviews before they are finalized and signed. This step is not a check on whether the supervisor's judgment about performance is appropriate. Instead, this HR check is to ensure that no statements have been made that could get the organization into trouble, such as an inadvertent promise about employment ("If you keep up this level of good work, we'll keep you through the grant period"). Particular attention should be paid to performance reviews that include any indications of a problem or dissatisfaction with performance, especially if there is a possibility of a termination in the future. The performance review will guide the organization's decision and, if the employee is later fired, may become evidence of the reasons for the termination.

Step 9. The supervisor and employee sign the final document. The signature section should make it clear that signing indicates that the employee has read and received the review. It does not mean that the employee has agreed with its contents.

Step 10. Place signed documents in employee files. If an employee writes a self-assessment or a response to the performance review, these documents also should be placed in the file.

Step 11. A higher-level supervisor should read the performance reviews. This last reading is not to look for legal problems, but instead helps a department head understand how better to support all employees in the department, not just those who report directly to him or her. In addition, this step helps the more senior supervisor assess how well the middle supervisor is managing. Proper supervision is a key function of many jobs, and looking over reviews allows senior personnel to assess the performance review skills of those who report to them and provide coaching as appropriate.

Strengthening Performance:
Supervision and Team Leadership

One-on-One Supervision.. 140

Dealing With Poor Performance.. 142

Legal Reminders for Supervisors... 142

The Important Role of Team Leaders.. 144

Coaching and Mentoring.. 147

    The Role of Coach in a Nonprofit... 147

    Mentoring—Enhancing Career Development 149

    Burnout... 149

Staff Training and Education.. 150

    In-House Training.. 152

    External Training... 153

    Continuing Education Opportunities.. 153

    Sending Staff to Conferences 154

    Learning through On-the-Job Training and "Apprenticeships"................ 155

    Job Expansion 156

    Career Path Development.. 157

    Use Internal Hiring to Promote Staff Development 158

Titles: More Than Just Words 159

Leadership Development.. 160

    Encourage Volunteerism by Staff.. 161

    Create Leadership Opportunities Within Your Management Team.......... 161

360-Degree Feedback.. 162

Meet Your Adviser

Sarah Gon
Title: Senior Human Resources Manager
Organization: Chinatown Community
Development Center
Location: San Francisco, California

What she does: Sarah oversees the HR functions for the organization of 130 employees, with two additional staff in HR. In addition, she manages the administration department.

What her organization does: We have a comprehensive vision of community development, which includes a quality environment, healthy neighborhood economies, and active volunteer associations. We are a community development organization that primarily serves San Francisco's Chinatown neighborhood. We play various roles, as community organizers, neighborhood advocates and planners, and developers and managers of affordable housing.

Best tip for the Accidental HR Managers: Join a local HR group to develop a network of HR professionals for legal information, to solicit suggestions, and to commiserate. Look for HR associations within specific geographic scope and industry, such as NCHRA for all employers, CompassPoint in the nonprofit industry, Bay Area LISC (Local Initiatives Support Corporation) in the affordable housing field, and SF EAC (San Francisco Employer Advisory Council), not an HR-specific group that hosts meetings on employment matters and provides an HR hotline. If your 501(c)(3) nonprofit agency opts out of the state unemployment insurance tax system, your vendor's services usually include HR advice.

HR lesson learned the hard way: Despite my reservations, a seasoned manager convinced me to immediately terminate a long-standing employee and confirmed the progressive disciplinary steps taken, albeit without HR. It was by far the worst termination scene I've experienced. The employee was unaware of any performance issues, was in complete shock, and broke down into tears. Supervisors think they've told an employee about ongoing issues and that performance expectations are not being met, but the manager more likely provided feedback, but didn't communicate overall performance concerns.

I've learned to become heavily involved in the disciplinary process, playing various roles such as neutral party during meetings, HR during counseling sessions, coach to the manager, and informal advisor to the employee. I try to balance managing the organization's liability, helping the manager, and being a fair and compassionate employer.

Song title that speaks to you about HR: "Perhaps, Perhaps, Perhaps," by Fashion Nugget.

I n much of nonprofit work, staff performance is at the heart of mission accomplishment. The performance of a great ballerina is art in and of itself, not just a cog in a ballet company's performance factory. And wonderful preschool teaching embodies the achievement of mission for a preschool; it's not simply a part of an employee's work objectives. In short, strengthening staff performance is at the core of strengthening organizational effectiveness and impact.

Nonetheless, in many nonprofits, staff training and development is neglected or, even worse, prescribed only for underperforming employees. If you are a supervisor, there are many simple techniques you can use to help strengthen the performance of those who report to you. Or, if you have HR responsibilities in your nonprofit, you can help supervisors bone up on their supervisory and staff development skills. In this chapter, we go over the various tools and strategies you can use to enhance performance management in your organization.

One-on-One Supervision

There are a startling number of books and seminars on employee supervision. The basic reality is that supervision is a relationship between two individuals: the employee and the supervisor. It is complicated like any relationship, even more so because it exists in the context of an organization and its structure, culture, and goals.

Among all the theories and "how-tos" out there, however, there are some straightforward principles that can help guide and manage this complex relationship. Here are eight of the most valuable ones that nonprofit supervisors can adhere to. Following these precepts will go a long way toward helping supervisors improve their performance as supervisors.

Supervision takes time. Supervisory and coaching activities take time—and not just around performance reviews, but every week and every day. How much time does it take? "More than you think it's going to take!" comments adviser Sarah Gon, HR Director of the Chinatown Community Development Center.

Establish and manage expectations. You will want to establish expectations for the employee's performance, what kinds of help you or others can provide, the range of authority the employee has, and how you and the employee will stay in touch. This is the core responsibility you have as a supervisor.

Adopt flexible supervisory styles that match employees' styles. Supervisors tend to think about their supervisory style as something they develop based on their own philosophy and personality. However, not all employees respond in the same way to instruction or supervision. One employee may do well with detailed instructions in advance while another may be most effective if given a chance to "jump into the pool" and work something out. As a supervisor, you want to have a portfolio of styles available, allowing you to use the supervisory style that fits a given employee's needs.

Schedule regular one-on-one meetings. Adviser Sarah Gon advises supervisors to have a regular standing meeting with each employee, whether weekly, every other week, or monthly (such as 8:30 a.m. the first Tuesday of every month). "It helps to have a forum for topics that are outside of day-to-day conversations," she says. "Allot an hour, but it may not take the whole time." Many employees appreciate a regular one-on-one. It can be especially useful for clarifying expectations and deadlines, and reducing the shocks that can occur during a performance review if you've had no opportunities to pause and reflect for an entire year.

Give feedback as soon as possible. A quick: "Your report did a great job of drawing out the key points" right after the report was submitted will inspire an employee more than a written comment six months later. Good or bad, immediate feedback is the most effective.

Support your staff with others in the organization or community. Sing the praises of your strongest employees to the management team. Stand up for them if they are criticized unfairly. At a meeting with clients or donors, introduce your staff with pride and explain their work and how well they do it.

Listen to your employees. Supervisors have a tendency to think of communication as a one-way street where they tell employees what to do. Remind them to listen as carefully as they give direction.

Get help when you need it. Most of the time, supervisors look for information about an issue only when problems come up. This is okay as long as they have a good overview of their role and awareness of the issues to watch out for. For example, supervisors don't need to remember all the steps in how to handle a termination or leave of absence, but they should know to go talk to HR before they make any promises or decisions about those things.

Dealing With Poor Performance

Many supervisors put off giving corrective or negative feedback until the employee's annual or scheduled performance review. But just as ongoing positive feedback helps employees, ongoing corrective coaching must occur as well. Sometimes, all you might need is a quick: "Please don't chew gum when you're on the phone with clients."

Often a supervisor will begin to have a nagging feeling that an employee is not performing at the necessary level. Perhaps a new employee just doesn't seem to be catching on as quickly as anticipated. Or a long-term employee seems to have become lazy or distracted. Rather than waiting for the next formal performance review, you'll have better luck correcting problems if you bring them to the employee's attention right away.

For more on performance and behavior problems, see Chapter 5.

Legal Reminders for Supervisors

It's all too easy for a supervisor to unintentionally create legal problems. In a moment of sympathy, frustration, or enthusiasm, a supervisor might say something that he or she later doesn't want to or can't make good on. You can minimize these problems by training supervisors about potential problem areas.

Here are some of the key things you should advise anyone in a supervisory role to remember during interactions with other employees or staff members.

Do not make any job promises. Never make commitments on behalf of the organization. Don't say: "If you show that you can handle this project, you will get more responsibilities and a raise." Better to say: "If you handle this project well, that may open the door to a discussion about expanding your role here."

Don't mention you've put in a promotion request before you've gotten it approved. Raising expectations only to dash them is a surefire way to end up with an unhappy employee on your hands and potential grounds for a lawsuit.

Do not threaten. It's appropriate to let people know there may be consequences if a particular behavior continues, but don't commit the organization to any type of action. Don't say: "If you don't improve your attitude, you're outta here." Better to say: "These rude and negative interactions with coworkers are inappropriate and must stop immediately."

Watch out for bullying. Teasing—whether about something personal like a hairstyle or a work matter like tardiness—can feel like good natured ribbing to one person but bullying and harassment to the person being "ribbed." Workplace bullying is persistent, aggressive, unreasonable behavior toward a coworker or subordinate. Make sure your supervisors are trained to identify behavior that might be considered bullying. If in doubt, supervisors should know to check with someone in HR.

Be alert to any type of harassment. In many nonprofits, there's a sense that "We're all on the same page," and people may not immediately recognize racial, sexual, religious, and other kinds of harassment. Make sure your supervisors are trained to identify any type of behavior that might be considered harassment. If in doubt, supervisors should know to check with someone in HR.

Be fair and treat people consistently. If your organization requires that vacation requests be authorized by a supervisor, the rule should apply to everyone. Nonprofits often ask employees to put up with difficult circumstances, and people are more willing to do so if they feel that rules are enforced and shared fairly.

EXAMPLE: Emily, an outstanding program staff person at Thornhill Homeownership Center, asked if she could work at home on Fridays for three months while her mother was visiting. Her supervisor, Joshua, was happy to accommodate her request. When Rachel, whose performance in the same job was just barely satisfactory, made a similar request, Joshua said no. Rachel complained to the executive director and because there were no clear guidelines for working from home, Rachel was granted her request. Afterwards, guidelines were drawn up for working at home privileges that would have made the criteria clear and usable.

Remedy situations quickly. If you've said or done something you aren't sure was appropriate, talk it over right away with your own supervisor or someone in HR. This conversation might reassure you that you handled things properly or provide the first step in preventing legal problems. Either way, you will have acted responsibly and will be learning for the future.

The Important Role of Team Leaders

In many nonprofits, work is often done in teams. As a result, a team structure may exist within a more formal supervisory structure. Often, the supervisory structure will fade into the background as the group works side by side on a project. The supervisor or team manager for the project becomes more of a team leader, whose primary responsibility is to oversee the project as a whole rather than supervising the performance or work of individual team members.

For instance, there might be a training manager leading a group that is putting on a conference. As work progresses, team members naturally make decisions, allocate assignments, and follow up with one another. The manager should neither insist on knowing everything that's going on, nor stand aside and leave the team unsupervised. The manager's role shifts from that of a supervisor focusing on the performance of individual team members to that of a team leader making sure the project is progressing on schedule and according to plan.

In any team management situation, the team leader can be most effective by acknowledging the subtle changes in work relationships and adjusting and following through on some "behind-the-scenes" actions such as:

- making sure that responsibilities are assigned to team members who are best suited for the work they have been assigned
- finding opportunities to give individuals challenging work that builds new skills
- encouraging team members to anticipate problems and suggest solutions
- keeping upper management informed at the right level of detail
- keeping the work activities aligned with the organization's goals, values, and practices, and
- ensuring that both the revenue and expense budgets for the project are met.

Some people move naturally between the role of individual supervisor and team leader. For others, specific training can help them understand the distinct roles and responsibilities. Especially in nonprofits where so much work is done in teams, training in team leadership skills is often overlooked. Be sure you support team leaders as a crucial way to support team performance.

In most nonprofits, teams are not always led by the supervisor of the group. For example, in a fundraising department, the development director may be a team member—but not the team leader—of the annual luncheon team. That team may be led by a person who reports to the development director.

The informal decision making and dynamics of teams may complicate the role of the supervisor. The supervisor must relinquish decision making to the team leader and the team, but must also ensure that the work is progressing properly and that inappropriate choices are not made. This complex situation (where the supervisor is working "for" the team leader on the luncheon while the team leader reports to the supervisor) can be confusing for supervisors. An important role for senior management and for HR is to help supervisors and team leaders understand the nuances and the value of teams and developing team leadership.

Seven Tips for Team Leaders

1. Make sure everyone on the team understands the goals for the year (or whatever time period you use). Ask team members to participate in setting the goals to involve them in the process and to make sure the goals set are clear, complete, and achievable.

2. Communicate progress to the team and work together to find ways to overcome obstacles. Make sure the team celebrates accomplishments.

3. Hold regular team meetings. For example, an accounting manager can hold a weekly Monday morning meeting of the accounting group. In the meeting, everyone can settle into the week by getting refreshed on immediate tasks (such as payroll on Wednesday), and everyone can check in on progress and goals for longer-term work (such as gathering data for a revision of the check-signing policy). When a team's members are frequently out of the office, a twice-a-month regular conference call can keep everyone connected.

4. Identify team learning opportunities. These could be software training, bringing in a department head or the executive director to discuss strategy, or taking the team to visit a similar department in another organization. Team learning not only builds skills and knowledge but increases team cohesiveness.

5. Draw the team's attention to the mission and matters outside the team. Teams often face inward and focus on tasks. An important role for the team leader is to draw the team's attention outside—to the needs of internal customers, clients, audience members, and the field (such as the international economic development field). Identify a constituency—such as the accounting department or gallery visitors—and ask the team to think of ways to support that constituency better. Help the team understand its role in the organization as a whole.

6. Be explicit about the team's decision-making authority. When a decision is being discussed, make sure everyone understands whether the team can make the decision or whether the team's discussion is intended to help you—as team leader—make the decision.

7. Hold the team accountable for its goals, its internal workings, and the way members support one another. Periodically ask the team to reflect on the degree to which it holds itself and its members accountable.

In organizations where a formal supervisory structure exists along with work that is being done in teams, you should identify team leaders and make sure their work as leader is reviewed. Anyone who supervises a team leader should include the results and productivity of the team in that person's appraisal, as well as how well the team is functioning. In nonprofits, supervisors are often team leaders, so they will need to be trained in team leadership and evaluated on their team leadership abilities.

Coaching and Mentoring

Traditionally, coaching and mentoring were activities that occurred, typically informally, between a supervisor (or another experienced employee) and a subordinate or new employee. These days, more and more nonprofits are putting formal systems in place or using outside coaches and mentors to train their staff, especially at the management level. Understanding the core ideas of coaching will help you develop your own system or approach for fostering these important relationships within your organization.

The Role of Coach in a Nonprofit

Think for a moment about the relationship between a coach and an athlete, and then think about the relationship between a supervisor and subordinate. Our society tends to think of a coach's role as helping athletes to achieve their inner potential and succeed, whereas too often it seems we think of supervisors as there to discipline or make sure a subordinate doesn't make a mistake.

In nonprofits, the supervisory role has the potential to be more like a coach than that of a disciplinarian. In fact, many nonprofit supervisors already instinctively act like coaches to their staff. They encourage, critique performance, and help employees focus and develop their skills. This type of "coach supervisor" helps individuals discover solutions for themselves rather than simply telling them what to do. Training supervisors in these kinds of coaching techniques can help them expand the skills and instincts they bring to their supervisory roles.

Some nonprofits hire external coaches to help them develop and manage their staff most effectively. You may wish to consider this arrangement if your organization has readily available financial resources. The employee most likely to benefit from an external coach is a proven, talented individual who has demonstrated commitment to the organization but has somehow gotten stuck, seemingly unable to overcome a particular deficiency on the job. Some large organizations partner an external coach with a midlevel manager who has shown significant potential to move into higher levels of responsibility.

Typically, professional coaches will come in and have a face-to-face meeting with the person they will be coaching, such as the executive director or a member of the management team. After that, meetings may be in person or over the phone, often for an hour or so a week.

There are different types of professional coaches, so make sure you know what you are looking for before you start your search. A technical coach with specialized knowledge, for instance, might be appropriate to help a specific employee in a certain area. If you have a fundraising coordinator who is relatively inexperienced, you might decide to hire a fundraising coach (perhaps a retired development director) to give that person the time and attention necessary to learn the proper skills for the job. This is different from hiring a fundraising consultant who helps management make decisions about fundraising strategies. A coach strengthens an individual's performance on the job but doesn't do the job.

CAUTION

Make sure any professional coach you hire understands the nonprofit world. An executive coach who usually works with midlevel managers in large electronics corporations may be of little help—and could possibly do harm—if hired to work with a midlevel manager in a shelter for abused women. Any coach you hire should be familiar with the nonprofit workplace and the field in which your nonprofit works. This can often be more important than the credentials or certification of the coach.

Life coaching is another type of coaching. This would most likely come up in the context of a life coach working with a program director to help the director think through how to be most effective on the job. The coaching might include some advice about leadership or management skills, but could also include other things like developing a personal exercise plan. Many coaches provide both management-oriented and life-oriented coaching. Be sure you know which you want and what the organization feels comfortable paying for.

Mentoring—Enhancing Career Development

A mentor does not play the same role as a supervisor and usually is not the same person. A mentor is a senior person in the organization—often from a different department—who is matched with a new staff member to help that person thrive and advance within the organization. In most nonprofits, mentoring is informal and occurs simply because an affinity develops between two individuals. But mentors also can be assigned by a supervisor or by the HR department in a more formal program.

If you establish a mentoring program, be clear about how mentors will be recruited and selected, how matches can be terminated if either party is unsatisfied, and how mentors will be trained.

Adviser Sarah Gon suggests that HR staff and nonprofit leaders find ways to "encourage informal mentoring without having to establish a formal program for mentoring." For interested staff, she provides information about what mentors do, such as monthly coffee meetings or introducing the mentee to others at a reception. She encourages senior staff to consider being more active and conscious as mentors. She also encourages new staff to talk to their supervisors or to HR to help identify an appropriate mentor.

Burnout

Everyone has a bad day or a bad week at work once in awhile. Sometimes depression or fatigue can cause an employee to be less productive for a longer period of time, even months. Burnout is more specific: it refers to the kind of tiredness, dullness, and irritability that comes from working at an unsustainable pace or zeal for a long period of time.

A person at risk for burnout may be impatient, jaded, always exhausted, or negative. In a meeting, nothing seems like a good idea. An employee who used to jump at the opportunity to leap a tall building now can hardly get out of the lunchroom.

People in nonprofit human services are particularly susceptible to burnout and compassion fatigue. When a person cares deeply about helping kids stay in school, there are bound to be discouraging or even despairing points. Advocates are also prone to burnout; if you're fighting everyday pesticides in food or for gay rights, you can wonder if you're making any real progress.

Performance or behavior problems that are attributed to burnout shouldn't be treated as more acceptable than problems from other causes. Try to help others recognize that an employee suffering from burnout may not be able to recover their energy and productivity, and may even need to leave the organization for their own wellbeing as well as for the organization.

If burnout is a common problem in your organization, consider ways to mitigate the stress and to help employees become more "stress hardy." For example, in some organizations, people in high-stress positions have paid, scheduled break time for reflection and renewal.

Staff Training and Education

"We do two things in the Army," says one Army officer who retired to run a nonprofit for people with disabilities: "We fight and we train." In the nonprofit sector, sometimes the term "continuing education" is more easily understood than "training," but both mean the same thing: structured learning strengthens performance.

Training and education are not only ways to enhance the performance of current staff, but also help attract new staff and keep existing staff satisfied and interested. Increasingly, people value gaining skills and experiences that will keep them competitive in the labor market.

For many people, the term "training" conjures up images of a dull instructor lecturing on a seemingly irrelevant topic in a crowded overheated room. However, done properly, a training session can not only build skills and knowledge, but can change a person's or a group's attitude.

Training is said to work best based on the following principles, with the acronym of "KASA:"

- knowledge
- attitude
- skills, and
- aspirations.

For example, sending people who answer calls at a cancer hotline to take a workshop on new cancer treatments would provide them with information about new treatments (knowledge), renew their enthusiasm for helping patients (attitude), help them listen for clues on whether a caller is ready to hear about new treatments (skills), and inspire them to learn even more (aspiration).

In another example, a program director might go to a nonprofit finance workshop and learn about balance sheets (knowledge), gain confidence in financial matters (attitude), learn new formats for end-of-year forecasting (skills), and get inspired to be financial leaders, not just financial managers (aspiration).

MYTH

If Employees Get More Skills, They're More Likely to Leave

A common worry among managers is that training people just gives them the tools and motivation to leave for better jobs.

Reality: In today's world, people change jobs fairly frequently and departures are normal and inevitable. Meanwhile, people enjoy jobs where they are constantly being challenged and offered opportunities for learning. If you improve the competitive skills of your staff, you will improve the overall effectiveness of your organization, and staff will appreciate the investment in them ... and as a result, stay longer.

In-House Training

Many organizations choose to do their training in-house, conducted by staff or outside trainers. Staff meetings can provide an excellent venue for mini training sessions. For example, you might have a monthly meeting for your entire staff that includes a 20-minute discussion on how to welcome visitors with disabilities or a brief presentation from accounting on timesheet coding.

One of the advantages of doing your training in-house is that the training can be closely tailored to the needs of your organization. For example, you can use the training to:

- train staff on a specific area, such as how to use a shared database or how to explain requirements to clients
- create greater cohesiveness in a team, department, or organization by providing the training participants with a shared experience, shared skills acquisition, and shared vocabulary for their everyday work
- address a concern that has come up within a work group, such as proper equipment maintenance, or
- convey your organization's message about mission, values, and norms.

EXAMPLE: A legal services nonprofit is inundated daily with calls from low-income people with a wide variety of legal needs and a high sense of urgency and emotional stress. The organization hired someone trained in emergency phone work to come in and teach the staff how to handle callers in distress, how to communicate effectively on the phone, and other skills. Even though the executive director never answered calls himself, he sat in the front row and participated in the training session. This demonstrated a commitment to learning, and a respect for the training content and speaker, and helped make the session feel like a group opportunity to strengthen skills.

External Training

Although there are many advantages to in-house training, for some things it's more valuable to draw on training offered outside of the organization. External training can:

- provide context for how similar work is done in other organizations
- give staff exposure to well-respected outside experts in the area in which they work
- expose participants to others with similar jobs, which can help develop a sense of professionalism and perhaps career aspirations, and
- provide networking opportunities to connect individuals and organizations.

In addition, sometimes being removed from your own work environment and the people you're usually surrounded by can lead to deeper reflection about your own work and performance than would otherwise occur if you never had that opportunity.

Budgeting for Staff Development

At Midtown Community Development Corporation, each department is given $500 per person per year to spend on staff development. The department head can use the funds (such as $5,000 for a department of ten) to bring training in-house, send individual staff to outside trainings or a conference, take the staff on a field trip, or anything else. "It doesn't mean that each person gets $500 worth of staff development," commented the HR manager. "The department head decides what individuals need and what the team needs and wants."

Continuing Education Opportunities

Another way to support staff development in your organization is to encourage enrollment in continuing education programs offered by colleges and universities. Some nonprofits can afford to give tuition support to promising or long-term employees. Others can be flexible with working hours so an employee can attend classes during the day or may allow a certain number of hours per week of class attendance to be treated as paid work time.

Particularly for organizations committed to hiring from low-income or low-skilled constituencies, supporting continuing education for employees can be crucial to retaining and developing staff. At the same time, it is highly congruent with mission. Helping a staff person obtain an associate of arts degree or helping a program manager obtain a Master's degree in business, for example, could be important ways of demonstrating commitment to staff development and also lead to better mission work.

Sending Staff to Conferences

Conferences are one of the few "perks" available to nonprofit staff. Even if a conference is just across town (rather than in the Bahamas), an employee can have an enjoyable and energizing time at a conference. In addition to the direct learning opportunities in conference sessions, employees learn about organizations doing similar work, what kinds of people are in the field, what jobs are available or seen as most desirable, and other relevant things going on in their world.

When you send an employee to a conference, be sure that policies on paid time and travel reimbursements are clear. Encourage the attendees to go to a variety of sessions, not just the ones on the topics most familiar to them. And let them know it's okay to use the time away for some personal development too, like exploring a new city or going to a speaker that seems interesting but not likely to cover much relevant work-related information.

Conferences also provide an opportunity for your organization to represent itself to others through the staff that you send. Your staff should know that they represent your organization. It can be exciting and inspiring for them to describe to others the work your organization does. They will get to see how people respond to them and the work you do.

Finally, conferences help employees develop their identities as members of a field or movement, not just of an organization's staff. For instance, a food bank manager who understands the context of the antihunger, antipoverty movement will be a better manager back at home by gaining the big-picture context of the work in which your organization is involved. This sense of context will help the food bank manager make better decisions: He or she may have a better idea of hunger trends at home, regionally, and even nationally; the funding picture may become more clear; and problem-solving is likely to become less daunting. Experience at conferences may also make the manager a happier, more inspired person.

Learning through On-the-Job Training and "Apprenticeships"

On-the-job training ("OJT") refers to learning that takes place in the course of doing the actual job.

Much of the work done in nonprofits is more skill-based (like carpentry) than knowledge-based (like sociology). While a carpenter may value classes and books, carpentry is learned primarily through apprenticeships. Similarly, a new language is learned partly in the classroom, but the most effective learning takes place by immersion and practice, practice, practice. However, OJT does not mean simply putting someone on the job and answering questions (or worse, criticizing missteps). Effective OJT is about apprenticeships: structured growth through new challenges with feedback, coaching, and testing at every step of the way.

> **EXAMPLE:** After each meeting they had with a corporate sponsor, Jamie and Marc would spend a few minutes debriefing. As her supervisor, Marc would point out what he saw as the best and worst things Jamie had said or done during the meeting and make suggestions for the future. This would lead to a discussion about Marc's actions and the reasons for them as well; Jamie found these brief coaching sessions immensely helpful as she learned more about working with corporate donors.

Job Expansion

In most nonprofits, someone who is willing and able to take on more responsibilities will be given as much or as many as he or she can take on—and then some. As a result, jobs change and expand over time. For many people who work in nonprofits, these new duties and the possibility of changing job responsibilities are what keep the work interesting and rewarding.

But such changes in duties are not always accompanied by an increase in authority or additional resources, or a change in title or job description. Often, it's not until someone's annual performance review that the person's job description is reviewed and changed to match reality. A person whose job has expanded over the course of the year should have those new responsibilities recognized at the right point with a clear revision of the job description and new duties.

Here's a common nonprofit scenario: Vanessa worked as an administrative assistant for the New Morning College Project, which helps low-income students with college applications and tests. When Erica, the development coordinator, went out on maternity leave, Vanessa was asked to manage some of the fundraising paperwork. She enjoyed it and started taking on more responsibilities. She wrote donor acknowledgment letters and eventually even wrote a short Letter of Inquiry. By the end of the year, Vanessa was working 50% as a development assistant and 50% as administrative support, and had received a modest pay raise. The problem was that this new job–50% admin/50% development—had not been posted as a vacant position and others were not given a chance to apply. There were charges of favoritism, and people resented Vanessa's new role. A lot of the ill will could have been prevented if the job vacancy had been posted internally so that anyone could have applied for the position. The job may have still changed over time because of Vanessa's eagerness to take on more and more responsibilities. But at least everyone in the organization would have been aware of and understood the process.

The lines between job expansion, the evolution of a job into a different job, and a promotion from one job to another can be very fuzzy. The expansion of a stellar employee's job can easily turn into the creation of a new job. You may also have a situation where someone's title changes even though the job remains essentially the same. This might happen, for example, to comply with government contract guidelines.

Keep on top of what your staff is actually doing and make sure that you follow proper channels when one of your staff member's role and responsibilities evolve. Follow the processes and policies you have in place for advertising and hiring. In short, make sure new jobs are posted and open to all staff and that if the actual work being done by anyone has significantly changed, the new work and responsibilities are recognized with appropriate changes in title, job description, and salary.

Career Path Development

In a large nonprofit, there are often well-worn paths for how employees advance. At a YMCA, for instance, a person might move from an entry-level position as a swim instructor to a supervisor of instructors, to a program manager, and from there to program director, then director of programs, then chief operating officer, and ultimately to chief executive officer at a different YMCA. But in most nonprofits, the small number of staff combined with rapidly changing programs means that career paths are nonexistent.

In either case, supervisors and HR staff should seek opportunities to discuss career paths with employees. In some cases, you can help an employee identify a position within your organization as a goal. In other cases, you may work with an employee who wants to be an executive director someday, and you can offer guidance in skills, networking, and degrees that might be helpful.

The question that supervisors can ask is: "What skills and experiences can I help you get on this job that will help you on your next job, whether here or somewhere else?"

Use Internal Hiring to Promote Staff Development

Knowing that an organization promotes from within is often valued by staff, and helps them think about developing their skills. A supervisor might ask a promising employee about desired positions within the organization and then help devise a plan for professional development that will help the employee get there. This benefits the employee, who is motivated to develop more skills and take extra steps to demonstrate worthiness. It also is good for the organization, which benefits by having motivated employees and by being involved in the development of its staff.

The best way to promote internal hiring is to make sure that whenever a job vacancy occurs, you "advertise" the job internally, either before or simultaneously with any outside listing. If you do it simultaneously, you could let staff know that no hire will be made within the first seven days. This gives all internal candidates a chance to express interest in the position before anyone is hired. At the end of the week, you could hire from among the applications received thus far or continue to accept applications. But all potential internal hires would have had an opportunity to be considered in the first instance.

> **EXAMPLE:** Jessica, a housing manager in an affordable housing organization, hoped to eventually be promoted to the position of senior housing manager. Her supervisor, Eric, agreed to get her the training necessary for HUD certification and to allow her to work at different facilities so that her experience would be broader. His engagement with her professional development and career goals not only resulted in a stronger employee, but strengthened Jessica's involvement and commitment to the organization. When a senior housing manager position opened up, she submitted her resume with other internal and external applicants and, much to her delight, was chosen for the job.

Titles: More Than Just Words

Despite the importance of job titles, not much attention is paid to titles for existing staff and how they may need to change over time. A person's job title has both an internal and an external function and is often very important to employees. Internally, a title must suggest both the content of the job and the level of authority. Externally, a title is a strong statement about clout and importance. You have probably heard someone complain, "I need a more official title so that people will take my calls."

Be consistent with titles. Don't use "administrative assistant" in one department if "administrative associate" is used for the same position in another department. If you have a president and vice presidents, have a vice president of finance rather than some other title like finance director. Use internal title changes to signify a change in an employee's job or authority. If a person is promoted above peers, for instance, having a new title will help make the transition clear to everyone.

At the same time that you balance the significance of a title for internal and external purposes, be aware of the dangers of "title inflation." An all-too-common phenomenon in nonprofits is to upgrade a person's title unnecessarily and perhaps inappropriately. It may be tempting to agree to a request for title change to satisfy a good employee and compensate for your organization's inability to provide a pay raise. But, there are negative ramifications to this. Other staff may resent a title that is seen as falsely important, and outsiders can feel tricked by an inflated title as well.

If you have gotten to the point where you feel that titles have run wild in your organization, perhaps with more "vice presidents" or "directors" than ordinary staff, consider a "title reset." It may be useful to review all job descriptions and titles and institute a new taxonomy.

Leadership Development

More and more nonprofit leadership development programs are becoming available to nonprofit staff, especially executive directors. And better news yet, you can often obtain outside funding for many of them.

Leadership development courses come in many formats, but usually take a small group of selected participants through a series of sessions. Employees with a lot of potential benefit enormously from nonprofit leadership development programs that focus on developing leadership skills. These skills include self-reflection, self-monitoring, choosing the right behavior, developing vision, understanding complex systems, identifying appropriate goals, and integrating personal vision and qualities with organizational vision and values. In addition to skills training, leadership programs provide excellent networking opportunities and out-of-the-office time for reflection.

Some leadership programs provide an overview of management topics, while others focus on personal growth and fulfillment. Some programs bring cohorts together, such as leaders of youth development programs or community clinic directors. Some integrate experiential learning and community learning into their programs. Not all programs make a distinction between management and leadership, even though these can be very different things. Think of the likely difference between a session on "how to do accounting" and one on "how to lead an accounting team."

You can help your staff find nonprofit leadership programs in your community and choose the program that will be most helpful to them. One manager might benefit most from a city leadership program run by the chamber of commerce, while another might thrive in a leadership development program for middle managers in affordable housing. Check out the different options and think about what is best for the person and what type of leader or skills you're trying to develop for your organization.

Encourage Volunteerism by Staff

Many corporations encourage their managers to serve on nonprofits' boards, partly for networking purposes, but also for leadership development. People who serve on boards learn group skills such as building consensus, mapping strategies, learning how to be persuasive, and promoting damage control. Nonprofits should also encourage and support staff to serve on the boards of other nonprofits or in community service leagues, such as the Rotary or Soroptomists. You will find that this type of work not only develops leadership skills, but that people who serve on boards of other organizations often develop a greater appreciation for their own organization and its management.

Create Leadership Opportunities Within Your Management Team

Although most nonprofits have management teams, few of them view management team meetings as opportunities for leadership development. Instead, management team meetings are usually dominated by budget discussions, staffing changes, and inter-program coordination. Try to find ways to develop leadership among management team members. One way to do this is to have management team members become leaders or heads of cross-department committees. For example, a management team member could be appointed head of the safety committee or a cultural competence task force. They would report back to the management team on that committee's performance. And, a supervisor or a coach could be appointed to review and critique their leadership skills, or this could be done by the management team.

Management teams also benefit from strategy discussions, particularly those that bring in information about trends and other organizations in the field. When managers understand the outside environment in which your nonprofit operates, that understanding can strengthen their ability to frame and communicate a meaningful vision for their team.

360-Degree Feedback

A circle has 360 degrees—and 360-degree feedback is a process in which input on performance is gathered from people who interact with an employee from many different angles. Sometimes this approach is called multisource feedback or multi-rater feedback.

People are frequently intrigued by the idea of 360-degree feedback, and it's discussed more than it is used. A common assumption is that 360-degree feedback is a component of performance review. But this extensive and time-consuming practice is best as part of an effort to advance the skills of individual staff members. The individuals who show great promise and who may be poised to take on more leadership are those who benefit most from 360-degree feedback.

Here's how it works. In a 360-degree feedback for a program manager, feedback forms would be completed internally by the manager's supervisor, subordinates, volunteers, and coworkers. In addition, feedback would be collected from external sources such as clients, partners in other organizations, and funders. At least some of the feedback is likely to be personal, contradictory, and from people without training in how to complete the form. Because responses are anonymous, it's not possible to explore a comment further or to ask for details. This is partly why 360-degree feedback works best for coming up with a training or staff development plan, rather than as part of performance appraisal.

Very seldom does a nonprofit conduct 360-degree feedback on all its employees in the same year. Instead, 360-degree feedback may be used for individuals who have been identified as promising leaders, or for people who have been on staff for a certain amount of time—say five years. This process of feedback is time-consuming for those completing the forms and for the supervisor and employee as they discuss the results and devise a staff development plan.

If you decide to use 360-degree feedback, you can draw up your own questions, using different ones for the different types of raters you'll be using. You will want to solicit ratings from enough people at different parts of the "circle" so that you have a full picture and are not relying on just one or two opinions—but you don't want so many raters that the process becomes unwieldy. There are generic 360-degree feedback forms available in books and on the Internet, and some Web-based companies have online survey services that collect, sort, and process the information. These online providers cost anywhere from $250 to $400 per employee being rated.

You will need to be careful and thorough as you analyze the feedback. It's important to decide whether all of the feedback or only some of it will be shared with the employee. Focus on comments that can help employees understand the perceptions of those around them, how those perceptions were formed, and how to respond. Work with the employee on developing a plan to address any concerns that were raised or to maximize potential that was identified in the feedback. Check back with the employee from time to time, as 360-degree feedback is often felt deeply and emotionally by recipients.

TIP
External and internal customer satisfaction surveys can also provide useful feedback. Many nonprofits have systems in place to obtain external customer feedback, whether through conference evaluation forms, surveys of people who receive home-delivered meals, or other means. This information is similar to what you get from 360-degree feedback. In addition, surveys of internal customers can be useful, although they are less common. For example, you can periodically survey staff to see how satisfied they are with the work of the computer support staff or various program departments. Such surveys are easy to do, depersonalize the feedback, and help remind staff that accountability to one another is an important part of everyone's jobs.

Steps in 360-Degree Feedback

1. Agree with the employee that a 360-degree feedback process will be used, explaining why this employee was chosen and the goals of the process.
2. Make a list of who will provide the ratings, with perhaps two to five in each of the following categories:
   - peers within the organization
   - direct reports
   - clients
   - volunteers
   - managers at level above employee
   - partners at other nonprofits, and
   - funders.
3. Develop questionnaires; send with instructions to raters.
4. Gather and analyze feedback.
5. Meet with employee.
6. Work with employee to develop and implement a development plan.
7. Check back with employee several times on the plan and on any thoughts that may have arisen from ongoing reflection on the feedback.

EXAMPLE: Lisa's supervisor Daniel felt she showed strong potential in her role managing a youth journalism program, and saw her as a potential program director or executive director someday (at a different organization). He suggested a 360-degree feedback to help her understand better how people perceive her strengths and weaknesses.

Two themes emerged strongly from the feedback. Managers who were senior to Lisa appreciated her commitment and her "touch" with young people. But Lisa was shocked by the harsh, negative feedback from the youth workers who reported to her, as she thought of herself as a great supervisor. She even stayed home from work for a few days as she couldn't bear facing the people who had criticized her (although she didn't know which of the youth workers had said what). Both she and Daniel learned a good deal from the feedback, but Daniel wondered if he had made the right decision. After all, he had known that Lisa's staff resented her but had wanted the feedback to come directly from them. In retrospect, he wondered if a less painful and shorter process could have produced the same results. ●

Terminations and Layoffs

Trying to Improve Employee Performance and Behavior 171

Before Firing—Steps to Take 174

Firing At-Will Employees 176

Termination for Cause 178

Firing "On the Spot" 179

Once You've Decided to Fire 179

    Nuts and Bolts: References, Health Benefits, and Other Matters 180

    Final Paycheck and IT Issues 181

    Letting the Employee Know: The Termination Meeting 182

    Communicating to Staff 183

Layoffs 184

    Preparing for Layoffs 185

    Pay Cuts Instead of Layoffs? 188

Handling Exit Interviews and Forms 188

    Holding Exit Interviews for Employees in Nonmanagerial Roles 189

    Holding Exit Interviews for Management Team Members 190

Avoiding Layoffs Through Furloughs 191

Temporary Layoffs 192

Postemployment Health Insurance 192

What Happens If an Ex-Employee Sues? 193

    Discrimination Complaints 194

    Other Types of Claims 195

    How It Ends Up 195

Who's Eligible for Unemployment Insurance 196

    Steps in the Claims Process 197

Providing References 198

Meet Your Adviser

Ellen Aldridge, JD
Title: Labor and Employment Risk Manager
Company: Nonprofits Insurance Alliance Group
(encompasses Alliance for Nonprofits' Insurance (ANI)
and Nonprofits' Insurance Alliance of California (NIAC))
Location: Santa Cruz, California

What she does: Pamela Fyfe and I are essentially a free help desk for our nonprofit insureds to assist them in navigating through complex employment issues. They call and email with questions about topics like pending employee discipline or terminations, how to manage leaves of absence, or how to conduct a harassment investigation. We give them advice about the law and the various options for handling the situation, and then they decide the course of action they want to take knowing the risks. We also write the "Ask Rita in HR" column for Blue Avocado.

What her organization does: We provide liability insurance to 501(c)(3) nonprofits. It makes business sense for us to help our members minimize potential loss. We also provide our member-insureds free or reduced cost risk management support, such as driver training, sexual harassment training, and many other services.

Best tips for HR managers including Accidental HR managers: If an employment lawsuit ends up in court, if you didn't tell them in writing, you didn't tell them. Next: When you put an HR question into Google, always put the state you're in because state laws are so different. Better yet, subscribe to an employment law database service—it's money well spent.

HR lesson you learned the hard way: You need to hear all sides of the story, including the manager and employee involved as well as neutral witnesses. You don't want to hear for the first time in a lawsuit that the employee who was terminated for excessive absenteeism told her supervisor that she had a medical condition!

Song title that speaks to you about HR: "The Long and Winding Road," by Paul McCartney. HR issues rarely take the straight path!

Meet Your Adviser

Pamela Fyfe, JD, MS
Title: Labor & Employment Risk Manager
Organization: Nonprofits Insurance Alliance Group,
encompassing Alliance for Nonprofit Insurance (ANI)
and Nonprofits' Insurance Alliance of California (NIAC)
Location: Santa Cruz, California

What she does: As an employment attorney, I help our member-insured nonprofits either prevent litigation or, if they are sued, help them do everything right so that the nonprofit wins. In a typical week, Ellen Aldridge and I advise about 45 nonprofits on a wide variety of employment issues ... all at no cost to them.

What her organization does: We're a nonprofit ourselves: a nonprofit insurance company exclusively for nonprofits. We serve our members. If you have Directors and Officers insurance through us you can call us as often as you like and we will give you the best advice we can. You don't have to take our advice, and it won't affect your rate or how we handle your claim.

Best tip for HR manager including the Accidental HR manager: The person in charge of HR is often a finance person. Finance people often think in "black and white," but employment issues can be gray, with dotted, not straight lines. So my tip is to be more flexible and practice patience. Many times a thoughtful patient approach will stop a lawsuit in its tracks.

HR lesson learned the hard way: One time an HR person called and said her executive director was about to fire someone who was over 60, and had been saying: "We don't want anybody that old." The HR person had been unable to convince the ED that it would appear to be age discrimination unless other steps were taken first. I've found this is pretty common: that the HR person can't convince the ED about how to handle an HR matter. I've learned to tell the HR person: "Blame it on me ... say that the NIAC employment specialist gave you this advice; have the ED call me and I'll take the heat."

Song title that speaks to you about HR: I love country music, the Beatles, and Paul Simon. I have to go with the Beatles: "We Can Work It Out."

Sooner or later, every nonprofit will have to fire or lay off employees: hiring mistakes happen; a long-time employee might slide into poor performance, or financial concerns could make layoffs necessary. All employee departures are accompanied by emotional turmoil. It's wrenching to see a well-liked, high-performing staff person leave for another city or another job. And terminations and layoffs are especially difficult. They're hard on the employees being let go, their coworkers, the people making the decision, and the people giving the news.

Terminations and layoffs are also a cause for concern because they can lead to lawsuits. Even though your employees may be at-will employees, there is still room for liability. An employee who has been let go might sue for wrongful discharge, harassment or discrimination, or improper classification (as an independent contractor or an exempt employee not entitled to overtime). In addition, the way the termination is handled can lead to legal problems if final pay was not timely or correctly paid, or if something defamatory was said in the process.

For many legal and other reasons, terminations and layoffs must be handled with care, paying particular attention both to employees' legal rights and protections and the emotions that are likely to be involved. This chapter can help you make sure that termination decisions are handled properly and legally.

Terminations for cause can be broadly cast into two categories: performance problems and behavior problems. Performance problems are related to an employee's failure to meet performance goals or standards, while behavior problems are related to violation of standards or rules of conduct. These can overlap; for instance, rudeness could be viewed as either related to performance or behavior. Keep in mind that at-will employees can be fired without specifying which behavior or performance problem is the issue, or any reason at all.

TIP

Firings and layoffs are different. Firing refers to an employee dismissal related to behavior, while a layoff refers to dismissal due to budget cutbacks, reorganization, or other reasons that are not related to employee behavior. Both are types of termination, although "termination" usually refers to someone being fired.

Trying to Improve Employee Performance and Behavior

Nonprofits seem to have an especially difficult time letting staff go. Some of the reasons for this reluctance to fire or lay off may be attributed to the following:

- Many nonprofits are grounded in a belief that people are capable of change. As a result, if an underperforming employee doesn't improve, the supervisor may keep wondering, "Maybe I haven't done enough yet, or found the right ways to motivate this person to improve."

- Nonprofits with constituents on staff find it especially painful to let them go. For example, a supervisor in a drug abuse clinic could well be reluctant to fire or lay off a former client who now works at the clinic, in part from worry that the person will go back to drugs if out of a job.

- Nonprofit staff typically care about coworkers and know about one another's personal lives. It can be hard to fire or lay off someone who has a child with a chronic illness or who may not easily find another job.

- Nonprofits worry that they won't find anybody better for the job, so they keep a problem employee in fear of being unable to hire a replacement that's better.

- Sometimes nonprofits are so skittish about lawsuits that they are overly reluctant to fire or lay off anyone, especially someone in a protected class.

Because of these concerns, firings are often done only as a last resort after considerable exploration of other alternatives. However, what if you've worked with an employee—given warnings and held one-on-one meetings—but don't feel like you're making progress? You are at the point where you think you are headed toward a termination. To avoid issues cropping up later about process, communication, and fairness, it's a good idea to hold a performance counseling session with the employee. With this meeting, you communicate a new level of seriousness to the employee.

In preparation for this meeting, you will want to prepare a written performance improvement plan ("PIP") for the employee that covers the following:

- a description of the poor performance or behaviors—be factual (as specific as possible) and brief
- specific, measurable performance targets, including quality standards and timeliness goals, if appropriate
- a process and timeline to discuss progress on the plan; include an interim check-in meeting
- any training, meeting, or other tools that will be provided to the employee to assist them meeting goals, and
- a specific consequence that is likely to occur if the goals or targets have not been met and sustained during employment. If the employee will be terminated if improvement does not occur within the specified timeline, say so.
- if employment at your organization is at-will, remind employees of this during the session and point out that employment can be ended at any time in accordance with this policy.

The employee, the employee's supervisor, and someone from either HR or the management team should be invited to the meeting. Allow the employee to go over the PIP and give comments or tell his or her side of the story. For instance, if you have gotten complaints about your housing manager from tenants in an affordable housing facility, give that person the chance to provide additional information about the circumstances. Whether or not you decide to investigate further, the employee will have had a chance to give his or her input.

After the session, create a final version of the PIP. Once you have it finalized, get it signed and dated by the employee, the supervisor, and the manager. Make sure you follow through on any interim or final check-ins that are in the plan and keep written records for yourself regarding progress or lack of progress on the PIP. These notes should include comments on positive steps and improvements as well as any continuing problems.

In some cases, employees will improve their performance after a counseling session and implementation of a PIP. In others, it may still be necessary to fire an employee—in which case the PIP will be useful documentation. Either way, having a session with the employee and creating a PIP will serve you well.

> **EXAMPLE:** Anna never thought she'd be fired. She was outgoing, got along well with her coworkers, and knew the job inside and out. Her supervisor felt that knowing the job too well might in fact be part of the problem, and had pointed out recent mistakes that Anna hadn't made in the past. "You may be getting overconfident about your performance," said her supervisor. "This many mistakes on the grant reporting forms can't continue." Anna just brushed off these comments. But when her supervisor called her to a performance counseling session that included the administrative director, Anna got a wake up call. This was serious. She agreed to a performance improvement plan and was glad to see that it included taking a workshop on burnout. She got her act together, brought her performance back to its previously satisfactory level, and felt good that she had done so.

TIP

Take language fluency into account. In a multilingual workplace, supervisors may not be completely fluent in the language in which an employee is most comfortable. Although this may work out informally most of the time, take special care with warnings and PIPs. Make sure that both the employee and supervisor fully understand each other and that the PIP is in a language familiar to the employee. Adviser Sarah Gon notes: "Sometimes a supervisor will be more comfortable in Chinese than in English while the employee speaks only English. Or the other way around. In these cases, I'll translate in a counseling session, and help the supervisor write the plan or the warning in the employee's language, whether that's English or Chinese."

Before Firing—Steps to Take

Some employee handbooks specify steps that must be taken before firing an employee. Others are less specific. Before terminating any employee, review your handbook to see what is required in your organization and follow any steps or procedures there. Even if you don't have any policies that spell out a process for termination, following the steps below can help protect your organization against lawsuits and ensure that the termination goes as smoothly as possible for you, the employee, and other staff:

- give verbal reprimands and warnings to the employee, explaining why the employee's behavior or performance is a problem and what the employee must do to turn things around
- place disciplinary memos in the employee's personnel file
- hold a counseling meeting with the employee identifying the performance problems and communicating what improvements need to be made
- draft a performance improvement plan and proper documentation of the counseling meeting
- follow the performance improvement plan steps
- review the employee's personnel file for any relevant background, paying particular attention to whether performance reviews document poor performance, and
- check to be sure the employee's performance or behavior problems are not related to any legally protected status.

Following these steps can help you show that the employee was treated fairly and fired for good reasons should you later face a wrongful termination lawsuit. In addition, you'll want to make sure the employee doesn't have grounds to claim the termination was illegal for any of the reasons discussed in "Illegal Reasons for Firing Employees."

MYTH

You Are Legally Required to Give Warnings Before Firing

People often think that your organization must include in its policies or employee handbook a process by which an underperforming employee receives progressively more severe warnings. Or, that even if your handbook doesn't include a progressive discipline process, you must follow some type of progressive discipline before firing someone.

Reality: There are no legal requirements for discipline procedures or personnel policies. You only have to follow progressive discipline steps if your policies say that you will.

Make sure your policies don't hamstring you by specifying detailed processes that may not always be feasible. Remember: if it's in your policies, you have to do it.

If in doubt, consult with an HR attorney or consultant before making a final decision to fire. If you have relatively little experience with terminations or if you think the employee may be likely to sue, get guidance before proceeding.

CAUTION

Calling a firing a "layoff" can be risky. Nonprofit managers would often prefer to lay off employees instead of firing them. It avoids confrontation and allows the employee to collect unemployment benefits. However, mischaracterizing a termination as a layoff can leave your organization vulnerable to a lawsuit. For instance, if you lay off an unsatisfactory employee (rather than terminate for poor performance or misconduct), and then hire someone into a similar position, the "laid off" employee may well question your motives: Your organization clearly didn't need to cut staff or eliminate the position, so the employee may wonder if you had discriminatory or other illegal reasons for getting rid of him or her. It's much better to be honest about the situation (don't give a reason that's not true). In other words, if you have reasons to terminate an employee for unsatisfactory performance, then terminate for those reasons.

Firing At-Will Employees

If your employees are employed at will, then you don't need "cause" or a reason to fire them: You can let them go for any reason or for no reason at all. For example, it may become apparent after you hire someone that the person isn't working out—and you are free to simply let that person go.

However, you cannot fire an at-will employee for reasons that are illegal under state or federal law. For example, you can't fire someone for whistleblowing or supporting a union or taking a legally protected leave. Similarly, you can't fire someone based on race, gender, or other protected characteristics. So, despite at-will status, you need to be careful when terminating an employee. To minimize lawsuits, have both an at-will statement and a legitimate, documented reason why you are taking a termination action.

MYTH

At-Will Employees Can't Sue for Wrongful Termination

Some people think employment at will protects an organization from wrongful termination lawsuits. Reality: This is not the case.

Although at-will employees can be terminated at any time for any reason (or without a reason), there are still many laws that protect employees from being fired. In fact, there are dozens of employment laws that specify illegal reasons for firing anyone, including employees at will. So employees searching for justification to claim an illegal firing will probably be able to find something they can argue.

Illegal Reasons for Firing Employees

Here are some of the most common illegal reasons for firing employees. Check this list before you terminate any employee to make sure that you are not firing someone for an illegal reason.

Note that this list touches on some of the most common issues, but is not complete.

Discrimination. Federal law makes it illegal to fire an employee because of race, gender, national origin, disability, religion, age (if the person is 40 years old or older), genetic information, pregnancy, having recently given birth, or having a pregnancy-related medical condition. In addition, states, local governments, and some government contracts will also prohibit firing someone because of their sexual orientation, HIV status, marital status, whether they are smokers, or other protected characteristics.

In other words, even if you fire an employee for no reason at all, that employee may believe, and claim, that the firing was based on one of the above illegal reasons, and therefore, that you committed illegal discrimination.

Retaliation. It is illegal to fire employees for asserting their rights under the antidiscrimination laws described above. You cannot fire someone for complaining about discrimination or harassment or for speaking out on behalf of a coworker who was discriminated against or harassed.

Whistle blowing. You may not fire an employee for complaining about illegal or unethical conduct by your organization. The federal Sarbanes-Oxley Act, known mostly for its regulation of for-profit companies, applies to nonprofits in only two instances, one of which is whistle-blower protection. (The other regulates the retention of litigation-related documents.)

Immigration status. Under the federal Immigration Reform and Control Act (IRCA), you cannot fire an employee based on lack of U.S. citizenship. As long as the employee is legally eligible to work in the United States, you cannot discriminate against an individual based on alien (rather than legal resident) status.

Illegal Reasons for Firing Employees (cont'd)

Violations of public policy. The laws and rules on what constitutes public policy vary, although most states agree that firing someone for refusing to commit an illegal act (such as falsifying payroll records) or exercising a right (such as filing a workers' compensation claim) is illegal. Under federal law, employees cannot be fired for supporting a union.

If you are considering firing an employee where it might be construed that it was for an illegal reason, consult an employment attorney before taking action. For more information, see *The Manager's Legal Handbook*, by Amy DelPo and Lisa Guerin (Nolo).

Termination for Cause

Terminating an employee "for cause" means ending that person's employment for a reason: failure to do the job adequately, violating policies or standards of conduct, or breaching the terms of an employment contract (if there is one). In some instances, the employee may have violated a specific policy such as one on confidentiality, or a nonspecific policy such as "professional behavior." Or, it may simply be a situation where the person is not progressing or is no longer performing at a satisfactory level.

TIP

Sometimes, the demands of the job may have outgrown the person. A bookkeeper, for instance, may have had the skills needed at the time he or she was hired, but may not have the accounting skills necessary now that the organization has grown in size and complexity. Rather than terminate this person for cause, it may be better to eliminate the position and create a new position that accurately states what's required in the newly complex organization, and lay off the bookkeeper.

Many people are reluctant to fire someone for poor performance or behavior. Instead, they wait for something truly egregious to happen before taking action. Don't wait. Inadequate performance or negative behavior not only hurts organizational mission, it also demoralizes others and can send the wrong message about tolerating poor work.

Reluctance to fire an employee because of personal sympathies or attachments can stand in the way of organizational achievement. Whether you are a supervisor, a manager, or someone with HR responsibilities, be objective with yourself and others if you see that type of thinking interfering with proper employee management.

Firing "On the Spot"

In some cases, it may be necessary and appropriate to fire someone on the same day that an incident occurs. For example, if a case worker hits a client, a driver backs up a van injuring a pedestrian, or a bookkeeper is caught forging signatures on checks, you won't want to wait. Go ahead and take action even if you don't have any other documentation on that employee to support your decision to fire.

When something like this occurs, let the employee know immediately that you are looking into the incident and will meet with the employee as soon as possible to discuss it further. Make sure the employee's supervisor is contacted, HR is involved, and—depending on the incident—the executive director, chair of the board, or anyone else who needs to know is advised. Write up a report of the incident and then hold a meeting with the employee. Someone from HR and the employee's supervisor should be present at the meeting. If you need time to gather facts and prepare for a meeting, you can place the employee on administrative leave.

If you have decided to terminate, let the employee know verbally and in writing that his or her employment is terminated effective immediately. You can decide whether the employee should take all of his or her belongings that day or if you will let the person back in at a future date to collect personal belongings. In some states, terminated employees must be given all accrued pay on the last day worked, so check your state's laws to see if this rule applies.

Once You've Decided to Fire

However you have gotten there, you have come to the conclusion that a certain employee has to go. You know that you are not firing for an illegal reason; you have followed your policies and proper protocol and you don't see any basis for a wrongful termination suit. So, what steps should you take now to terminate the employment?

Nuts and Bolts: References, Health Benefits, and Other Matters

Before having the termination discussion with the employee, make sure you have thought through what you want to provide the person upon departure:

Timing of departure. It's usually best to get a terminated employee out of the picture as quickly as possible, maybe even that same day. If you want to give someone a bit of a cushion, offer two weeks of pay but don't let the person continue coming to work; they may feel resentful and the person's presence is often demoralizing to other staff. The exception might be for a long-tenured, trustworthy employee who knows that he or she is no longer doing a satisfactory job. You might consider letting that person stay a week to wrap things up and say goodbye.

References. Let the employee know what your policy is on giving references for employees who are fired. If your organization has a policy of releasing only employment dates, make that clear. If your organization doesn't give references or gives them only under certain circumstances, let a terminated employee know what will happen in his or her case.

Health benefits. Because health care coverage is so important, this is usually one of the first things a terminated employee will ask about. Some nonprofits offer to foot the bill for continued insurance coverage for a few months. For more on this topic, see "Postemployment Health Insurance," below.

Severance pay. You are not legally required to offer severance pay to an employee who has been fired, unless you have made this commitment in your policies. In some cases, you might want to make an offer of severance pay contingent on the employee signing a release agreeing not to sue the organization. If you offer such a release, work with an employment attorney on the wording and how much time you will give the employee to decide whether or not to sign it.

Termination letter and employee change form. Prepare a termination letter to give to the employee. If your organization uses employee change forms, complete one and ask the employee to sign it acknowledging the change in status.

Sample Termination Letter

Dear Daniel:

Your job at the Waterfall Nonprofit Center will be terminated effective on November 30, 20xx. Please return all equipment, keys, and other organizational property immediately. Human Resources will provide you with information about continuing employee benefits and your final paycheck, and can answer other questions you may have. [*Alternatively, include this information in the termination letter itself.*]

If there are ways I can help you in this transition, please let me know. I wish you the best of luck in the future.

Sincerely, Alyssa Stone

_____

Additional Sample Language:
[As you know, we have held three work improvement meetings with you and given you written warning letters about improving your performance as a condition of you continuing to work here. There has not been an acceptable improvement evident in your work. As a result, I must inform you that your work is not up to the standards required of our staff in the position you hold, and your employment with the Waterfall Nonprofit Center is terminated, effective immediately.]

Final Paycheck and IT Issues

Some states require that a terminated employee receive a paycheck on the last day of work, and some require that accrued vacation be paid that day, as well. Work with your payroll department in advance if you need to have these checks prepared.

Talk with your organization's IT staff about disabling the employee's computer password, email access, and voicemail. Don't give an unhappy employee an opportunity to download confidential documents or send an angry blast through the email system. Immediately after the employee is notified, change outgoing voicemail and email in order to direct inquiries to the appropriate person.

If you have reason to believe that the employee might become violent or vengeful, make arrangements to have the employee escorted from the building if it becomes necessary.

Letting the Employee Know: The Termination Meeting

Don't keep an employee in suspense. Let the person know you want to meet right before the meeting. Don't say: "I want to talk to you tomorrow at 11 a.m." Instead, wait until you can say, "I want to talk with you; can you come to my office in five minutes?"

Don't start the meeting with small talk. Be direct and get right to the point: "I'm afraid I have some bad news for you. As you know, we've struggled around improving your performance, but it just hasn't worked out. Your employment is terminated as of today."

Don't try to be a friend, but be compassionate: "I'm sure this isn't news that you want to hear and you'll need some time to let it sink in. Here's a memo that explains the next steps" (such as talking with HR about health coverage). "Why don't you read it and see if you have any questions I can answer."

Some nonprofit managers feel so bad about having to fire someone and are so nervous about a confrontation that they give inappropriate and unwelcome advice such as: "This will turn out to be the best thing for you." Another common error is to apologize and set up the grounds for a lawsuit, saying something along the lines of: "I'm just as much at fault for not being able to give you better mentoring."

Remember that employees are probably never going to agree with you that they should be fired, so don't try to convince them of it. Don't bring up anything new about their performance or behavior in an effort to explain why they are being fired. This will leave you open to the charge that "You never said anything about that to me before." If the employee argues with your decision, stay calm and simply say, "It looks like we're going to have to agree to disagree. You think your performance is adequate, but I don't agree."

As soon as the meeting is over, write down what happened. Note what you said and how the employee responded. Keep a record of any issues left up in the air (for example, if the employee asked to continue to use the organizational laptop for a few weeks).

> **EXAMPLE:** Andrew was firing someone for the first time in his life and he felt terrible, especially because Caitlin was such a sweet person. During the termination meeting, he kept saying how awful he felt, how miserable he was that this was happening, and on and on. Caitlin looked him in the eye: "I'm the one getting fired, and you want me to feel sorry for YOU?" Caitlin turned out to be as resilient as she was sweet. She said she had known this was coming and that it was probably good for her to be moving on. Andrew was just about to thank her for making him feel better about firing her, but he stopped himself.

Communicating to Staff

Staff will want to know right away if an employee has been terminated. As tempting as it may be to stay silent, don't delay making the announcement. In some organizations, it's possible to call a meeting where you can explain what happened. In other organizations, it may be necessary to make the announcement via email.

However you inform employees, let them know who has been terminated and as of what date. Do not explain why the employee was fired. Some employees may be angry and protest that the termination is unfair. Don't try to explain it to them by telling them about the sexual harassment incident or the poor performance reviews. You can say that you are protecting the employee's confidentiality by not discussing it further. Stay neutral and don't express either anger or relief.

Be sure to let staff know who in the organization is responsible for distributing that person's work and responsibilities.

Layoffs

In the rapidly shifting world of nonprofit funding, layoffs are often a necessary decision for an organization facing budget cuts. Because personnel is usually the costliest item in the budget, often the only way to cut expenses significantly is to cut staff. And, nonprofit staff understands the logic of layoffs: Perhaps a government contract wasn't renewed or the annual mail appeal didn't bring in as much money as expected.

It will be up to senior management to decide who will be laid off and on what date. However, an important HR component is making sure that the layoffs don't put the organization at risk and that the transition goes as well as possible. Layoffs require a type of change management, comments adviser Lisa Morton. "You need to help the people leaving to transition out, and help the people staying to manage in a changing situation."

Check your employee handbook for policies that address layoff or severance pay, and find out whether employees who will be laid off are on any kind of protected leave (such as family or medical leave, workers' compensation leave, or pregnancy disability leave). Get advice from an HR attorney or other expert before laying off these employees. Although you have the right to do so if they would have lost their jobs anyway (that is, even if they hadn't been on leave), these situations sometimes lead to lawsuits.

If you are laying off three people from a group of seven with the same job, check past performance reviews to make sure you are not open to claims of discrimination. Check to be sure that the criteria you use don't adversely affect a protected classification, such as those over 40 or any racial or gender group. In all cases, document the "why" of each decision you make, perhaps with business necessity as the main theme and merit and seniority or a combination of both as additional considerations.

Preparing for Layoffs

It's generally better to announce a deeper layoff all at one time than to lay off a few people at a time in dribs and drabs. The staff who remains shouldn't be working in daily fear of losing their jobs. As you prepare to announce layoffs, consider the staff who will be laid off, those that will stay on their jobs, how to manage the work with fewer staff, and whether and how to let others outside the organization know about the layoffs.

Involve the board of directors. In most nonprofits, the board of directors will want to be informed of or involved with layoff decisions. If the layoffs involve only a few employees on a large staff, it may be okay to simply notify the board of the decision. In other cases, the board should be consulted prior to announcing layoffs. Check with the executive director to see what board involvement is appropriate. Even if there is no requirement to involve the board, doing so may help board members respond appropriately to staff or community concerns raised about layoffs.

Comply with the WARN Act. Determine whether your nonprofit is subject to either federal or state Worker Adjustment and Retraining Notification (WARN) regulations. Enacted in1988, the WARN Act is generally applicable if you have 100 or more employees, and if you will be laying off 50 or more employees or ⅓ of your workforce. The Act requires that you provide layoff notices 60 days in advance to employees and certain government agencies, as well as other steps. For more information, see the U.S. Department of Labor Employment & Training Administration site at www.doleta.gov (enter "WARN Act" in the search box).

Even if your organization is not subject to the WARN Act, it's a good idea to let staff know that your organization is facing financial concerns well ahead of when you make any layoff decisions. Most staff will probably be aware of financial problems, but make sure that they know the seriousness of the problem and that management is considering different options, including layoffs.

Consider offering severance pay and extended benefits. Think about what you will provide to each employee who is being laid off. For example, you might be able to provide one week of severance pay to staff who have been employed for three or fewer years, and two weeks to those whom have been employed longer. There may be some employees whom you ask to stay on for a few weeks, while others whom you'll need to have leave more quickly.

Some nonprofits can afford to pay health benefits for a few months to employees who are being laid off. You should also help employees understand how to apply for COBRA benefits and what their options are for continued health coverage (see "Postemployment Health Insurance," below).

Explain your policy on references. Let employees know what they can expect in terms of references for future prospective employers.

Prepare last-day paychecks. As with terminations, some states require you to give employees their final paychecks (and sometimes their accrued vacation) on their last day of work. If this is the case in your state, talk with your accounting department to have the checks prepared.

Distribute FAQs about layoffs. If you are laying off several staff, prepare an FAQ (Frequently Asked Questions) sheet for them and their supervisors, including information on how long their insurance benefits will continue, COBRA options, and unemployment insurance information. (Most states require that you provide information on how to apply for unemployment benefits.) Let them know if there is other support the organization can provide, such as temporary continued use of an organizational email address (with access to internal documents disabled).

Prepare supervisors to deliver layoff news. Rather than have an outside consultant give the news, have the employee's supervisor talk with each employee who is being laid off. Coach supervisors on how to be sympathetic without making any promises on behalf of the organization. Give them a chance to discuss their own feelings about the layoff decision and think out loud about how they will handle the layoff interviews.

In particular, give managers a chance to think about how they will reallocate the work in their departments and transfer any specific clients that are assigned to staff being laid off. In some instances, vulnerable clients who have longstanding relationships with a staff person will need help transitioning to work with a different employee. And with fewer staff in your organization, managers will have to decide which work won't get done or can be done differently, and how remaining tasks can be redistributed among continuing employees.

Decide what day of the week is best for announcing the layoffs. There are different schools of thought about this issue. If you lay off staff on a Friday, they will have the weekend with family and friends to recover. Alternatively, you can lay off staff on a Wednesday and give them a chance to finish the week, which allows them time to say goodbye, transfer their work, and receive the sympathy of their coworkers.

Schedule all layoff interviews for the same time. Arrange for all interviews with people being laid off to be made during the same morning or afternoon. No one who is to be laid off should hear the news from a coworker.

Inform the rest of the staff. Immediately after layoff interviews have taken place, make an announcement to all staff letting people know who has been laid off and who is responsible for managing the redistribution of work. Be prepared to explain why layoffs were necessary and how the organization plans to move forward.

After layoffs have been announced, managers may be tempted to retreat to their offices and look buried in work. Instead, encourage them to circulate with the staff, ask and answer questions, and demonstrate confidence.

Nonprofit staff will often react with anger and protests over layoffs, citing a variety of concerns. Some may feel that there will be too much work for the remaining staff; some will feel the selection process was unfair; some will worry about clients who are attached to particular staff; some will feel so badly for those being laid off that they can't help but protest. Listen to what people have to say but don't overreact. Employees typically can't turn their attention to going forward until the laid off staff have left. Only then can staff express their relief at still having jobs, and take up their work with a positive attitude and hopefully, confidence in the organization's improved financial viability.

Pay Cuts Instead of Layoffs?

In a financial crunch, employees may raise the issue of giving everyone a pay cut rather than laying off staff. Sometimes staff may suggest putting the proposal to a vote. Anticipate how you will answer this question before it arises. In some organizations, such a move is in keeping with the culture and is financially feasible. For example, if by giving all employees a 10% pay cut you can prevent layoffs, this choice may work as opposed to a situation where all employees would have to take a 30% cut in order to prevent layoffs.

If you choose to avoid (or reduce) layoffs this way, set a timeline for reviewing this decision and reconsidering the choice. Otherwise, the organization's salary scale will have gone down permanently, making it harder to keep the best employees and harder to attract new quality staff when the time comes to do so.

In making the decision, the fundamental question is whether pay cuts or layoffs better serve the organization's constituents and its cause, now and in the future. The answer to this depends on the organization, the particulars of the financial circumstances, and the people involved. Although shared pay cuts may feel more democratic and compassionate than layoffs, layoffs may be a better choice for the organization's flexibility and positive financial future.

Handling Exit Interviews and Forms

In an exit interview, employees typically feel much freer to share their thoughts, providing valuable information for the future. You can not only find out how the job could be improved, but because an unhappy employee gets a chance to be heard, sometimes an exit interview allows them to get closure on the relationship and they don't feel as compelled to have their say in court. And the notes taken during an exit interview may be useful if there is a lawsuit and the employee has a different story in the future about the reasons for departure.

Never force or require an employee to participate in an exit interview or complete an exit form. But when a person resigns or is terminated, ask if he or she would be willing to do so.

Exit interviews should not be conducted by an employee's immediate supervisor. Instead, have someone from HR or a higher level of management talk with the departing employee. This person can bring a neutral tone to the interview. Also, involving someone from higher management lets the employee know that the exit interview is being taking seriously.

Holding Exit Interviews for Employees in Nonmanagerial Roles

If an employee agrees to an exit interview, you can either conduct the interview in person or ask the employee to complete a written questionnaire. If you do it in person, the interviewer can ask questions and take notes. In a few instances, they may be useful in a wrongful termination suit that is filed later on.

Here are some sample questions for employees who resigned or were asked to leave:

1. What did you find the most rewarding or satisfying about your job?
2. What did you find the most frustrating about your job?
3. Were there any procedures or rules that made your job difficult?
4. Would you recommend this organization to a friend as a good place to work?
5. Do you have any suggestions on how to structure the job differently for a new person?
6. Supervision is an important part of how an employee experiences a job. Are there things you would have liked your supervisor to have done differently?
7. Do you think that this organization does high-quality work for its clients/patrons/members/etc.?
8. Is there any work that needs to finished or transferred that you have not already discussed with your supervisor?

If the person decided to leave and was not fired, you can ask the following additional questions:

9. What are your primary reasons for leaving?

10. Is there anything we could have done to prevent you from leaving?

Remind the employee that confidentiality policies continue after his or her employment ends. Confidential matters about clients and organizational information must continue to stay confidential.

At the end of an exit interview, thank the employee for participating and let him or her know that the discussion will help make the organization a better place to work for others in the future.

Holding Exit Interviews for Management Team Members

When dealing with the departure of management team members—or anyone who reports to the executive director—have the board chair or another board officer conduct their exit interviews. This provides the board with an inside view of the executive director's work and strengthens the board's ability to hold its executive accountable in an informed way. Sometimes an issue will emerge—perhaps an executive director's alcohol problems or fudging data for a grant report—that might not have been discovered otherwise. Board exit interviews also send a signal to the whole staff about accountability and the responsibilities of the board of directors.

The board chair can choose which board officer will conduct an exit interview. For example, it may be appropriate for the board treasurer to hold the exit interview with the chief financial officer, or the board chair might hold the interview with the development director. The results of the interviews can help inform the next performance review of the executive director and suggest ideas for the board to discuss with the executive director.

Avoiding Layoffs Through Furloughs

When salary expenses need to be cut—but not by very much or for very long—nonprofits sometimes consider furloughs. In other cases, some staff may be laid off while remaining staff are given furloughs. A typical furlough would be to close the office two days per month and reduce everyone's pay proportionately.

In some cases, nonprofits allow employees to choose their furlough days. Or, they might provide a combination where, for example, the office is closed two days per month and the employee can choose another furlough day each month.

For nonexempt staff, a furlough results in fewer hours worked each pay period, which means less pay. For exempt staff, furloughs are a bit more complicated. As a general rule, exempt employees cannot be paid for less than a full week in any week in which they worked at all. What you do instead is to reduce their full-time salaries. So if exempt employees take off one day per week, reduce their full-time salaries by 20%. This solution does not work for short-term furloughs (such as week or two) but is applicable if you expect furloughs to last awhile.

Be clear whether employees will continue accruing vacation and receiving benefits at their full-time levels (typically yes) and whether an employee taking a furlough on a holiday will still be paid for the holiday (typically no). Some noncitizen employees on H1-B visas may need to work a certain number of hours per week to maintain their eligibility to work in the United States. And remind employees whose wages are being garnished or who have deductions for child support that these amounts may be affected.

If you choose to institute furloughs, keep in mind that staff often continue to work as many hours as before, so encourage them strongly to make use of the time off that they are entitled to. Have supervisors and work team leaders work with their groups to find ways to reduce their workload and to encourage staff to take advantage of the time off.

When you announce furloughs, establish a time when the issue of furloughs will be reconsidered, perhaps in three months or six months. It's important not to allow furloughs to continue indefinitely without considering whether other options are better long-term choices.

Temporary Layoffs

Nonprofits tend to consider only permanent layoffs. But sometimes short-term layoffs can be effective for saving jobs while protecting the organization's financial status. For example, there may be an unexpected two-month gap between the completion of one government contract and its renewal. In the past, you may have been able to keep paying people who worked on such contracts all the way through the gap. But there's an alternative: You can lay them off and, at the same time, let them know that if the renewal comes through, you may be calling them back. However, phrase this carefully—you don't want to overpromise in case things change. And check your state laws regarding accrued vacation. You may have to pay all accrued vacation if you lay off for a week or more even if you plan on rehiring.

Instead of a temporary layoff, some nonprofits choose to close operations for a short period of time. You can pick a slow week (perhaps Fourth of July week or school spring vacation). Closing for a full week allows the organization to save on both exempt and nonexempt payroll. Remind exempt employees that they cannot do any work that week— even checking their work email—lest they trigger a legal requirement to pay them for the full week. Some employees may find this a relatively easy cut to accept, but for others a one-week closure may result in a loss of pay that is untenable. Give employees the option of using their accrued vacation pay during the shutdown or taking the week off as unpaid leave; otherwise you may be required to pay out all accrued but unused vacation.

Postemployment Health Insurance

Regardless of whether they are fired or laid off, many employees' primary concern will be what happens to their health insurance coverage. Knowing this, some nonprofits offer to pay for continued coverage for a few months as a measure of good will and to give the former employees some peace of mind and time to explore alternatives.

Check with your employee benefits' insurance broker regarding whether and how you can continue to cover laid-off staff.

There are also federal and state laws that require employers under certain circumstances to offer the option of continuing health care coverage for employees who have left.

A federal law known as the Consolidated Omnibus Budget Reconciliation Act (COBRA) applies to employers who offer a group health plan and have 20 or more employees. Among other things, it requires employers to offer former employees the option of continuing their health care coverage for up to 18 months if they quit or are fired for any reason other than gross misconduct. Employees can also exercise this option for a spouse and dependents.

Most states also have laws that give former employees the right to continue group health insurance after they leave a job. In other words, complying with COBRA may not be enough if your state's law requires more. State protections are generally more detailed and more generous to workers than COBRA. In addition, even small employers (with fewer than 20 employees) that don't fall within COBRA may have to comply with state laws.

In most cases, the company that administers your health plans will also handle COBRA notices, so consider talking to them ahead of time about how employees can best connect with them on COBRA matters.

To learn more about COBRA, and to get information and forms, go to www.dol.gov/ebsa/COBRA.html.

What Happens If an Ex-Employee Sues?

At some point your nonprofit—like employers of all types—may be sued by a former employee for wrongful termination. If you use the principles and practices in this book, you will reduce the chances of a lawsuit, but you may not be able to prevent one altogether. (Anyone can sue, even if they ultimately lose.) So: what do you do when it looks like a lawsuit is on its way?

If you have reason to believe that either a current or former employee is thinking about suing your organization, talk with an employment lawyer or consultant. They can advise you on steps to take and ensure that you are not overlooking anything important you need to do. In addition, if your organization carries employment practices liability and/or directors and officers liability coverage, notify your insurance broker.

Discrimination Complaints

One avenue former employees can take is to file a complaint of discrimination or harassment with the Equal Employment Opportunity Commission (EEOC) or a similar state agency. Depending on the state your organization is located in and the nature of the complaint, employees must file their complaint within 180 or 300 days after termination. Most states have Fair Employment Practices Agencies (FEPAs), in which case an EEOC complaint is automatically filed with the relevant state FEPA. Your organization will receive a notice from the EEOC or the state agency that a complaint has been filed against it.

The government agency has several options in responding to the complaint. It can dismiss the charges if it does not find any evidence of discrimination or harassment. It can ask the two parties to try to settle their differences through mediation. Or, it can investigate the charges and, if it finds your organization has violated a federal or state fair employment law, can try to reach a settlement with you. If that does not turn out to be possible, the agency may file a lawsuit against you or give the employee a right-to-sue letter, allowing him or her to file a lawsuit.

Someone who has received a "Notice of Right to Sue" has 90 days to bring a civil lawsuit against your organization. You and your attorney can try to work with the former employee and attorney to see if you can reach a settlement. Otherwise, the lawsuit will be taken to court.

Along the way, there will be several points at which your organization will have choices to make. It's always a good idea to have an employment attorney or consultant working with you as early as possible in the process.

RESOURCE

The Equal Employment Opportunity Commission's website has comprehensive information for both employees and employers: www.eeoc.gov.

Other Types of Claims

Not all wrongful termination lawsuits are based on charges of discrimination. For example, an employee might sue for wrongful termination based on whistleblowing, refusal to commit an illegal act, or another illegal reason (see "Firing At-Will Employees," above for more on illegal reasons to fire).

In addition, an employee can bring a lawsuit based on your organization's failure to follow the procedures in the employee handbook or personnel policies. If, for example, your employee handbook states that four written warnings—each acknowledged in writing by the employee—are required prior to termination for cause, and you have do not have signed receipts by the employee for each warning, the employee may be able to sue for breach of contract. As a reminder, two principles are very important to follow: Include only those processes in the employee handbook that you can and will follow, and make sure to carefully follow all processes in the handbook.

Regardless of the type of claim, if you receive notice that an employee has filed a complaint or is bringing suit, get the advice you need. Connect with an employment attorney or consultant to be sure that you respond legally and effectively.

How It Ends Up

Wrongful termination claims and lawsuits can take different tracks and progress to different ends. An employee may lose steam and allow the claim to expire. Your attorney may help you negotiate a settlement with the former employee. Or, the case may end up in court and a jury decides the matter. Your organization cannot control the outcome of a lawsuit, but your decisions along the way will be important to make thoughtfully and with expert advice and guidance.

> **CAUTION**
>
> **Get help if you think you will be sued.** This chapter is meant to give you a sense of the most common scenarios for lawsuits, but is far from a complete or comprehensive look at employment-related lawsuits. If you believe a lawsuit may be brought against your organization, bring the issue to the attention of senior management and speak with an employment attorney.

Insurance and Employment Lawsuits

Claims are not cheap. The Nonprofits Insurance Alliance Group reports that about 1% of the nonprofits they insure will file a claim under Directors and Officers (D&O) liability insurance coverage, and that about 95% of these are wrongful termination, discrimination, and other employment related claims. The average settlement in cases that settle is $28,000, and the average legal cost of defending a claim is $35,000.

If your organization does not have D&O coverage, talk to your insurance broker or carrier about different types of coverage and costs.

Who's Eligible for Unemployment Insurance

Employees who lose their jobs through no fault of their own are eligible for unemployment benefits. An employee who is laid off due to financial cutbacks is clearly eligible for unemployment benefits. But there are also some instances in which an employee is eligible for benefits after having quit or having been fired for cause.

For example, if an employee leaves the job because of intolerable working conditions (such as being sexually harassed) or because the job is a serious threat to the employee's health, most states allow the individual to collect unemployment. In addition, employees fired for cause can claim unemployment benefits if they were terminated because they were deemed not to be a good fit for the job for which they were hired. In most states, however, an employee who is fired for misconduct will not be able to receive unemployment benefits.

These eligibility requirements are important to understand because an individual's former employer must complete a government form indicating why the employee left the job.

Steps in the Claims Process

Although the processes for unemployment insurance compensation vary from state to state, some general principles apply. Unemployment claims typically proceed through the following steps:

1. The former employee files a claim with the state unemployment office. That office then sends you written notice of the claim and you have a time period (usually seven to ten days) in which to file a written objection if you wish, stating that you do not think the former employee is eligible for unemployment benefits.

2. The state agency makes a determination of whether the former employee is entitled to unemployment compensation benefits. If the state determines that the worker is eligible for benefits and if you have not contested the claim, your involvement as the former employer ends and the employee will begin receiving benefits.

3. If you have contested the claim, a hearing officer (sometimes called a referee) from the state unemployment agency will listen to you and the former employee and make a decision. This hearing often takes place by phone.

4. Either you or the former employee can appeal the referee's decision to an administrative agency. Finally, either side can ultimately appeal to the state court system, but this is rarely worthwhile for either the employer or employee.

At some point you will probably have a former employee who was fired for misconduct or poor performance file for unemployment insurance, claiming that the termination was a layoff. Some nonprofits contest questionable claims because they want to set the record straight and because they don't want their unemployment insurance premiums to go up. Others just let it go because fighting a claim can be time-consuming and expensive, and usually results in angering the former employee. You will have to decide what is best for your organization.

Providing References

Your nonprofit will have to decide what to say to other employers who call for a reference for one of your former employees. Of course, with employees you liked, you will want to tell the whole glowing truth to any prospective employers. But if the employee was fired or was unsatisfactory, you face a more difficult task. In a few cases, employees who receive a negative reference have sued their former employers for defamation, charging that the negative reference was false and made it difficult for them to get new jobs. Defamation is a personal injury claim that can be brought against both your nonprofit and the individual supervisor who gives the reference.

To avoid problems, most nonprofits adopt a policy of giving "just the facts, ma'am" to prospective employers. You can give an individual's employment dates, title, and salary at the time of departure and leave it at that. There are no obligations for you to tell more. If you choose to say more, keep it to a minimum and stick to the facts.

It's tempting to want to give positive references to great employees and just the bare facts for employees who have been fired. But doing so means that by saying, "We don't give references," you are really saying that an employee has been fired. Instead, be consistent on what level of reference is given.

An easy way to manage references consistently and fairly is to choose one person in the organization—perhaps the HR manager or the deputy director—to be responsible for all references, and tell staff to direct requests to that person. ●

The HR of Volunteers

Managing Volunteers 201

   The Traditional Model: A Director of Volunteers...201

   The New Model—By Department...202

   Consider Using a Volunteer Advisory Council..204

Defining Volunteer Jobs..205

   Drafting Volunteer Job Descriptions...205

   Common Volunteer Positions 206

Recruiting Volunteers...210

   Look Within Your Community..210

   Online Advertising..211

   Volunteer Centers 212

   College Volunteer Centers...212

   Third-Party Placement Organizations...212

   Court-Ordered Community Service "Volunteers"..214

   "Work-Study" Volunteers...216

Screening Volunteers..216

Getting the Right Insurance Coverage for Volunteer Activities....................219

Preparing for Your Volunteers' First Day 220

Creating Leadership Positions for Volunteers...222

Volunteerism Practices and Policies for Volunteer Board Members...........223

Thanking Volunteers...224

Professional Development for Managers of Volunteers....................................226

Meet Your Adviser

Amy Smith
Title: President
Organization: HandsOn Network
Location: Atlanta, Georgia

What she does: Amy manages a team of 30 that produces signature national days of service (such as Martin Luther King, Jr. Day and 9/11 Day), and supports 250 HandsOn affiliates in 16 countries. Her team develops tools and resources for volunteers, nonprofits that involve volunteers, and self-organized volunteer groups.

What her organization does: HandsOn Network is the largest volunteer network in the world. As the volunteer-focused arm of Points of Light Institute, HandsOn works with 70,000 corporate, faith, and nonprofit organizations that bring about meaningful change in communities through volunteer action.

Best tip for HR managers, including the Accidental HR manager: Don't forget about professional development for yourself. One good program is the CVA: Certification in Volunteer Administration, which involves study in many areas of volunteer management practices and principles, and a comprehensive exam.

HR lesson you learned the hard way: Not paying enough attention to whether a person who has the right skills is also a person that can fit into our environment. We're a very fast-paced environment—almost like a start-up—and you might get called at 9 p.m. about something that has to be done that night. Or, you have to be able to adapt quickly. I ask candidates, "How do you work in these types of situations? I pay attention to their body language and see if they get nervous as I talk."

Song that speaks to you about HR: I have a young child so these days I'm listening to children's songs: "Talk of the Town," from Jack Johnson's Curious George CD. I like the lyrics: "The hours just don't seem enough to put it together."

Volunteers are part of the workforce in more than 80% of American nonprofits. In fact, many nonprofits have more volunteers than paid staff, in some cases putting in more total hours than the nonprofit's paid staff do. American volunteers contribute more than 15 billion volunteer hours to their communities, the equivalent of 7.5 million full-time staff hours.

Volunteers are clearly a huge "human resource" for nonprofits, yet their HR concerns are often overlooked. Although all-volunteer organizations (AVOs) are important contributors to our society, this chapter considers the HR of volunteers in the context of a nonprofit with paid staff. We'll begin with how volunteers are managed by staff.

Managing Volunteers

Although nearly half of staffed nonprofits have designated a staff person to be responsible for volunteer matters, volunteer responsibilities are typically only part of this person's job This may be one reason that the HR of volunteers is seldom taken as seriously as the HR of paid staff. This can create a downward spiral, in which volunteers get frustrated because their needs (or existence) are paid little attention to, and so they quit; while the nonprofit staff gets frustrated at how little sense it makes to train volunteers who soon quit; and so on. Even if you have only a few volunteers, it's worth taking the time to think through how you will manage them to maximize the effectiveness of this important resource.

The Traditional Model: A Director of Volunteers

Traditionally, volunteers have been managed by a director of volunteers or volunteer coordinator, whose job is to recruit, screen, and assign volunteers to various tasks or departments. For instance, the director of volunteers at a senior center might recruit volunteers, interview them, and then place some with the lunch program, some with the recreation program, and some with reception. The director of volunteers continues to act as a kind of supervisor, however, by monitoring attendance, providing recognitions and thanks, and, when necessary, "firing" volunteers.

This model works successfully for many organizations because the responsibility for volunteer management clearly rests with one person, who is or can become an expert in volunteer utilization. Although the day-to-day work with volunteers is done by managers and coordinators in the various departments, the director of volunteers is the overall supervisor of volunteers, whom staff can turn to if an issue comes up with a volunteer.

As nonprofits have become more conscious of the high skill levels needed to recruit and manage this strategic human resource, stature and pay have been rising for directors of volunteers. After all, if the volunteer hours were valued at what it would cost to pay staff to do the same work, the director of volunteers may well be bringing in far more resources in dollar value than the development director. Rather than seeing volunteer management as a tangential benefit, organizations are increasingly investing in volunteer management by hiring volunteer directors at the level of the development director or the HR director.

The New Model—By Department

More and more, the traditional model for volunteer management is giving way to one where volunteers are seen as a strategic component of a workforce that combines paid staff, volunteers, and independent contractors. In this framework, volunteers are recruited and managed by the departments where they are assigned to work.

Using the same senior center as an example, volunteers would be managed as follows: The lunch program director would recruit and put volunteer cooks and servers to work, the recreation director would recruit volunteer performing artists, and the office manager would recruit and supervise volunteer receptionists. In short, just as program directors hire and manage paid staff in their departments, they also recruit and manage volunteers in their departments.

There are several advantages to managing volunteers by department or work group. Because a program director knows what types of work volunteers are needed for, the director also often knows best where to find people with the necessary skills and experience, and how to interview candidates for the position.

The program director is also in the best position to integrate the new volunteer into the workforce. Another benefit to this structure is that volunteers respond positively to being specifically recruited as volunteer coaches, volunteer cooks, visiting artists, and volunteer receptionists rather than simply as "volunteers."

In this model, someone still has organization-wide responsibilities for volunteers, and this position parallels the HR position: a volunteer coordinator who supports managers in the same way that the HR director supports managers. This volunteer coordinator—the "HR director for volunteer human resources"—can also be titled the director of volunteer involvement.

Typical responsibilities for a director of volunteer involvement in this structure include:

- first-day paperwork and personnel files for volunteers
- assisting managers with job definition and recruitment
- researching local volunteer resources and establishing relationships with volunteer centers
- encouraging program directors to involve volunteers in new and expanded ways
- assisting program directors in thanking and acknowledging volunteers
- assisting the development director in seeking ways to develop volunteers as donors
- advocating for a strategic integration of volunteerism into all levels of the organization, and
- developing organization-wide volunteer recognition programs if appropriate.

Whichever structure your organization decides to use, there are some special HR principles about dealing with volunteers that differ from those for paid staff. Whether you are the organization's director of volunteer involvement, the HR manager, or a program manager, understanding the "HR of volunteers" will help you be more effective with these crucial human resources.

> EXAMPLE: "At Clover Performing Arts Center we have two theaters, four stages, a school building, a gift shop, and a large number of special events," says president Kyle Anthony. "We have a very big volunteer force, and the volunteers are all managed through the departments, since the departments know what the volunteers need to do."

Consider Using a Volunteer Advisory Council

An additional management tool to consider is an internal volunteer advisory council, comprising management staff, nonmanagement staff, and volunteers. The central role of this council is to consider how volunteers will be recruited, trained, put to work, and recognized, and to propose any advisable changes to management. The council may perform other functions as well, such as recognizing staff who excel at partnering with volunteers and creating volunteer positions with more responsibilities.

As an example of how this works, a senior center nonprofit might have the following people on its council:

- a board member
- the executive director
- the volunteer director
- the recreation program manager
- the office manager (who supervises reception volunteers)
- two volunteers from the lunch program
- two volunteer receptionists, and
- one musician who volunteers with the recreation program.

The council might meet only twice a year. At those meetings, the group would take up various topics, such as volunteer titles, using social media to recruit volunteers, volunteer-staff interactions, or a need for lockers that volunteers could use. They might surface complaints or suggestions from volunteers or from staff and make recommendations for changes. In some organizations, to send a message about the value of volunteer input, the volunteers elect representatives to the volunteer advisory council.

A volunteer advisory council often provides other benefits for organizations, such as raising the profile of volunteers among the staff, connecting the board of directors to volunteerism in the organization, and serving as a cross-departmental means for communication and relationship-building.

Defining Volunteer Jobs

Many nonprofits have well-established roles for volunteers who want to contribute to their organization. The availability of volunteers also provides an opportunity to expand or take on new activities that wouldn't be possible without volunteer labor. For example, a concert hall might be able to put on performances for niche audiences due to hundreds of volunteer ushers and ticket-takers. If it were to pay such staff, it would be limited to presenting only mainstream performers that can draw very large audiences. Or an organization that works with emotionally disturbed children may be able to have a smaller teacher/child ratio because both paid staff and volunteers work with the children.

But volunteers shouldn't be seen simply as free labor. Involving volunteers can be an important way to build a constituency that can support the organization's cause. For instance, a high desert conservation organization might find that it costs about the same to pay a garbage company to clean up the desert as it costs to recruit and deploy volunteers to do the same thing. Yet volunteers may do a more careful job, and their involvement will keep them engaged as voters in a wide variety of open space and wildlife conservation efforts as voters and in other ways.

Drafting Volunteer Job Descriptions

Volunteers appreciate having clear job or project descriptions. A clearly defined role or description gives volunteers the confidence that the job is realistic and within the scope of their skills and commitment. Just as HR managers help staff supervisors define job descriptions, a volunteer coordinator or director of volunteers can help supervisors develop volunteer job and project descriptions.

When writing job or project descriptions for volunteers, be sure to include the following:

- the title of the position (Instructor or Volunteer Faculty is better than just "Volunteer")
- the types of activities involved and job responsibilities
- the location of the job
- the schedule of days and hours
- the expected time period for the project or commitment
- required skills
- training provided, if any
- perks, if any (such as a parking lot pass), and
- the name of the contact person.

You might consider structuring some jobs so that they can be done part time by students. That way you can recruit from an eager and well-educated pool that might not be available for full-time work. Similarly, structuring some jobs as temporary projects—a three- or six-month project, for example—may make it an attractive option for some retirees or others who are not able or willing to commit to an indefinite period of service.

Common Volunteer Positions

To help you think creatively about how to maximize volunteer involvement with your organization, we'll look next at the most common volunteer positions in nonprofits.

Direct service volunteers. Through direct service, volunteers participate in activities that directly benefit the organization's clients and audiences. Direct service volunteers read to children, deliver meals, foster abandoned cats, maintain hiking trails, prepare tax returns for low-income people, write antidiscrimination legal briefs, usher film festival attendees to their seats, lead Camp Fire troops, and perform a myriad of other community-building activities.

Sample Volunteer Position Description

Literacy Coach

Title of position: Reading and Writing Coach

Activities and responsibilities: Tutor one-on-one with adult who is developing English reading and writing skills. Complete brief written progress report each month.

Location and schedule: Madrone Community Center, regularly scheduled 1.5 hours per week

Period of time for the project or commitment: Six-month commitment. Time required: In addition to the coaching time, planning and preparing materials for the session will take time as well.

Required skills: Prior teaching experience not required. Reading and writing coaches must speak English well and read/write English at the 12th grade level or higher. Good listening skills, ability to be patient and respectful of learner's situation and goals. Punctuality a must.

Training provided and/or required: Successfully complete two-hour Reading & Writing Coach workshop. Materials provided.

Perks: Four-hour parking pass downtown one day per week. A $30.00 gift certificate at Madrone Bookstore.

Contact person on staff: Katia K., Literacy Program Director, katia@madronecc.org or 712-555-1234.

Direct service volunteers sometimes participate in work requiring little or no training—such as filling food bags or weeding marshes. But volunteers also take on responsibilities that require substantial training. As examples, volunteers at hospices, in theater productions, at rape crisis centers, at zoos, and in programs for autistic children can do their work only if they have made substantial time commitments to training and ongoing supervision. Consider posting direct service volunteers as temporary commitments (such as two months), after which a volunteer can renew for another period, rather than simply setting them up with no established end.

Volunteers also bring unique value to the services they provide. Think about it this way: If Big Brothers were paid, they would be babysitters. Instead, Big Brothers are people who have chosen to spend their free time helping out with kids who may need guidance. In the same vein, volunteers who bring their dogs to visit nursing homes bring more than just friendly dogs; they bring a sense of caring and personal giving that changes the service itself and the impact of the service on recipients.

> EXAMPLE. The Sunlight Hospice cares for residents who have diagnoses of six or fewer months to live. While a substantial medical staff is there to keep patients comfortable, a great deal of the work is done by volunteers, who care for both the patients and their families. To maintain high standards of integrity and expert care for people in such vulnerable situations, Sunlight Hospice requires potential volunteers to complete a series of ten two-hour training classes, and then pass a screening interview. While such requirements may appear burdensome to some prospective volunteers, they respect the standards for care that the Hospice maintains.

Direct service volunteers usually volunteer in person, but moderating online discussion groups, online mentoring, and website management are ways that people can perform direct service volunteer work "virtually."

Administrative volunteers. Some people want to support an organization or a cause, and feel that the best way for them to do so is in an administrative role. This includes positions like newsletter editor, a translator for written materials, membership secretary, and so forth. Structuring administrative work for volunteers usually means creating part-time positions (such as two hours per day maintaining an animal rescue website). Some organizations successfully recruit volunteer bookkeepers, CFOs, file clerks, inventory specialists, retail sales help, and other volunteers.

Pro bono work and skills-based volunteering. Many professionals do consulting-like projects (and sometimes ongoing work) for nonprofits on a pro bono basis. Examples of this type of volunteerism include a lawyer providing legal help with a new lease, an IT consultant helping to choose database software, or an interior design professional advising on workspace layout.

Fundraising volunteers. Most fundraising volunteers work on time-limited projects, such as auctions, gala dinners, annual mail appeals, and walk-a-thons. More rarely, volunteers write grant proposals, head up planned giving campaigns, and draft fundraising letters. Some organizations form separate entities to raise money. For example, a neighborhood health clinic might form Friends of the Free Clinic, a separate organization whose sole purpose is to fundraise for the Clinic. A Hospital Auxiliary or Alumni Auxiliary might put on a large event, such as a garden or home tour or gala-type dinner that might take an entire year to stage.

Political action volunteers. Sometimes it's important to get 100 people to attend a city council hearing to speak out on a zoning issue or five people to go to the state capitol to talk with legislators. Volunteers can get involved in one of two ways with political events: They can attend the event and they can help organize the event from the ground up.

Policy volunteers. Researching policy issues and drafting policy papers is often welcome work for volunteers in the same field, such as an environmental scientist who volunteers with a toxics organization.

Board of directors. The governing body of a nonprofit—the board of directors—is nearly always composed of volunteers. As a body, the board is responsible for the financial oversight of the organization, hiring and overseeing the CEO or executive director, and making key decisions in areas such as the general direction of the organization, its revenue strategy, and its main programs. As individual board members, these strategic volunteers often advise the management staff, raise money, recruit volunteers, and represent the organization to the community.

Recruiting Volunteers

Although it would be great if volunteers were delivered by storks, it usually is more effective to deploy specific recruiting techniques. In some ways, recruiting volunteers parallels what you have to do to obtain job applicants, but there are differences as well.

In particular, while paid jobs are typically advertised one by one, volunteers are often recruited en masse (such as volunteer race monitors for the leukemia walk-a-thon). This difference in recruiting reflects the contrast between paid jobs, which are typically full time, and volunteer jobs, which are typically temporary or very part time, and between paid jobs that require specialized skills and volunteer jobs that require less training.

But just as posting an ad that says, "Staff Wanted" is likely to result in a hodgepodge of applicants with varied skill levels and interests, a sign that says "Volunteers Wanted" is less strategic than a more targeted effort. You'll want to be thoughtful both about how you describe what you're seeking and where you post listings.

Look Within Your Community

Most organizations find it effective to recruit volunteers from their communities and constituents. After all, these are people who already understand what your organization does and support your efforts. Placing "Help Wanted" ads in your lobby, on your website, Facebook page, and in your newsletter are ways to attract inquiries from a highly targeted group of people who already know—and probably like—your organization. Be specific about what positions are open and the times needed: "Volunteer Chefs Needed One Morning Per Week" is better than just "Volunteer Kitchen Help Needed." Also let your current volunteers know you are looking for more volunteers. They may well be delighted to bring friends and others to join them as volunteers in your organization.

An often-overlooked source of volunteers is your current donors. Donors have shown interest in the organization's work and may be intrigued by being more actively involved—or by being involved in a way that doesn't involve more money. (Often the increased closeness to your organization created by volunteering means that they're likely to continue making financial donations as well.)

> **EXAMPLE:** A shelter for homeless families holds an open house once a year when donors can visit the facility, meet the staff, and visit with a few of the families. This year they sent a letter to donors asking for volunteers to greet visitors at the upcoming open house. To their surprise a long-time donor volunteered who had never even attended an open house. "I didn't like the idea of going to the open house when it was being done for my benefit," she explained. "I want to help."

Often an organization will want volunteers who are connected to specific communities. For instance, the American Heart Association knows that African American volunteers can do a better job of reaching African Americans at risk for heart disease than white volunteers. A tutoring center may want young volunteer tutors because it has found these volunteers have more success with their students than older tutors.

The volunteer coordinator or director can help with targeted recruiting of volunteers by finding out about volunteer placement organizations in the community and by working with other staff to identify ethnic or other relevant media in which to advertise, the best groups to approach, and other ways to find volunteers from particular cultures or with particular skills.

Online Advertising

Many volunteer centers and college volunteering centers also maintain websites where nonprofits can post volunteer job openings and volunteers can search for interesting opportunities. In addition, you can post information on national sites including:

- HandsOnNetwork.org
- Idealist.org
- VolunteerMatch.org
- Craigslist.com (look in "Community" then in "Volunteers").

> **TIP**
> **No-shows are common among volunteers who signed up through online nonprofit referral sites.** You can improve responses enormously by responding to any inquiries you receive from sources like this by first asking the volunteers to answer some questions about themselves, including why they want to volunteer for your organization, what they expect to do as a volunteer, and the best times and ways to contact them. This email exchange will weed out the impulsive individuals who just clicked without thinking much, and will give you valuable information with which to greet the prospective new volunteer in person.

Volunteer Centers

Most communities have a volunteer center with information about local volunteer opportunities. Sometimes these centers sponsor volunteer fairs and other recruitment activities. Work with your local center to learn how it can help you, perhaps with posting positions, connecting you with a local corporation looking for employee volunteer opportunities, and so forth.

Check whether such a center exists in your community. Many local centers and bureaus are affiliated with the national HandsOn Network/Points of Light Institute (www.handsonnetwork.org), although these centers have different names and may be housed in other organizations, such as United Ways.

College Volunteer Centers

Colleges and universities frequently have centers that encourage volunteerism by students, through service learning projects as well as through one-on-one placements.

Third-Party Placement Organizations

In addition to the more traditional method of finding or recruiting volunteers, the volunteer managers at your nonprofit also should be aware of third-party organizations that recruit volunteers and place them in nonprofits for temporary periods of time.

A relationship with a third-party organization can provide a steady stream of eager volunteers, even though the volunteers generally remain identified with or loyal to the "placing" organization rather than the "utilizing" organization. For instance, a group of Hewlett-Packard volunteers may work one day a month at a food bank, but continue to consider themselves Hewlett-Packard volunteers rather than food bank volunteers.

Some third-party volunteers receive a salary or stipend from the third-party organization, like AmeriCorps VISTAs, and are then assigned out to work at a nonprofit.

Some sources for checking into third-party volunteers include:

AmeriCorps VISTA and AmeriCorps regional volunteers. Recruited and paid (about $11,000 per year) by the National Committee for Community Service (NCSS), there are several types of AmeriCorps volunteers who can be placed at nonprofits for full- or part-time engagements that typically last a year.. Be sure to seek out both the national and regional offices of AmeriCorps, which can provide different services and types of volunteers.

RSVP. Retired Senior Volunteer Program (RSVP) is a federal program that places volunteers who are 55 years or older with nonprofits and government agencies. Most communities have RSVP programs; some are located in volunteer centers or senior centers, while others are stand-alone organizations. You'll find other programs for older volunteers under Senior Corps (which itself is under the Corporation for National and Community Service), including the Foster Grandparents and Senior Companions programs. Both offer stipends for volunteers.

Corporations. Many corporations have employee volunteer programs—in some cases even paying employees their regular salaries for time spent on volunteer work. Contact local corporations to learn whether they make volunteer opportunities available to their employees. If you already have volunteers from a corporation or receive donations from a corporation, consider proposing a special program where corporate volunteers work in teams, such as "UPS Day at the Watershed."

Service clubs. Associations such as Rotary, Kiwanis, Soroptomists, AAUW (Association of American University Women), and the National Council of Negro Women often take on volunteer projects with community organizations. In addition to reaching out to such organizations, having senior staff join a nearby service club is an efficient and effective way to meet the leaders in a community and to recruit both individual volunteers and teams of volunteers.

Churches and religious organizations. A spirit of service in many congregations leads individuals to volunteer. In addition, churches often become involved with projects and nonprofits involved in community work.

> **EXAMPLE.** The Faith Collaborative Home is a homeless shelter for families that employs relatively few staff. All the meals—21 each week—are prepared and served by one of the eleven congregations participating in the collaboration. Each week one congregation takes responsibility for shopping, cooking, serving, and cleaning up. These volunteer congregation members not only make the Home financially stable, they are able to exercise their service and faith together, and the collaboration helps strengthen the community as a whole.

Sororities and fraternities. If you have nearby sororities and fraternities, approach them for group volunteer projects. For example, a sorority might "adopt" your organization and build a float featuring your work for a Main Street parade, or a fraternity might commit to washing the cars of volunteer food deliverers four times a year.

Court-Ordered Community Service "Volunteers"

Under some court sentencing programs, people can choose to do community service instead of (or in addition to) paying a fine or serving time in prison. Community service might also be offered as a condition of parole or probation. For example, a court might order someone to do 80 hours of yard work at a nonprofit summer camp as an alternative to serving time. Or, a court might sentence a bookkeeper who committed fraud to "volunteer" for a specified time period as a bookkeeper for a nonprofit (with safeguards, of course). Court-ordered volunteers come from a wide range of skills and educational backgrounds.

While some court-ordered volunteers may not be highly motivated, others welcome the opportunity to give back to their communities. A surprising percentage of them even continue volunteering after they have fulfilled their legal commitment. Some organizations rely on a steady stream of court-ordered volunteers to do a multitude of tasks—from groundskeeping at a nonprofit school to sorting materials at a recycling center to providing legal counseling for tenants. Some nonprofits like to work with court-ordered volunteers because they see it as a way to help these volunteers get jobs in the future by providing them with the opportunity to learn skills and have a work reference, if appropriate.

If you're interested in finding out about these types of volunteers, contact a local volunteer center: it may manage a court-appointed program already, or be able to refer you to the courts or organizations that do. Courts require special paperwork for alternative sentencing volunteers, and you'll need to work with the referring court when enrolling such a volunteer. If you are working with court-ordered volunteers for the first time, also contact a nearby nonprofit with experience for advice, sample policies they may have developed, and tips on how best to utilize the volunteers.

> **EXAMPLE:** Finance director Sarah was resistant when her executive director suggested that she accept a bookkeeper through the court-ordered service program. After all, the bookkeeper had been convicted of embezzlement. However, her exec pointed out that controls would be in place and that bookkeeping was the skill that the volunteer had to offer. Sarah agreed to try out the volunteer, and was very pleased to have a full-time, highly skilled bookkeeper for nearly a year.

"Work-Study" Volunteers

If your organization offers classes, workshops, or other kinds of learning opportunities, consider creating "work-study" volunteer positions. For example, a volunteer may be able to take yoga classes in exchange for spending an equal number of hours doing registrations or maintaining a website for the organization that holds the classes.

Screening Volunteers

When you take on volunteers, you also take on potential risks and liability. Make sure you do the proper screening and background checks for any volunteers you involve. This is an important part of protecting your organization as well as your clients, staff, and others who participate in your activities. In this section, we'll discuss three types of screening: fingerprinting, background checks, and reference checks.

Fingerprinting. Most states require fingerprint checks for volunteers who will work with children (under 18 years old) and, in certain circumstances, for those working with the elderly or those with disabilities. The laws typically apply to school volunteers, mentors (such as Big Sisters), and anyone who will be working with minors. Even if you are not required to do so by law, you may still want to do some type of background check on prospective volunteers. But make sure you have a clear policy in place and check everyone who'll be applying for certain categories of volunteer positions to avoid angering people and opening your nonprofit open to charges of discrimination and invasion of privacy. (Some states have laws restricting the use of fingerprinting to doing a criminal records check on job applicants.) If you are thinking about requiring fingerprinting or another check on a regular basis for volunteers or staff, check your state laws. If you decide to do fingerprinting, you can set up an account for this service with a nearby fingerprinting shop (most UPS stores offer this service).

EXAMPLE. At one Florida church, an outgoing young man volunteered as a Sunday School teacher and became friendly with some of the boys and their parents, some of whom started asking him to babysit. He was later charged with sexual molestation and lascivious behavior, and the parents of the molested boys sued the church. Fingerprint screening would have revealed a record of sexual misconduct that would have disqualified him from teaching at the church.

Background checks. If volunteers will be working with children, substantial amounts of money, or any vulnerable population such as frail seniors or people with disabilities, you should require background checks. In fact, your state's law may already require such checks. Let prospective volunteers know that screening is required for certain volunteer positions, and that your organization will pay for the service. Although some "qualified entities" (defined differently in different states) can use FBI fingerprint services at low cost, it's often easier to work with a commercial background screening service. These companies usually conduct background checks using the name, date of birth, Social Security number, and other identifying information.

A "comprehensive" screening service will use a state database search, its own internal records, and a search of counties that have not reported crimes (or not reported recently) to their respective states. A search like the latter might reveal charges and dispositions that were not reported to the state or national repositories—but can never be truly comprehensive, since the record-keeping systems are themselves imperfect. Be especially wary of generic online background screening sites, which may not follow federal legal requirements such as the Fair Credit Reporting Act privacy protections. For example, federal law requires that the person receive a copy of the report, be notified of negative information within the report before your nonprofit takes an adverse action in response to it (such as refusing to let the person volunteer there); have a chance to dispute the information in the report; and receive assurance that your group will use the report only for the purposes for which you ordered it.

Remember that criminal background checks do not always include fingerprint checks. For volunteers who will be working with minors, a separate fingerprint check is important.

In all cases, the right to check criminal and arrest records or to use fingerprinting for these purposes may be limited by state law.

Finally, some insurance carriers have more favorable rates for their insured nonprofits that do background checks on all their volunteers. Ask your carrier or broker if they make such a rate available, and whether they can make a discounted rate for an online service available to you.

Sample Reference Check Form for Prospective Volunteer

1. Prospective volunteer's name and affiliation (if any) _____
_____

2. Reference's contact information _____
_____
_____

3. How long have you known this person and in what capacity? _____
_____

4. What do you consider this person's strengths? _____
_____
_____

5. What suggestions do you have for our staff in engaging this person successfully? _____
_____
_____
_____

6. Our organization delivers meals to elderly or house-bound people at their homes. Would you recommend this person as a volunteer in this type of setting? _____
_____

> **RESOURCE**
>
> **Need more information?** A comprehensive article on background checks for volunteers and staff can be found at www.blueavocado.org (enter "criminal records checks" into the search box.

Reference checks. Particularly in situations where volunteers will be working with money or with people in vulnerable situations, reference checks are a useful screening tool. As part of the initial paperwork, ask prospective volunteers for two references, preferably one from previous volunteer experience and the other from an employer, coworker, or teacher. You can either conduct reference checks by phone or in writing. We provide a sample form below that can be used for either method.

Getting the Right Insurance Coverage for Volunteer Activities

Imagine a situation where both a volunteer and a staff person at your nonprofit are standing on a scaffold as they paint your building and the scaffold falls. As an employee, the staff person most likely has workers' compensation insurance and may also have medical coverage and disability through you, the employer. The volunteer, however, may have no such coverage. A volunteer who cannot return to work due to such an injury may feel forced into suing your organization to make ends meet. Your organization might end up having to pay for medical costs, lost wages, and other expenses stemming from the incident. And of course, you'll feel terrible.

Another area where you may be vulnerable is if you are sued by a disgruntled or injured client or patron because of something done by a volunteer. For example, someone might sue your organization if, while being helped from a wheelchair to the toilet by a minimally trained volunteer, the client fell and was injured. The volunteer is protected from liability under the federal Volunteer Protection Act (provided his or her actions constituted negligence and not gross negligence or willful misconduct). However, your nonprofit is not protected by the Act, and could be sued by the client.

You should make sure you have insurance to cover your organization in both these situations—workers' compensation insurance and/or disability insurance for volunteers working on your behalf and general liability or other insurance that covers liability for actions by volunteers. Ask your broker for quotes for both these types of insurance and make sure the coverage is adequate for your circumstances.

If you have volunteers who drive on behalf of your organization, you will also need to make sure you have insurance to cover liability in the event of an accident. Volunteers can make enormous contributions through driving-related activities: delivering meals to shut-ins, taking elderly and disabled people to doctor and legal appointments, picking up donations, and getting to volunteer activities. Suppose a volunteer for your agency gets into a car accident while using his or her own car to deliver surplus food from a restaurant to a homeless shelter?

As a first step, before any volunteer drives a vehicle to carry out any activities on behalf of your organization, you should require proof of a valid driver's license. In addition, if volunteers will be using their own cars, you should ask to see proof of up-to-date car insurance in an adequate amount. Check with your insurance broker if you have any questions about what constitutes adequate coverage.

While the volunteer's own car and medical insurance may pay for auto damage and any medical bills related to the accident, many nonprofits choose to obtain their own coverage for these types of incidents. Several national insurers specialize in insurance for nonprofits—such as the Nonprofits Insurance Alliance Group and First Nonprofit Insurance—and as a result, are familiar with insurance for volunteers. Your broker may not be aware of these insurers but you should make sure you get quotes from these companies.

Preparing for Your Volunteers' First Day

Volunteers expect to be welcomed on their first day—an important thing to remember before you start asking them to complete a bunch of paperwork. Make time for some personal conversation and introductions. Then it helps to give them a "welcome packet" of information from the organization, which includes the materials described below.

Start your packet with a volunteer enrollment form or agreement, which should request the following information:

- name, address, telephone, cell phone, and email addresses
- emergency contact information
- simple statement of anticipated volunteer position or activities
- based on planned activities, documentation where appropriate, such as driver's license and car insurance if the volunteer will be driving, evidence of certification as a phlebotomist if the volunteer will be drawing or testing blood samples, and so on
- signature acknowledging receipt of any organizational property such as keys, GPS unit, cookies to be sold, or other equipment or supplies.

In addition, it's helpful to give some or all of the following materials to volunteers (make yourself a checklist, so you don't forget any of them):

- welcome letter from the chair of the board of directors
- staff contact for when a volunteer is in the field and has a question
- staff contact in case the volunteer is ill or can't come as scheduled
- emergency staff contact for off-hours calls if necessary
- information about the organization, such as brochures, annual reports
- calendar of events, including any special events for volunteers and donors (in some organizations volunteers are invited to donor events)
- reimbursement form (if volunteers can request reimbursement for purchases and expenses)
- guidelines for tax deductions for which volunteers may be eligible, and
- where appropriate, a policy or procedures statement—perhaps requiring the volunteer's signature—such as an affirmation of the confidentiality policy, or the procedure for turning in cash after a fundraising sports night.

Creating Leadership Positions for Volunteers

Volunteers are often inappropriately stereotyped as unskilled "envelope stuffers," always working under someone's direction and control. This is far from the truth. Volunteers can be leaders and managers in organizations as well as hands-on doers. And just as paid staff value the opportunity to move up within an organization, many volunteers want to advance to volunteer positions with more responsibility and authority. In addition, there are many kinds of leadership work—typically high profile, high impact—into which high-level volunteers can be recruited directly.

Some examples of leadership work for which you will want to recruit high-level volunteers:

- leading a high-profile fundraising campaign
- serving as a spokesperson for a cause
- organizing a coalition of nonprofits and churches
- chairing a community planning process sponsored by your organization
- representing your organization and others in a class action court case, or
- being part of a turnaround oversight body for a struggling organization.

You can also promote volunteers from within your organization to supervisory and leadership positions among other volunteers. An experienced and faithful volunteer cook at a soup kitchen, for example, can be promoted to "Wednesday Head Chef" and given responsibilities for menu creation and supervising the volunteer crew. Volunteers who host international visitors can become "Lead Hosts" for groups of visitors, assigning them to family hosts and organizing group activities for them. Although staff is sometimes reluctant to ask volunteers to do more or more demanding work, remember that asking a volunteer to do more is an authentic way of communicating the value of the volunteer and his or her contribution to your organization. If, for instance, you have high school students volunteering as tutors for middle school students, they will see it as a recognition of their value if they are asked to come in another day per week. Of course, it's also important not to demand more of your volunteers than they are comfortable giving.

You can try to cultivate the upward movement of volunteers within your organization by offering training opportunities. Staff often will stay longer at a job if they feel they are getting good experience and learning new skills. The same is true for volunteers. For example, one of the reasons that people volunteer as museum docents is that they will receive education about the art on display. Hospice volunteers are honored by being chosen for "advanced training" in hospice care. Your group can reward and train your fundraising volunteers by offering them the opportunity to take a grantwriting class.

Finally, don't forget that some volunteers may be good candidates for the organization's board of directors. Operational and on-the-ground volunteers often have insights into how things work that can strengthen the oversight and strategic work of the board.

Volunteerism Practices and Policies for Volunteer Board Members

Members of the nonprofit board of directors are a special and unique type of volunteer. They are there to represent the public interest, ensuring that the organization manages its funds in pursuit of its mission. They lead and direct the organization and, in some cases, take on responsibilities as advisers, fundraisers, helpers, and ambassadors to your community. Board members are usually recruited by other board members and senior staff, rather than through the director of volunteers. Additionally, support to these volunteer members is provided by the executive director, the development director, the executive assistant to the CEO, or someone other than the volunteer director.

When bringing on new board members, it's a good idea to provide them with a board binder or manual that discusses their responsibilities toward the organization and the community. These binders should include some HR-like materials, such as:

- contact information for other directors and key staff

- a conflict of interest form policy and disclosure form, which should be signed by the new board member, and
- after-hours contact information for the executive director or appropriate person in case of emergency.

Make sure to pay attention to HR issues related to your board in the same way you pay attention to these issues with staff. While it's become common knowledge that staff needs and appreciates training opportunities, that the organization benefits from exit interviews with departing staff, and that people are more productive when they get evaluations, these sound HR procedures are seldom used with board members. Executive directors and board chairs should consider the "HR of the board" and attend to the development and full utilization of the board and board members.

> ⓘ **TIP**
>
> **Consider reference checks for board members.** If a prospective board member is not well known to at least two of the current board members or senior staff, a personal reference check will help assure you that this person is appropriate to be in a leadership position in your organization. Board members have access to a good deal of confidential information and can exert significant influence in the organization. Sincere board candidates will appreciate an organization that takes appropriate, courteous precautions with its volunteers.

Thanking Volunteers

All too often, nonprofits bungle the job of thanking volunteers, either by not thanking them at all or doing so inappropriately. Although it may seem like a matter of common sense, thanking volunteers in a meaningful way is frequently overlooked by both staff and other volunteers. The person responsible for volunteer involvement should encourage managers and others who supervise or work with volunteers to thank them, personally and often. You could consider doing an organization-wide thank-you program as well.

MYTH

Volunteers Should Be Treated Like Staff

Adviser Amy Smith of HandsOn Network notes the pendulum on thanking volunteers has swung too far. While it used to be thought that volunteers should never be criticized and didn't need job descriptions, she sees a problem with treating them the same as paid staff. "You can't just tell them to do this and this and get it done by 5 p.m. Volunteers have chosen to come and donate their time, and they need to be managed and appreciated differently from staff," she says.

There are many ways you can thank volunteers, from giving out "One Year of Volunteer Service" pins to writing up a complimentary profile in your newsletter to offering special experiences, such as a "behind-the-scenes" tour of the aquarium. The best volunteer acknowledgments are those that are specific to the individual or to the work accomplished. If a volunteer brings his own bottle of root beer to the job every day, surprise him with a case of gourmet root beer. A modest gift certificate to an electronics store given to a volunteer computer instructor by the head of computer training is likely to make that person feel particularly appreciated. Sometimes volunteer gifts are donated to an organization by a local business or supporter. One senior center received donated certificates from a nearby doughnut shop for "one thank-you doughnut" for the staff to give to volunteers.

These small gifts demonstrate that the staff isn't just performing a generic "volunteer recognition" chore, but genuinely has noticed and appreciated the volunteer as an individual.

Remember that volunteers—like any group of people—have different points of view and different preferences. Some volunteers will be delighted by a box of chocolates, while others will feel insulted, or even offended that organizational funds are being spent on such things. Do your best to thank people in a way that seems appropriate for the individual and the circumstances.

Make sure your volunteers don't get thanked for the wrong thing. This can be a problem when staff acts as if the volunteers are there to help them as opposed to the people or community the nonprofit serves. For example, a staff person at a nonprofit theater might say to a volunteer usher: "Thank you for helping me out tonight." A message that better conveys the volunteers' true achievement is: "Thank you for helping the audience members tonight." Similarly, instead of: "I don't know what we would do without you," say "I don't know what our patients would do without you."

When staff thinks of volunteer work as menial or even grunt work, they are likely to thank volunteers for getting it done rather than for contributing to the organization's mission. If you hear a staff person say, "Thank you so much for helping us with this mailing—it saves us a lot of time," suggest that they say instead: "Thank you for helping with this mailing—we've gotten a lot of important nutrition information out to people today."

Changing the way that staff talk to volunteers is just one area where a designated director of volunteer involvement can make a difference in the effective utilization of volunteers.

Professional Development for Managers of Volunteers

All staff that supervise volunteers—not just the volunteer coordinator or director of volunteers—can benefit from learning opportunities, whether workshops, conferences, webinars, or newsletters. In addition to the resources listed below, volunteer managers may be especially interested in the credentials offered by the Council for Certification in Volunteer Administration: CVA (Certified in Volunteer Administration) and CAVS (Certified Administrator of Volunteer Services). The materials are helpful for anyone, not just those seeking credentials.

RESOURCE

For more information on volunteer management, the following resources are recommended:

- Alive: Association of Leaders in Volunteer Engagement, a new (2009) organization of professional volunteer program managers: www.volunteeralive.org
- Blue Avocado columns have both practical and provocative articles on volunteerism (www.blueavocado.org/category/topic/volunteerism) and boards (www.blueavocado.org/category/topic/board-cafe).
- Directors of Volunteers in Agencies (DOVIA), an association of staff who work with volunteers. National directory at www.energize.com/prof/dovia.html
- Energize Inc., a company that trains, consults, and publishes research and opinion pieces at www.energizeinc.com, and manages 3-Volunteerism.com that offers volunteer managers useful files, printable training materials, and commentaries
- HandsOn Network provides tips, strategies, and tools on a wide variety of volunteer recruitment, engagement, and management issues: www.handsonnetwork.org.
- Idealist Volunteer Management Resource Center collates tools and resources and provides networking opportunities for volunteer managers: www.idealist.org/en/vmrc.
- National Service Resource Center, administered by ETR Associates, provides training and technical assistance to organizations with volunteers: www.nationalserviceresources.org.
- OurSharedResources.org is a user-generated compilation for volunteer managers with downloadable forms, manuals, position descriptions, and more
- ServeNet aggregates relevant content for volunteer managers: www.servenet.org.
- VolunteerMatch.org offers articles and webinars as part of their volunteer-nonprofit matching site. ●

Bringing in Outside Help:
Independent Contractors

Employee or Contractor? 231

    Frequently Asked Questions About Independent Contractors 232

Benefits and Drawbacks to Hiring Independent Contractors 233

    Benefits to Hiring Independent Contractors 234

    Drawbacks to Hiring Independent Contractors 235

Criteria for Classification 236

    The Relevant Factors 237

    What If You Goof? Investigations and Penalties 238

Independent Contractor Questionnaire 240

Creating an Independent Contractor Agreement 243

Managing Independent Contractors 247

Paperwork for Independent Contractors 249

Meet Your Adviser

Sarah Gort
Title: Director of Operations
Organization: CompassPoint Nonprofit Services
Location: San Francisco, California

What she does: Sarah oversees three areas—HR, finance, technology—and she is also on the Management Team for the organization. "In my HR role, I'm the 'sole provider,' while in finance and technology, I oversee staff. In all three areas, I'm overseeing the long-term strategy for the department as well as the day-to-day operations. I also convene the HR Network, which brings together peers in the nonprofit sector in the Bay Area."

What her company does: We intensify the impact of fellow non-profit leaders, organizations, and networks as we work together toward social equity. We do this through convening, training, consulting, research, and publishing. Our focus is the greater Bay Area but our reach and scope is across California and the country.

Best tip for HR managers including the Accidental HR manager: On a previous job, I was the accidental HR person in a staff of 24 and 10% of my time was allocated for HR. When I left ten years later, there was a staff of 250 and an HR department of five that reported to me along with the finance and tech departments. As the organization changes, you have to be comfortable with your own strengths and with hiring people who know more than you do. Find people whose strengths complement yours.

HR lesson you learned the hard way: When an organization is growing a common mistake is to promote somebody who isn't ready for it. I promoted someone who had the tenure, had a good amount of experience, had a great heart, but wasn't ready for a new level of responsibility.

Song title that speaks to you about HR: "I Want to Be Ready," by Ben Harper.

I n the "olden days," nonprofits thought of their personnel as being paid staff and volunteers. Outside consultants or independent contractors were used only occasionally, typically for specialized professional activities such as legal work or graphic design. For example, a nonprofit might bring in an outside consultant to design a newsletter and then staff or volunteers would do the production work to complete it.

Things have changed. Today, nonprofits use independent contractors and other outside consultants in ongoing, significant, and central ways. It wouldn't be unusual to have an outside consultant design a newsletter and have another outside consultant write and produce it on a monthly basis. Or, a nonprofit might have an independent contractor serve as chief financial officer hired on retainer for ten hours per week. And let's not forget the workers that we usually think of as "contractors," hired to repaint your facility or landscape the green space at your entryway. So, even though people think of HR in terms of paid staff, a nonprofit's human resources—especially in today's world—must include independent contractors as well.

Employee or Contractor?

When you hire someone to do work for your nonprofit, you will need to classify that person as either an employee or an independent contractor. In fact, you should make this decision at the outset, before you start looking for candidates. Why is this classification so important? Because the IRS and other governmental agencies keep a close watch on employers who use independent contractors. By hiring independent contractors, employers avoid a host of obligations that they otherwise have with employees, such as paying Social Security and Medicare taxes, withholding state and federal income taxes, paying for workers compensation and unemployment insurance, and providing employee benefits like sick time or health insurance. So, state and federal agencies are not only protecting workers, they have a vested interest in making sure that employers aren't skipping out on their tax and other obligations by calling workers independent contractors when they should really be classified as employees.

Frequently Asked Questions About Independent Contractors

What is an independent contractor?

Independent contractors (sometimes referred to as consultants or freelancers) are independent businesspeople who perform services for other people or businesses. In other words, they are people who do work for a company but are not its employees. Independent contractors are paid for work produced (for example, $5,000 for a grant proposal), whereas an employee might be paid a salary or hourly wage to work as a grantwriter.

Figuring out the difference between employees and independent contractors is not always easy, and the answer often depends on who is asking the question.

What are the benefits to a nonprofit of using independent contractors?

Because employers don't have to pay taxes or provide benefits (such as health insurance) for independent contractors, it can be less expensive and involve less paperwork to use them. It's easier to increase or reduce time with independent contractors and easier to stop using a contractor than to lay off staff.

A nonprofit can deploy a wider range of expertise in smaller increments than would be possible with staff. Additionally, many individuals ask to be paid as independent contractors because they do not want income and payroll taxes withheld from their earnings.

What are the drawbacks to the nonprofit of using independent contractors?

An employer doesn't have the same right to control independent contractors as it does employees, nor can a company expect the same type of loyalty from independent contractors. In addition, independent contractors can sue your company if they are injured while working for you, while employees cannot. From a practical standpoint, a key risk to paying someone as an independent contractor is that the person will be reclassified as an employee by a government agency, and your nonprofit will be subject to substantial fines.

Do we need to use any special paperwork to hire independent contractors?
You can greatly reduce the chances of a worker being reclassified as an employee by requiring the person to fill out an independent contractor questionnaire, provide copies of business licenses, and sign a written independent contractor agreement.

Do we have to use a written agreement with independent contractors?
With a few exceptions, the law does not require you to use a written agreement with an independent contractor. Still, it's a good idea to write things down, for a number of reasons.

Who owns the rights to the intellectual property we hire an independent contractor to create for us?
Unless the work falls into one of nine categories defined by law, the intellectual property rights to work an independent contractor creates will belong to the independent contractor, not to your nonprofit. This is true even if you hired and paid the independent contractor specifically to create the product for you. But you can ensure that you own the copyright by using a written contract with the independent contractor.

> **TIP**
> **Corporations—including nonprofit corporations—do not need to be classified as either an independent contractor or employee.** If, for example, you pay a for-profit employment agency for a temp accountant or a nonprofit organization for consulting services, you do not need to be concerned with classification, nor do you need to report the payments on Form 1099. They are simply paid as corporations using the corporation's tax identification number.

Benefits and Drawbacks to Hiring Independent Contractors

"We use a lot of independent contractors," comments adviser Sarah Gort of CompassPoint Nonprofit Services. "They let us bring in just the right amount of time and access a broad range of expertise. But there are definitely pluses and minuses." For every plus, there is an equally important drawback. In the end, you'll probably want to hire both independent contractors and regular paid employees, but remain careful about which kinds of work are done by each type of worker.

Benefits to Hiring Independent Contractors

Independent contractors require a smaller cash outlay than employees. Although an independent contractor may charge more to do the work than you would have to pay an employee, the independent contractor's fee will be the only cost to your nonprofit. With independent contractors—as opposed to employees—the hiring nonprofit doesn't have to:

- pay the employer's share of federal or state payroll taxes, including Social Security and Medicare taxes
- withhold any state or federal income taxes
- pay workers' compensation insurance or unemployment insurance
- provide employee benefits (such as health insurance, paid sick leave, paid holidays, and retirement benefits), and
- provide facilities, equipment, or training (unless the project requires otherwise).

In addition to the monetary benefits, nonprofits gain flexibility by being able to hire independent contractors for specialized work without the obligations of full-time staff. For example, if you want to present workshops in schools using performance educators (such as a person dressed as Ben Franklin teaching electricity), you can hire independent contractors and pay them by the workshop. This gives you a lot of flexibility and allows you to deploy a wider variety of educators than you could using only your own employees.

Employers also have less exposure to lawsuits from independent contractors than from employees. Most antidiscrimination laws and wrongful termination laws are all designed to protect employees, not independent contractors. In addition, employees have the right to unionize; independent contractors do not.

Nonprofits that hire independent contractors also have less exposure to lawsuits from third parties. Although your nonprofit is liable to third parties for anything an employee does on the job, it is not liable for what an independent contractor does unless you had some part in causing the injury or accident. For example, if you gave an independent contractor poor directions about how to set up the information booth for your festival, you could be held liable for any resulting injuries to the public. Or, if you hired an unlicensed caterer to cater your special event, participants who got food poisoning could sue your organization as well as the caterer

Drawbacks to Hiring Independent Contractors

The primary drawback of classifying any worker as an independent contractor is that a government agency will audit your organization and reclassify the worker as an employee. According to *Business Wire* magazine, the government loses about $20 billion a year in taxes because more than half of the workers classified as independent contractors in the country should be characterized as employees.

Government audits of independent contractor classification are often triggered by an independent contractor filing for unemployment insurance or workers' compensation, which are benefits exclusively reserved for employees. If a government agency decides that your organization has misclassified a worker, you will owe all of the back taxes associated with that worker, plus interest on those taxes and penalties. This could add up to a hefty sum. In addition, the worker might be entitled to overtime and back pay, as well as any unpaid unemployment or workers' compensation benefits.

Aside from legal concerns, there are other possible drawbacks to using independent contractors. These folks aren't part of the organization; they don't have the loyalty or investment of staff. They are unlikely to contribute to team development or organizational strategy, and they don't put in extra unpaid hours as nonprofit exempt staff so often do.

Because independent contractors are often paid significantly more than staff on an hourly basis, the use of nearly full-time independent contractors can also result in resentment from staff. Make sure that staff knows the status of independent contractors with whom they are working, and why they are classified differently. (Explaining that, "Their higher hourly rate isn't really so high when you realize that they don't get benefits, and have to cover their own office space, trainings, and other overhead," can help.)

> **TIP**
> **Pay particular attention during a unionization drive or if you're under a union contract.** If your organization is undergoing a unionization drive, union members will be extra alert to see if you are overusing independent contractors to avoid hiring staff who would be part of the bargaining unit. Overuse of independent contractors can inflame unionization efforts and, if a union contract is already in place, spark a dispute with the union.

Criteria for Classification

The government agencies that oversee the classification of employees and independent contractors on the federal level are the IRS and the federal Department of Labor (DOL). The agencies on the state level will probably have names like the unemployment compensation board, the state workers' compensation insurance agency, the state tax department, and the state department of labor. (Yikes!) Unfortunately, there is no single, uniform litmus test for how employers should properly classify employees versus independent contractors. The rules vary from one government agency to another. Whichever agency decides to investigate will look at a number of factors and make a decision based on its own criteria and the whole factual picture.

The IRS is probably the most important agency to satisfy when it comes to proper classification. Under the IRS test, workers are considered employees if the place they work for has the right to control the way they work, including the details of when, where, and how the job is accomplished. In contrast, the IRS will consider workers independent contractors if the place they work for does not manage how they work, except to accept or reject the final results. In other words, with an independent contractor, the hiring organization or company has the right to tell the worker what work needs to be done (the end product desired) but not how to do it. With employees, the hiring organization or company controls both what needs to get done and how it gets done—what equipment or tools are used, the workspace, the hours, the methods, and so on.

The Relevant Factors

The IRS and other agencies consider a number of factors when deciding whether a worker is an independent contractor or employee. The agency is more likely to classify a worker as an independent contractor if the person:

- can earn a profit or suffer a loss from the activity (rather than always earning a set amount of money)
- furnishes the workspace, equipment, and materials to do the work (as opposed to using workspace, equipment, and materials provided by you)
- is paid by the job (rather than by the hour or month)
- has more than one client at a time (rather than working only for your nonprofit)
- can set his or her own working hours (as opposed to working according to an established schedule), and
- has control over how the work is done.

On the other hand, a worker is more likely to be classified as an employee if that person is paid by the hour, can be fired at any time, receives training and instructions from your nonprofit, works full time and receives benefits, has the right to quit without incurring any liability, and provides services that are an integral part of your nonprofit's day-to-day operation.

> **RESOURCE**
>
> **Need more information on proper classification?** For more on the Department of Labor's classification rules, see the DOL's website at www.dol.gov. For more on the IRS rules, see the IRS website at www.irs.gov.

> **TIP**
>
> **A133 audits often examine employee classifications.** A133 audits (also called single audits) are required if you have $500,000 or more in federal funds during the year. As part of an A133 audit, the auditor has to verify that any federal dollars received were used properly. Because of this, an auditor doing an A133 audit is likely to look more deeply than in a regular audit into whether you are properly classifying employees/contractors and exempt/nonexempt. Adviser Sarah Gort notes: "They often look at whether contracts and workplans are in place and whether 1099s were filed accurately."

What If You Goof? Investigations and Penalties

One of the most common liability problems for nonprofits is misclassification of employees as independent contractors. The penalties for improper classification can be severe and expensive. Government investigation into independent contractors is typically triggered by one of the following:

- an application for state unemployment insurance benefits by a person who had been paid as an independent contractor (independent contractors are not eligible for unemployment)
- a complaint filed to a state labor department (often for overtime), by a person who was or is being paid as an independent contractor but who believes that employee status would be more accurate
- an audit by a state or local government agency related to a contract with the nonprofit being audited
- end-of-year payroll reports that show high expenses paid to independent contractors as compared to salary expenses, or

- an IRS investigation into an independent contractor who has not been paying income taxes.

A government agency does not, however, need to be prompted by anything at all to investigate whether an independent contractor has been properly classified as such. The issue can arise during a routine audit or review.

> **EXAMPLE:** The Clean Food Initiative paid its full-time deputy director as an independent contractor. Originally, the director had been a part-time, occasional field organizer, but his job gradually evolved into deputy director, and he liked maintaining independent contractor status. When the state agricultural agency conducted a routine review of its contract with the Clean Food Initiative, the visiting official noted the $85,000 payment to the Deputy Director and determined that the position was really an employee position. Although the state agency was pleased with the work of the Clean Food Initiative, they had to give them a "provisional" rating on management, and the Initiative had to pay back taxes and penalties on the misclassified amounts.

If an agency determines that you have inappropriately classified someone as an independent contractor, you may be required to pay (for the period in question):

- both the employer's and the employee's share of Social Security and Medicare contributions
- federal and state income taxes that should have been withheld from the employee's wages
- federal unemployment tax
- minimum wage (if the worker's pay divided by hours fell short)
- overtime (if the contractor worked extra hours and should have been classified as a nonexempt employee)
- where applicable, state unemployment compensation taxes, and
- if the individual was injured on the job, workers' compensation benefits.

In short, it's worth paying attention to proper classification!

EXAMPLE: The Racha Preschool maintained an informal "pool" of substitute teachers who could fill in for staff teachers for reasons of illness, vacation, and so forth. These substitute teachers were paid by the day as independent contractors. This made payments easy, because the school didn't have to add a teacher to payroll every time someone came in to do a day of work. But when one of the substitutes hadn't been called in a while, she filed for unemployment benefits, saying that she had been laid off.

The unemployment claim sparked an investigation into the preschool's classifications, and all of the substitute teachers were declared to be temporary employees, not independent contractors. The rationale for the decision was that the substitutes worked at hours set by the preschool, the work occurred on the preschool's site using the preschool's equipment, and most of the substitute teachers did not do substitute teaching anywhere else. Racha Preschool ended up having to pay $80,000 in back employment taxes. Needless to say, they now treat all substitute teachers as temporary employees and put them on the payroll, even if it's just for one day.

Independent Contractor Questionnaire

A good safeguard against problems with improper classification is to have independent consultants complete a questionnaire before you contract with them. Design the questionnaire to elicit information that will help establish that the independent contractor is a separate business entity and not an employee under your control. Make sure all managers with authority to contract with independent contractors understand the significance of these questionnaires. They should require any prospective independent contractors to complete the questionnaire and then have it reviewed by someone in HR before a contract is signed. You can also use this form if you are not sure whether a vendor is incorporated or not.

Sample Independent Contractor Determination Form

Independent Contractor Determination Form

Instructions: This form must be completed and signed by individuals with whom our nonprofit is considering signing a contract as an independent contractor. The form should be reviewed and signed by the staff person who is proposing the contract, and must be approved by the HR Manager prior to the contract being signed.

Name _____

Business mailing address _____

Business telephone and fax _____

Email _____

Do you maintain an office separate from home? ❑ yes ❑ no

Fictitious business name _____

❑ I do not have a fictitious business name

Is your business: ❑ Sole proprietorship ❑ Partnership ❑ Corporation ❑ LLC

Tax ID number _____

Professional licenses held (copies attached) _____

Business insurance carried _____

	Yes	No
Do you currently work for this nonprofit as an employee?		
Have you been an employee of this nonprofit within the last 12 months?		
Will the nonprofit provide you with workspace, materials, or equipment?		
Will the nonprofit determine your hours of work?		
Will the nonprofit reimburse you for expenses incurred in the work?		
Will the nonprofit provide supervision of your work rather than relying on your expertise?		
Will the nonprofit furnish you with business cards, professional stationery, and invoice forms?		

Sample Independent Contractor
Determination Form (cont'd)

❏ Proceed to developing agreement with independent contractor.

❏ This individual should be classified as an employee. Please see HR.

❏ This person's status as an independent contractor requires more investigation. Please see HR.

_____   _____

Independent contractor   Date

_____   _____

Nonprofit Organization   Date

_____   _____

HR manager approval   Date

TIP

Make sure you have good internal processes in place for verifying independent contractor status. "Too often the accounting department only hears that someone has hired an independent contractor when the invoice comes through for payment," says Sarah Gort, "But HR hasn't had a chance to review whether independent contractor status is legitimate. Managers who supervise people with the authority to hire independent contractors need to hold those people accountable to following the process for proper classification."

The answers to these questions will help you accurately assess whether the worker is an independent contractor or not. However, none of the questions is conclusive evidence of the worker's status. Each answer is just one factor among many you should consider when deciding how to classify the worker.

RESOURCE

Your regular financial auditor may be a good advisor about employee-contractor classification. In addition, you can find the rules and instructions from the IRS in IRS Form SS-8, *Determination of Worker Status for Purposes of Federal Employment Taxes and Income Tax Withholding* and the attached instructions.

Creating an Independent Contractor Agreement

For most types of projects, the law does not require you to enter into a written contract with an independent contractor. You can orally agree to the terms of your arrangement, and in most cases that oral contract will be enforceable in court. However, just because you can do something doesn't mean you should. Oral agreements can lead to costly misunderstandings and disagreements, because there's no clear written statement about what the independent contractor is supposed to do, how much your organization will pay, the timeline for the work, or what happens if a dispute arises.

A written agreement can also help establish a worker's independent contractor status by showing the IRS and other agencies that both parties intended to create a contracting arrangement, not an employment relationship.

Below is an example of a contract between a nonprofit and an independent contractor, referred to as the "Consultant." When creating a template for your own organization, be sure that you take your organization's situation and the relevant state laws into account. For more information and other sample independent contractor agreements, see *Consultant & Independent Contractor Agreements*, by Stephen Fishman (Nolo).

Independent Contractor Agreement

This Agreement is made between Mission Nonprofit, Inc., ("Client"), with a principal place of business at Chicago, Illinois., and Jordan Lee ("Consultant"), with a principal place of business at Oak Park, Illinois. The consultant is an independent contractor and not an employee of the client.

1. Services to Be Performed

Consultant agrees to perform the following consultant services on Client's behalf:

As per attached workplan, conduct prospect research for government, foundation, corporate and individual grants, and contracts for research projects related to independent living for people with disabilities. The work will be completed by June 15, 20xx.

2. Payment

In consideration for the services to be performed by Consultant, Client agrees to pay Consultant $10,000. The first payment of $2,500 will be paid at the satisfactory conclusion of Phase I in the workplan, and the remaining $7,500 will be paid upon receipt of a satisfactory final report completed before September 30, 20xx. Consultant will submit invoices to client in order for payments to be processed. A signed W-9 will be submitted with the first invoice or before.

3. Expenses

Consultant will be responsible for all expenses incurred while performing services under this Agreement.

4. Materials

Consultant will furnish all materials, equipment, and supplies used to provide the services required by this Agreement.

5. Independent Contractor Status

Consultant is an independent contractor, and neither Consultant nor Consultant's employees or contract personnel are, or will be deemed, Client's employees. In its capacity as an independent contractor, Consultant agrees and represents, and Client agrees, as follows:

Consultant has the right to perform services for others during the term of this Agreement.

Consultant has the sole right to control and direct the means, manner, and method by which the services required by this Agreement will be performed.

Consultant has the right to perform the services required by this Agreement at any place or location and at such times as Consultant may determine.

Consultant has the right to hire assistants as subcontractors or to use employees to provide the services required by this Agreement.

The services required by this Agreement will be performed by Consultant, consultant's employees, or contract personnel, and Client will not hire, supervise, or pay any assistants to help Consultant.

Neither Consultant nor Consultant's employees or contract personnel will receive any training from Client in the professional skills necessary to perform the services required by this Agreement.

6. Business Permits, Certificates, and Licenses

Consultant has complied with all federal, state, and local laws requiring business permits, certificates, and licenses required to carry out the services to be performed under this Agreement.

7. State and Federal Taxes

Client will not:

- withhold FICA (Social Security and Medicare taxes) from Consultant's payments or make FICA payments on Consultant's behalf

- make state or federal unemployment compensation contributions on Consultant's behalf, or

- withhold state or federal income tax from Consultant's payments.

8. Fringe Benefits

Consultant understands that neither Consultant nor Consultant's employees or contract personnel are eligible to participate in any employee pension, health, vacation pay, sick pay, or other fringe benefit plan of Client.

9. Workers' Compensation

Client will not obtain workers' compensation insurance on behalf of Consultant or Consultant's employees. If Consultant hires employees to perform any work under this Agreement, Consultant will cover them with workers' compensation insurance and provide Client with a certificate of workers' compensation insurance before the employees begin work.

10. Term of Agreement

This agreement will become effective when signed by both parties and will terminate on the earliest of:

- the date Consultant completes the services required by this Agreement

- November 30, 20xx, or

- the date a party terminates the Agreement as provided below.

11. Terminating the Agreement

Either party may terminate this agreement at any time by giving 30 days' written notice to the other party of the intent to terminate.

12. Exclusive Agreement

This is the entire agreement between Consultant and Client.

13. Intellectual Property Ownership

Consultant assigns to Client all patent, copyright, trademark, and trade secret rights in anything created or developed by Consultant for Client under this Agreement. Consultant will help prepare any papers that Client considers necessary to secure any patents, copyrights, trademarks, or other proprietary rights at no charge to Client. However, Client will reimburse Consultant for reasonable out-of-pocket expenses incurred.

Consultant must obtain written assurances from Consultant's employees and contract personnel that they agree with this assignment. Consultant agrees not to use any of the intellectual property mentioned above for the benefit of any other party without Client's prior written permission.

14. Resolving Disputes

If a dispute arises under this Agreement, the parties agree to first try to resolve the dispute with the help of a mutually agreed-upon mediator in Chicago, Illinois. Any costs and fees other than attorney fees associated with the mediation will be shared equally by the parties. If the dispute is not resolved within 30 days after it is referred to the mediator, any party may take the matter to court.

15. Applicable Law

This Agreement will be governed by the laws of the state of Illinois.

Signatures

Client: Mission Nonprofit, Inc.

By: _____

Sally Ann Bremerton, Executive Director

Date: _____

Consultant: _____

Jordan Lee

Taxpayer ID#: _____

Date: _____

MYTH

If Someone Wants to Be Paid as an Independent Contractor You Can Treat Them Like One

As you might have suspected, the widely acted-upon belief that a person who agrees to be paid as an independent contractor rather than as an employee can be classified as one, is just plain wrong.

"He insisted on being paid as an independent contractor," said one executive director. "He gets benefits through his wife's job, so he doesn't need to be an employee. If he agrees to it, it's okay, right?"

Actually, no. Someone who wants to be paid as an independent contractor is probably less likely to complain about this status (or make a claim for unpaid overtime, unemployment compensation, or workers' compensation). But there are many other ways for the arrangement to come to the attention of government auditors. And a worker who initially asked to be paid as an independent contractor might have a change of mind after a serious workplace inquiry or long spell of unemployment. The bottom line: The wishes of independent contractors or their written statements or agreements regarding their independent contractor status are not factors that will be considered in determining their classification.

Managing Independent Contractors

In nonprofits, contracts with outside consultants are typically initiated by someone on staff, such as a program director, facilities manager, or development manager. However, someone in HR or finance should be responsible for checking the independent contractor's classification. One way to do this is by using an independent contractor questionnaire as described above. Once someone has been hired, follow-up should be done by the manager in charge of that person's work—usually the person who initiated the contract, not HR or another department like finance. That person should also be the one who approves invoices from the independent contractor and submits them to accounting for payment.

Once you have hired an independent contractor, it will be important to introduce the person to your organization and do anything else necessary to maximize the effectiveness of the contractor's work. There are certain good practices you should adopt in this regard. First, make sure that the independent contractor and the rest of your staff know the point person at your organization for the independent contractor. This is the person who can approve invoices for payment, interface with staff as necessary, and answer any questions that come up. If staff and independent contractors will be working together, take the time to let everyone know "who is what," and what their roles and responsibilities are. In addition, there may be certain restrictions that apply to independent contractors that others should be aware of. For example, you might allow staff to use the copier machine, but not independent contractors.

A pitfall of working with independent contractors is the need to control the contract: "Everyone starts to get used to independent contractors," remarks adviser Sarah Gort. "Accounting is used to paying their invoices; staff is used to seeing them around. It gets too comfortable and they just keep getting paid."

Remind staff who are overseeing contracts with independent contractors that while they cannot tell contractors how to do their work (as you can with staff), they can and should hold independent contractors accountable for quality, timeliness, and completeness. If the staff person responsible for the independent contractor is not satisfied with the person's work, they should talk to someone in HR or finance and delay or withhold payments until the issue is resolved.

Independent contractors are an indispensable component of the workforce for most nonprofit organizations today. With just a little effort, you can keep your organization on the right side of the law, and help staff keep independent contractors as productive and on-time as your mission needs them to be.

Paperwork for Independent Contractors

It's a good idea to have a file for each independent contractor, These files can be maintained in the contracts department (if you have one), the finance department, or the HR department.

Each file should contain:

- the independent contractor questionnaire
- any supporting documents to the questionnaire
- a W-9
- the contract or agreement
- any correspondence related to the contract, such as added work or extension of deadlines.

TIP

Don't neglect to file Form 1099 reports for your independent contractors. By February 15 of each year, anyone who has paid an independent contractor $600 or more during the previous calendar year must issue an IRS Form 1099-MISC to that individual and send a copy to the IRS.

Many organizations find it convenient and affordable to have 1099s issued by their payroll services or use an online 1099 service (often about $3 per 1099).

RESOURCE

For a more comprehensive look at working with independent contractors, see *How to Safely & Legally Hire Independent Contractors*, by Stephen Fishman (Nolo eGuide) (includes sample forms).

The Board's Role in HR

The Board's Oversight of the Executive Director 253

The Board's Oversight of HR 256

Guidelines for the Board's Role in HR 257

Creating a Board HR Committee or Task Force 257

Reviewing Personnel Policies and the Employee Handbook 258

Approving (or Commenting on) the Salary Schedule 258

Ensuring Salary Scale Compliance 259

Establishing Employee Benefits 260

Role in Hiring 260

Monitoring Diversity 260

Deciding When Layoffs Are Necessary 261

Responding to Complaints and Grievances 261

Dealing With Serious Concerns About the Executive Director 261

Conducting Exit Interviews 262

Meet Your Adviser

Terrence Jones, MA, MFA
Title: President and CEO
Organization: Wolf Trap Foundation for the Performing Arts
Location: Vienna, Virginia (just outside Washington, DC)

What he does: As the head of "America's National Park for the Performing Arts," Terrence D. Jones is not only responsible for this large and multifaceted nonprofit, he is a national and international leader in thinking about the arts.

Jones is responsible for the management and strategic planning of the Foundation's annual budget which is in excess of $28 million. The organization has 80 full-time employees and hundreds of part-time employees and volunteers, and presents more than 270 performances each year.

Since joining the Foundation in 1996, Jones has commissioned more than 70 new works from such renowned artists as jazz greats Don Byron and Max Roach, composer Philip Glass, multimedia artist Robert Wilson, and choreographers Elizabeth Streb and Ann Reinking.

What the Foundation does: The Wolf Trap Foundation for the Performing Arts produces and presents a full range of performance and education programs in the Greater Washington area, as well as nationally and internationally. Wolf Trap includes the Filene Center, the Barns at Wolf Trap, the Children's Theatre-in-the-Woods; and a wide variety of education programs, including the Wolf Trap Institute for Early Learning Through the Arts and the Wolf Trap Opera Company.

HR lesson you learned the hard way: It's important to make the tough calls. I have learned that it pays to follow your instincts. A candidate may look terrific on paper, interview well, and come highly recommended from the department head. However, if your gut tells you that the candidate is not the best fit for the job, more than likely they're not.

Song title that speaks to you about HR: "Don't Stop Believin'," (Journey, 1981).

The nonprofit board of directors has two crucial and distinct roles to play in the realm of HR. First, it is responsible for the hiring, compensation, performance review, and terminating of the executive director. In addition, the board is in charge of overseeing HR functions, to ensure that they are handled properly. These two roles require board members to put on different "hats" as they carry out their responsibilities. On the one hand, they are doers: acting collectively to hire, evaluate, support, set the salary for, and sometimes fire the executive. On the other hand, they are overseers: monitoring staff HR work and authorizing policy changes.

In both roles, board members will need to be assisted by the executive director and HR staff. The board will need data, suggestions for processes, and often nudging (or even pushing) to get its work done.

The Board's Oversight of the Executive Director

In most nonprofits, the only staff person hired by the board is the chief executive—commonly titled the executive director or the CEO. If a nonprofit starts as an all-volunteer organization, the board must first decide whether or not to hire an executive director, and then, if they decide to do so, proceed to hiring. The executive director is then responsible for seeing to the hiring of the rest of the staff, and only the executive director reports directly to the board.

In some cases, the board may be responsible for hiring more than one person in the organization. For example, in a performing arts organization—such as a dance company or a theater—there may be two top positions, an artistic director and a managing director. Typically, the board would hire for both these positions, and each director would report directly to the board. There are a few other instances in which more than one position would report directly to the board. For example, a research institute might have a CEO and a director of science or a primary care clinic might have an executive director and a medical director, and each of these persons would report directly to the board.

In addition to hiring, the board of directors has several responsibilities for employees who report directly to it: performance review, establishing compensation, and termination. In each of these areas, the board is likely to use a system that is different from the systems in place for other staff. For example, a nonprofit might have a detailed process for its regular employees to set performance goals and then be reviewed against those goals. But in the same nonprofit, instead of setting individual goals for the executive, the board might rely on a combination of organization-wide achievement and its own direct observations as the bases for performance review.

> EXAMPLE: At the Cricket Performing Arts Center, CEO Martin Gonzales each year sits down with the board chair to review the organizational goals and focus on his responsibilities to accomplish those goals. At the end of the year, the board meets in executive session to discuss Martin's performance and then the board chair meets with him to discuss his review. "There isn't a form we use," comments Martin. "Some board chairs write a letter, some do notes, whatever is most comfortable for the chair that year. Then it goes into my personnel file."

Providing guidelines for boards about how to hire and evaluate executives is beyond the scope of this book. But staff with responsibilities for HR should know that the systems are likely to be different.

RESOURCE

Where to find online resources on executive review. Examples of performance review processes and forms to be used in nonprofit executive director evaluation can be obtained from Bridgespan (www.bridgespan.org), Blue Avocado (www.blueavocado.org), or Boardsource (www.boardsource.org).

In addition, the board may ask for assistance from staff in developing a system for executive review or gathering information on comparable salaries. In such cases, the executive may assign a person on staff with HR responsibilities to complete such tasks. Here are some common ways in which HR staff support the board's management of the executive director:

- providing examples of how other organizations conduct executive director performance reviews
- during efforts to recruit a new director, providing administrative support to an executive search consultant hired by the board
- if the board is conducting the search themselves, providing administrative support to a board (or board-staff) committee
- obtaining comparable job descriptions and compensation data from similarly-sized organizations in the same field, and
- providing the CEO's salary history to the board.

Documents related to the CEO's job—whether job description, salary authorization, performance reviews, or other material—should be signed by the board chair and the executive, and placed in the CEO's personnel folder.

> **EXAMPLE:** Ten years into the executive director job, Sandra had never had a performance review by the board of directors. The board's philosophy had been to focus on organizational performance; because they were pleased with how the nonprofit was doing overall, they felt the executive was doing a good job. But this year both Sandra and the new board chair, William, decided that a performance review would be a good idea. But how to start?
>
> Sandra and the HR manager worked together to compile a packet for the board. It included Sandra's job description (of ten years ago!), her salary history, and the salary histories of the two other highest-paid staff. In addition, they obtained three sample processes for board appraisal of the chief executive, including a board satisfaction survey, a mapping of individual and organizational achievement against individual and organizational goals, and a 360-degree assessment. William and the board officers decided to use a board satisfaction survey, modifying the sample they had to suit the organization's circumstances. As a first performance review, Sandra and William

were pleased with the process. Sandra's job description was revised, and she and the board agreed upon a set of goals for the coming year. The board was on its way to better performance review—and more strategic support—of their executive.

The Board's Oversight of HR

The role of the board of directors in human resource administration is frequently a sticky issue for nonprofits. Should the board approve all salaries, or just the executive director's? If a staff member has a grievance, should it go to the board? How can the board's finance committee members, for example, be helpful in hiring accounting staff, but not usurp the hiring role of the executive staff? How can a board member appropriately give feedback to the executive director on the behavior of a staff person?

MYTHS

(1) The Board Should Stay out of HR; (2) The Board Should Approve All Staffing Decisions

Some nonprofits operate on the theory that the board should have no say in HR matters beyond hiring and firing the executive director. Others think the board must approve all personnel changes, including raises, benefits, title changes, and layoffs.

The bottom line is that no absolute rules govern the role of the board. In each organization, a negotiated balance develops and evolves as personalities and circumstances change. Rather than assume that the board must or can't be involved in a decision, the board's leaders and the executive need to discuss situations as they arise and together determine the most appropriate and most beneficial role for the board to play.

Boards tend to be at one extreme or another: Some insist on approving every raise for every staff member, while others never see a salary report. Where on this spectrum a board stands is typically related to the level of confidence they have in their executive. As a board loses confidence, they step in closer. As they gain confidence, they step back.

This chapter proposes specific guidelines for board oversight that don't take away from the executive director's authority or responsibility. The board can approve various policies such as salary ranges without interfering with the executive's ability to manage.

Guidelines for the Board's Role in HR

However the board structures its oversight of HR administration, it needs an explicit process to exercise that oversight. The guidelines below provide such a process. They follow the principle that the board as a whole governs (not manages) the organization, while individual board members can be helpful advisers to staff.

Creating a Board HR Committee or Task Force

The board can establish a committee or an as-needed task force that works with HR staff. The committee or task force makes recommendations to the board for approval (rather than deciding matters on its own).

The most common choices are:

- a standing (permanent) human resources committee
- a human resources task force (that is, a temporary committee)
- a board-staff standing committee, or a
- board-staff task force.

Committee members might include the staff human resources director (if there is one) or executive director, and/or non-board volunteers such as a human resources attorney. If there are non-board members on the committee, their role should be limited to that of nonvoting, advisory members, or else the committee's recommendations should come back to the board for approval. In some cases, the HR committee is also responsible for developing plans and strategies for appropriate recruitment and utilization of volunteers, while in other organizations the human resources committee looks only at paid personnel.

The scope of the committee's work typically encompasses personnel policies, hiring practices, salary schedules and compliance, and benefits. In many organizations with small boards, the work is done by the finance committee.

Reviewing Personnel Policies and the Employee Handbook

The executive director is responsible for ensuring that personnel policies and procedures are disseminated and implemented, and that the policies are reviewed as appropriate by the board. Individual members of the HR committee may be able to offer human resources expertise in making suggestions.

Every two years or so, the human resources committee (or task force) should review the policies with staff and, if appropriate, draft changes or a complete revision. Board approval of the personnel policies and employee handbook at that point ensures that the board has reviewed key elements such as benefits, staff development strategies, and equal opportunity measures.

Approving (or Commenting on) the Salary Schedule

The executive staff normally drafts a rate schedule (salary ranges for each position or category), which is then reviewed by the human resources committee. This ensures that the board has considered the strategic matters related to salaries: whether the schedule is in line with the organization's values, whether it achieves appropriate internal equity or differentiation among positions and departments, whether specific positions are appropriately placed on the scale, whether compensation is in line with that at similar organizations, and/or whether the compensation supports (rather than hinders) the organization's ability to recruit qualified staff.

The salary schedule is sent by the committee or task force to the whole board for approval. In this way, the executive staff remains responsible for salaries, but the range of salaries is approved by the board.

In some organizations, this work can be done by the finance committee as part of its work on the budget.

Ensuring Salary Scale Compliance

Once a year, the human resources committee should review the specific salaries of the staff (by name and position) against the organization's salary schedule. The purpose is to ensure that no one is being paid outside the range for that person's position. The committee's job is to protect against favoritism and ensure compliance with the salary schedule, not to review whether a particular employee deserves a particular salary.

> **EXAMPLE:** At the Marble Education Foundation, the executive director felt strongly that staff salaries were a management matter and that the board should only see the total expense for all salaries together. The board was okay with this until a departing development director complained in an exit interview with the board chair about the salary of the executive assistant. After a lengthy battle with the executive director, the board finally insisted on seeing a list of individual salaries for the staff of 11. To their surprise, they saw that the executive director's assistant was being paid significantly more than the development director or the program director. Further investigation uncovered other staff complaints about favoritism. The board didn't want to get too involved in the details, but they felt they needed to do something. They decided they could and should establish salary ranges for all positions and ask the executive director to keep salaries within those ranges. Charging "micromanagement," the executive quit, an action met with relief by many on the board.

Establishing Employee Benefits

The benefits schedule, health insurance, long-term disability insurance, 401(k), and so forth are reviewed annually. Doing this review is a necessary part of the budget process, as costs are being projected for the coming year.

To back up this process, the human resources committee should review the benefits package at least every two years and suggest changes (additions or subtractions), along with an explanation of their financial implications, to the executive director, the board's finance committee, or both. In particular, board attention to benefits provides oversight on long-term financial commitments to staff, overly generous paid time off policies (such as uncapped PTO), and policies that unreasonably benefit some staff more than others.

Role in Hiring

In some cases, at the request of the executive director, one or two board members may help with hiring. A common example is the board treasurer helping to interview and select the chief financial officer (CFO) or accountant.

It should be made clear to everyone involved that the final decision will be made by the staff person to whom the new hire would report. In these situations, individual board members are acting as advisers to staff.

Monitoring Diversity

If an organization has established goals or principles regarding a staff that is diverse in race, ethnicity, gender, age, disability, sexual orientation, or other characteristics such as status as clients, there will be an HR role to play in implementing the policies and goals. A diversity committee or the HR committee can assist with making sure that recruitment efforts reach out effectively (for example, through the ethnic press). It can also be on the alert for indicators of weak management of a diverse workforce (such as a string of resignations from Latina nurses). Additionally, such a committee can help monitor progress toward goals.

Deciding When Layoffs Are Necessary

A management decision to lay off staff usually reflects a financial situation that should already have been shared with the board. In this context, the steps that management is taking to deal with that financial situation—whether those include instituting layoffs, pay cuts, new income strategies, or others—should be discussed with the board. The board should either bless or put a hold on such management actions.

Although in most staffed organizations the decision of who to lay off and when and how to do so are management decisions, it's critical for the board and management to be in sync about how the organization is responding to financial problems.

Responding to Complaints and Grievances

Employees who want to file a grievance should first go through any procedures written in the employee policies manual. If an employee has exhausted the grievance process and that process has been documented, individual employees may be permitted (if it is so written in the policies) to raise a grievance to either the board chair or the board's human resources committee, which then acts as the final arbiter.

This may be especially appropriate where the complaining employee reports to the executive director and has an unresolved complaint about the executive director.

Dealing With Serious Concerns About the Executive Director

Sometimes a staff member has a serious charge against or concern about the executive director, such as the illegal or improper use of funds, sexual harassment, discriminatory behavior, improper accounting methods, or a concern about the executive director's mental health, abuse of drugs, or absenteeism. The normal grievance process most likely doesn't provide an adequate avenue for dealing with such issues, and you wouldn't want an employee's first move to be filing a complaint with the state attorney general (in the case of possible criminal activity). To fill the gap organizations can permit staff members to raise such concerns with the board chair.

With this arrangement, other board members who hear such complaints then have a responsibility to direct the staff person to the board chair. By making the board chair the sole recipient of such charges, the board can prevent a disgruntled staff member from trying to develop allies on the board against the executive staff, and can provide a way to bring an organizational matter to the attention of the board as a whole.

Conducting Exit Interviews

Exit interviews with departing members of the management team should be conducted by one or more board officers. Exit interviews with senior management staff are a way the board can maintain an independent perspective on executive performance and provide information useful both for oversight and for making suggestions to the executive director.

Each organization will want to choose its own guidelines on the sensitive and important issues described in this chapter. Striking the right balance between board's and the executive director's authority may initially be challenging, but it's far from impossible. In the end, sorting this out will strengthen your organization while making life easier for board members and staff.

Unions and Nonprofits

What Is a Union? 266

Laws Governing Unions 266

Who the Union Represents 267

How a Union Contract Is Created: Collective Bargaining 268

What's in a Union Contract 269

How Union Drives Work 270

HR Under a Union Contract 272

Employees Who Are Not Part of the Union 273

Day-to-Day Union Representation:
   Business Agents and Shop Stewards 274

Meet Your Adviser

Mark Masaoka
Title: Director/Policy Coordinator
Organization: Asian Pacific Policy and Planning
Council
Location: Los Angeles, California

What he does: Mark brings together the various Asian Pacific Islander (API) communities and their nonprofit organizations to advocate for API communities in Los Angeles County. Mark is also a former business agent for Service Employees International Union (SEIU) Locals 660 and 399 working with public sector and nonprofit hospital workers, and was an elected officer in the United Auto Workers Local 645.

What his organization does: The Asian Pacific Policy and Planning Council (A3PCON) is a coalition of nonprofits that works as an advocate, convener, and clearinghouse on issues affecting API communities in Los Angeles County, such as language access, housing, mental health funding, and more.

Best tip for HR managers including the Accidental HR manager: Screen classes and trainers carefully. Some training for new supervisors is great and some is terrible. I've wasted time going to generic "management" workshops or bringing in trainers that looked good on paper but they were not what we were looking for.

HR lesson learned the hard way: Disciplining people in community nonprofits is tougher than in for-profit situations. Employees are motivated, in part, by community service and they expect people to respect and appreciate this commitment. To some, this translates into thinking they shouldn't be criticized, or they should get special understanding with personal issues. You can't ignore this issue. You have to understand where people are coming from and address the concern. It requires a different type of conversation.

Song that says something to him about HR: Springsteen's "Working on a Dream." We're all working on dreams.

Whether or not your nonprofit's employees (some or all of them) have joined or formed a union, you need to know something about what's involved and what to expect. If there is already a union in your organization (or more than one), a good many HR practices and policies will be determined by the union contract.

If no union yet operates at your nonprofit, there is always the possibility that some employees will try to organize one. In that case, you will need to respond intentionally, thoughtfully, and legally.

In this chapter, we'll discuss the role of HR in a union environment as well as provide an overview of how union organizing drives play out, particularly in community-based nonprofits.

Other than hospitals and universities, few nonprofit organizations have unions. But unions and nonprofits have had many decades of complicated interaction. In some cases, unions and nonprofits have joined forces to push for workers' rights and safe working conditions. In other situations, nonprofits have opposed unions that have lagged in providing racial and gender equality or supported certain candidates for political office.

Try not to fall into the easy trap of being pro-union or antiunion in general, rather than considering how a particular union might operate in a particular nonprofit. Whether you are working under a union contract or in an organization where a union drive is occurring, it will be important to keep people focused on what policies and actions are best for your particular constituents and community.

Unions Are Nonprofits . . . But a Different Type

Unions are nonprofit organizations, although of a different type than those we generally think of. Unions are classified as 501(c)(5) nonprofit organizations, whereas charitable nonprofits are 501(c)(3) organizations. As a 501(c) organization, unions are exempt from paying corporate income taxes, but because they are not (c)(3) organizations, donations to unions are not tax-deductible to donors (although union dues are tax-deductible by members if they itemize).

What Is a Union?

In the United States, labor unions represent groups of employees in their dealings with their employers concerning matters such as wages, working conditions, and grievances. There may be more than one union at one workplace, as each might represent different employee groups at the same organization. For example, at a hospital, the nurses might be represented by a nurses' union (such as National Nurses United), and other staff by a hospital workers union (such as Service Employees International Union or SEIU).

Although unions are very common in government agencies, they are much less so in for-profit corporations, and even rarer in small businesses and in nonprofits of all sizes. In fact, outside of hospitals and universities, it's rare for a nonprofit to be unionized.

Most nonprofit managers, HR staff, and boards of directors have probably not even considered whether or not a union drive is likely to occur, or whether having a union would be good or bad for the organization. As a result, if a union drive starts, they are starting from scratch in sorting through various complex and emotionally laden issues.

What is clear is that nonprofit HR can be managed well with a union and managed well without a union. Nonprofit HR can also be managed poorly with a union and managed poorly without a union. Knowing more about unions can help you be better at HR in either situation.

Laws Governing Unions

The National Labor Relations Act (the NLRA) is the primary law governing the rights and obligations of employers, unions, and individual workers in the workplace. The National Labor Relations Board (the NLRB) is the federal agency that conducts unionization elections, and investigates and rules on charges of unfair practices by both employers and unions. You can learn more about these laws and the NLRB at the NLRB website (www.nlrb.gov) and in *The Manager's Legal Handbook*, by Amy DelPo and Lisa Guerin (Nolo).

In addition, your state, city, or other local governing body may have passed laws related to unions.

Who the Union Represents

A union can represent only employees who are part of what is known as a bargaining unit. A bargaining unit consists of a group of employees at a particular workplace who do similar types of work and have common concerns about wages, hours, and working conditions. Job classifications in the bargaining unit are determined by industry practice, but which job positions will be included in the bargaining unit, and which will not, is an important part of union organizing. Only bargaining unit workers have a right to vote on whether to be represented by a union, so the size and composition of the bargaining unit can be a hotly contested issue.

A bargaining unit generally won't combine professional with nonprofessional employees, nor will it include workers with significantly different job duties, skills, or working conditions. Instead, you would have different bargaining units within one organization representing different groups of workers. For example, in a unionized family service agency, you might have social workers included in one bargaining unit and administrative support staff included in another. The two bargaining units might be in the same union or in different unions.

Managers and supervisors, which typically include top management and senior management staff, cannot join a union. Under the NLRA, the employees who have the authority to take certain actions—like hiring, promoting, disciplining, or rewarding—cannot be part of a collective bargaining unit. Whether middle managers can join a bargaining unit will depend on their level of responsibility, including the degree to which they exercise independent judgment in their actions. This is an area where the rules are in flux.

The union is required to represent everyone who is in the bargaining unit—regardless of whether or not they've joined the union (although most will probably be members.) Union dues are usually deducted from employees' paychecks and remitted directly to the union. Union members have the power to elect union officials and vote on internal union matters. Unions often offer other benefits to members such as participation in credit unions, discounts to Disneyland, and so forth. The members also vote to approve (or reject) the contract that the union negotiates on their behalf with their employer.

Employees have the legal right to refuse to join a union and an employer can't require an employee to become a union member. Those who haven't joined cannot vote on the union contract. However, non-member employees may have to pay some portion of the union dues, depending on the nature of their objection to the union, and applicable state law.

How a Union Contract Is Created: Collective Bargaining

From an HR or management perspective, one of the important consequences of having a union operating in your nonprofit is that you'll need to engage in what's called collective bargaining. This term refers to the negotiation process between the union (on behalf of the employees it represents) and the employer, in order to work out the employment terms and working conditions of the bargaining unit members. The agreement reached through this process is the union contract, also called a collective bargaining agreement. The contract must be approved by a vote of the members of the bargaining unit.

To begin the negotiation process, the union and management each select a team of people to represent them. On the union side, this will consist of union leaders, a professional union negotiator, and a few employees from the bargaining unit at your organization. On the organization's side, the team typically includes members of the management team, a representative of the board of directors, and an attorney or a professional negotiator.

If you are the HR manager, you may be asked to be on the management negotiating team in a support role, which may involve attending meetings, taking notes, following up on questions that arise, and gathering data for the team. It's usually best if the HR representative stays out of direct participation and avoids heated confrontations during the contract negotiations. The best role for HR in this process is to help the management team by providing an informed, calm perspective on what's going on, while maintaining a cordial, working relationship with the employees on the union team. That way, after the negotiations are over, HR won't be viewed by some employees as the "enemy," and can more smoothly assume a positive role in implementing the new contract.

What's in a Union Contract

The contract between the union and the organization usually sets out a number of rules and processes that govern the relationship between the employees and the employer. For example, salaries and job descriptions for union employees are established under the contract rather than being negotiated on an individual basis. Every few years, the union and the organization's management negotiate a new contract, which establishes the salaries for all the employees represented by that union. Under the contract, employees are paid according to the category they fall into and corresponding pay scale. An employee who is promoted into a different category would receive a pay increase, but notice that this is different than negotiating a pay increase directly.

If there is a dispute between an employee and a supervisor, the union contract lays out in detail the procedure for how to file a grievance, such as disputes over disciplinary action, content of a performance review, or the process used for authorizing overtime. The contract will spell out how the union will be involved, and what process everyone will need to follow for resolution. In many contracts, if certain types of disputes cannot be resolved by mutual agreement, there will be procedures to take the case to an outside arbitrator.

In addition, the number of holidays and vacation days per year, health benefits, and termination procedures are all spelled out in union contracts. Once the contract is in effect, management has little leeway in making changes until the next contract negotiation period.

If you have HR responsibilities in an organization with one or more union contracts, you will need to be very familiar with all aspects of the union contract. You'll also want to make sure that all supervisors are well-trained in keeping to the roles that the contract spells out for them.

How Union Drives Work

In the United States, the rights of workers to organize a union in their workplace are strongly protected by law. Decades of hard-fought, bitter campaigns between unions and management have resulted in detailed laws and processes governing unionization.

Efforts to unionize a workplace often begin with unhappy employees. In both for-profits and nonprofits, employees may be unhappy with compensation, working conditions, or rules and requirements. In nonprofits, additional common triggers for unionization efforts are a distrust of management and unmet expectations regarding staff participation in decision making.

If employees are interested in organizing a union, one or more of them might contact a local union chapter and ask for information and help. The union will then send an organizer to speak with the workers who contacted them.

A union can represent only workers who have already formed a bargaining unit (of employees at the workplace who do similar work and have common concerns). The goal of the group organizing the union effort will be to get a majority of their fellow bargaining-unit coworkers to sign cards authorizing the union to represent their unit. At that point, the union will ask the employer to recognize the union voluntarily. Some nonprofits choose to do so and proceed to contract negotiations with the union.

In other cases, the nonprofit's board and management are against unionization. In that situation, the union can ask the NLRB to hold a secret election in the workplace, as long as it has signed authorization cards from at least 30% of the bargaining unit employees. If the union receives a majority of votes cast, it will be certified to represent the employees. Even if cards have been signed, such elections don't always favor the union. Perhaps 30% of employees will vote for the union, but it won't receive a majority of votes on election day. Even if more than 50% signed cards, it's possible that some did so only because they felt pressured into signing. Or, some of them may have been pro-union at the beginning of the drive, but since changed their minds.

The NLRB will nullify the results of an election if the employer engages in conduct that tends to interfere with the employees' right to freely choose—or reject—a union, without fear of reprisal. If you do have an election, you'll need to learn what type of activities are considered unfair labor practices in that context and make sure you refrain from any such conduct during an election campaign.

After the secret vote, if the union receives a majority of votes cast, the NLRB will certify the union to represent the employees, and contract negotiations will begin. If the union vote fails, the union drive is over, and any pro-union employees would have to start all over with getting cards signed.

If the union issue goes to a vote, it is likely to cause a great deal of tension within the organization. The election period can last several weeks or even longer. Some employees will be strongly pro-union, others will be uncertain, and some will be against the union. Funders, clients, patients, donors, elected officials, and others may get involved. The union may make public charges against the organization that seem unrelated to labor-management issues, such as unaddressed occurrences of sexual abuse or misuse of funds by management. It is crucial that during this time management—including HR staff—pay strict attention to NLRA rules about elections and other matters to avoid legal charges of unfair labor practices. In addition, close employee scrutiny of HR practices and morale concerns will elevate the role of HR to a higher-profile, immediately strategic role.

After a vote—whichever way it goes—it can take months or even years for the anger and suspicion that may have developed on all sides to subside. Deciding whether or not to unionize can be a very divisive and emotional issue and it can take a long time to heal. Both senior management and people with HR responsibilities will need to make a priority of getting HR functions on track and rebuilding the workplace climate.

If you think a union drive may be starting at your organization, speak with the executive director and management team. They will want to discuss the matter early, learn more, and, with the board of directors, thoughtfully consider the organization's response.

RESOURCE

For further information on the impact a union drive might have at your nonprofit, see: *A House Divided: How Nonprofits Experience Union Drives,* by Jeanne Bell and Jan Masaoka (Support Center for Nonprofit Management, 1998).

HR Under a Union Contract

In some ways, HR is much simpler when there is a union contract in place (particularly if it covers most of your employees). Nearly every HR function—from hiring to wages to layoffs—will be covered in the contract. For example, if an employee covered by the contract asks for a raise for having done exceptional work, the supervisor can simply point to the union contract. It will doubtless have spelled out the process for salary increases, which probably will not allow individual raises outside of job reclassification.

As another example, if an employee's performance starts deteriorating significantly, a supervisor cannot terminate the employee without going through the processes described in the contract. If, in representing HR, you talk to a supervisor who is furious with an employee and wants to fire the person immediately, you will need to point to the contract and explain what's possible and what isn't.

Adviser Mark Masaoka of the Asian Pacific Policy and Planning Council in Los Angeles is a former business agent for the Service Employees International Union (SEIU). "A common grievance is the addition of higher-level duties to an employee's work. Another is when an employee says, 'I'm given too many things to do; I can't do them all, and I'm being written up for not finishing something.'" He notes that staff in nonprofits may be interrupted frequently and asked by other staff to help out on various tasks such as a strong nurse constantly being asked to help turn heavy patients. In another example, a Chinese-speaking preschool teacher may be frequently asked to translate for parents, teachers, and the newsletter, and as a result may not be getting his or her own work done on time. Mark's advice for supervisors: "In writing, let an employee know what are the most important things to accomplish and the priorities for their time. If helping other staff with their jobs is interfering with someone's own work, the issue has to be turned back to the supervisor to decide which should come first."

> **TIP**
> **Seek expert and peer advice for help with union-related issues.**
> If your organization has a union, management will likely have an ongoing relationship with an attorney or consultant experienced with managing in a union context. Be sure that you know when and how to reach out for advice in any area where you feel uncertain. HR and management staff in other nonprofits with unions are often good partners in developing a philosophy, policies, and practices that are practical and in line with nonprofit missions. You can find other unionized nonprofits through local nonprofit networks as well as at the local chapter of the Society for Human Resource Management (SHRM).

Employees Who Are Not Part of the Union

Even if you are a "unionized" nonprofit, not all of your employees will be covered by the union contract (or contracts). Certain types of workers, like managers and supervisors and independent contractors, cannot join a union. For these nonunion staff, the union contract will provide context, but it does not mandate practices. So you will need to develop HR practices and policies for those employees who are not covered by the union contract.

> **TIP**
>
> **Use different terms for HR policies for your union and nonunion employees.** To maintain clarity, refer to HR policies relevant to employees covered by a union contract and other policies by different terms, such as Contract HR for employees covered by a union contract and Central HR for those who are not. Distinguishing the two types of employees by name—and even having different HR staff for the two groups in a large organization—helps remind employees that different rules and procedures will apply depending on which type of employee they are.

Day-to-Day Union Representation: Business Agents and Shop Stewards

On a day-to-day basis, there may be many issues and questions that arise related to the contract or to an employee under the contract. If you are the HR person, you will want to become familiar with the shop steward and the business agent (also called a business representative).

Employees within the bargaining unit will elect a shop steward from among their fellow members. The shop steward will continue to work as an employee at your organization, but also serve as an unpaid representative of the union members in dealing with employee grievances or seeking enforcement of the union contract.

In contrast, business agents are on the full-time staff of the union; one will be assigned to your nonprofit. Both shop stewards and business agents handle employee grievances and other day-to-day matters. For example, if an employee believes he or she has a grievance such as unfair treatment, that person will often first discuss the issue with the shop steward, or can choose to reach out to the business agent first. The shop steward and the business agent will help determine whether the matter is an actionable offense (a violation of the contract). If so, the business agent will help initiate the grievance procedures as set forth in the contract, typically a progression from lower to more senior levels of management.

In many instances, the business agent acts to help both the employer and the employees. The business agent can help defuse minor complaints and even point out to some employees that they are at fault, not the supervisor. Business agents can help make the grievance process efficient and fair. In a few instances, however, business agents have been known to aggravate small complaints and turn minor disputes into major battles. As a result, you will want to maintain good relations with the business agent and stay in frequent communication.

Some Key Points to Remember in Union Shops

- Conduct hiring for union positions in accordance with the procedures laid out in the union contract.
- Maintain clarity between HR for employees covered by a union contract and HR for those who are not.
- Handle performance reviews, disciplinary action, and terminations and layoffs in strict compliance with the terms set out in the union contract.
- Train supervisors on their responsibilities under the union contract. A mistake by a supervisor may not only damage a situation between the organization and an employee, but can set off a prolonged dispute with the union.
- Be familiar with the employees and union representatives who formally represent the bargaining unit, and stay in good communication with them.

RESOURCE

For more information on legal aspects of unionization, see the website of the National Labor Relations Board (www.nlrb.gov) and *The Manager's Legal Handbook,* by Amy DelPo and Lisa Guerin (Nolo).

Creating a Safe and Productive Workplace Environment

Protecting Employees' Health and Safety..280

    Frequently Asked Questions About Health, Safety, and the Law................282

The Workers' Compensation System..283

    Workers' Compensation Benefits 283

    HR's Role in the Claims Process..284

    Workers' Comp Fraud and Abuse..284

Ergonomics and Preventing Repetitive Strain Injury (RSI)...............................285

If Jobs Involve Driving..287

    When Employees Drive Organization-Owned Vehicles...................................287

    When Employees Drive Their Own Vehicles..288

Employee Use of Cell Phones..289

Smoking in (or Near) the Workplace...290

Employee Abuse of Drugs or Alcohol..291

    Alcohol Use at Work..291

    Off-Hours Drinking..291

    Legal Drug Use 292

    Illegal Drug Use...293

    Whether to Test Employees for Drugs...293

Preventing Harassment and Bullying..294

    Sexual Harassment..294

    Sexual Orientation Harassment...295

    Other Kinds of Harassment and Discrimination...295

Bullying...296

Steps Toward Combatting Harassment and Bullying............................297

Workplace Violence..298

Shaping Your Organizational Culture..300

Recognizing Good Work..301

The Multicultural Workplace...302

Managing Employee Expectations..304

Policies for Email and Internet Usage 306

Email...306

Instant Messaging..307

Facebook Pages, Blogs, Tweets, Diggs, and More...............................308

Workplace Romances 310

Dress and Grooming Codes..312

Off-Hours Conduct 314

Community and Political Activity...315

Moonlighting..316

Gaining Insights From Employee Climate Surveys........................317

Meet Your Adviser

Sonia M. Pérez
Title: Senior Vice President, Strategic Initiatives
Organization: National Council of La Raza (NCLR)
Location: New York, New York

What she does: Sonia manages both external and internal strategic initiatives and affiliate member services and is currently overseeing an internal look at infrastructure and systems.

What the organization does: NCLR affiliates and the national organization work to improve opportunities for Latino communities in the United States. The national staff of 150 work in their Washington, DC, headquarters and in five regional offices.

Best tip for HR managers including the Accidental HR manager: Don't underestimate the strength of your organization's culture. We have had very, very few HR problems because we maintain a professional approach to work; we stress ethics and values, and for many things we use an honor system rather than official policies and procedures.

HR lesson learned the hard way: If you've committed yourself to this work, it isn't just a phase in your life: it is your life. We have to pay attention to people and HR so that people can stay in this work long-term.

Song title that speaks to you about HR: "You Gotta Pay Attention." Because you have to.

D on't underestimate the importance of providing a safe, supportive environment for your employees—particularly in the nonprofit sector. Nonprofit employees experience many of the same stresses that other employees do. However, nonprofit staff often has the additional stress of working all day with elder abuse victims or people looking for housing, or they may be out canvassing door-to-door in a neighborhood where they may not be well-received. The very commitment that many people bring to nonprofit work can also make some of them feel frustrated, as it can seem that they are never doing enough. In these circumstances, a supportive workplace is particularly important. It can not only offset some of the emotional and physical work-related stress, it also reflects a core value of most nonprofits: respecting the people in the organization.

In this chapter, we focus on the areas where a person with HR responsibilities is most likely to have the authority to bring about change in the workplace environment and culture. This includes policies for harassment and bullying, email and Internet use, and dress codes. We also discuss health and safety rules, employee recognition, drug and alcohol problems, and multiculturalism.

Protecting Employees' Health and Safety

Maintaining a safe and healthy workspace is not only important to your nonprofit and its constituents, it's required by law. As an employer, you have a legal obligation to provide a safe workplace. Federal and state laws impose safety standards as well as posting, reporting, and record-keeping requirements for all employers, not just nonprofits.

The major federal health and safety law—overseen by the Occupational Safety and Health Administration—is the Occupational Safety and Health Act (OSHA). OSHA requires employers to provide a workplace that is free of "recognized hazards" likely to cause serious harm to employees. Under the Act, employers must conduct safety training sessions to educate employees about safety rules and the proper use of materials and equipment. This may sound like a rule that's meant for factory workers, but consider whether, for example, your employees are working on ergonomic desk setups, encountering toxins in an art studio, or moving supplies to a conference site.

OSHA imposes a number of paperwork obligations on employers to write up and maintain reports, injury logs, and training records. Some of these are applicable to all employers, while others exempt certain types of organizations. All employers are required to display the federal "Job Safety and Health Protection" poster in their workplace. This poster contains information on employee rights related to workplace hazards. Most states require employers to display posters on state safety laws as well.

Federal rules and free posters to download are available at the OSHA website at www.osha.gov. Go to "Publications" to download posters for printing or to order a preprinted poster. Be sure to also contact your state department of labor for state health and safety requirements.

TIP

Check with your payroll service for updated posters. The most recent federal and state labor law and OSHA posters may be available from your payroll service for no charge or at an inexpensive subscription price. There are also numerous commercial providers that offer subscriptions for under $100 per year and promise to provide all applicable posters.

Consider forming a safety committee for your organization. When employees are involved in safety and health, they become not only more observant of safety rules, but they come up with important suggestions for the organization. Only an employee, for example, might know that the gate latches on the rescued dogs' enclosures are very hard to open from inside, creating dangers for staff and volunteers when a dog becomes aggressive.

You can create a committee comprising a cross-section of the staff. The committee can meet quarterly, develop a calendar of safety workshops, help with safety drills, and make suggestions on how to encourage employee health and wellness. A safety committee may also earn you a modest discount on your workers' compensation insurance premium.

Frequently Asked Questions About Health, Safety, and the Law

What kinds of penalties are imposed on employers that violate health and safety laws?

Penalties range from minimal to major fines, depending on a number of factors, including the employer's record of violations, the severity of the violation, and whether the employer acted in good faith.

Can an employee who is injured at work sue us for damages?

Usually, an employee who suffers a work-related injury is limited to the benefits provided by workers' compensation; that is, the employee may not sue the employer for the injuries. If the employer willfully or recklessly caused the injury, however (for example, if the employer knew about the hazardous condition that caused the worker's accident but didn't do anything about it), then the employee may be able to bypass the workers' compensation system and sue for damages.

Do we need special rules about using cell phones while driving?

Yes. Studies have shown that using a cell phone while driving increases the risk of accidents. Employees who dial, talk, or text while driving not only create a safety hazard, they also create a legal risk for your nonprofit, which might be liable for any harm they cause if they are having a work-related conversation or driving for work. To minimize the dangers, every company should have cell phone rules for employees.

Can we fire an employee for being an alcoholic?

No. You cannot fire or discipline an employee merely for being an alcoholic. You can, however, fire an employee for drinking at work or appearing at work under the influence of alcohol. You can also fire or discipline an employee for not meeting the conduct and performance standards that apply to all workers.

> **TIP**
>
> **Get a free on-site consultation from OSHA.** Every state has an OSHA-funded agency that provides free consultations on workplace health and safety issues. An expert will come and walk through your worksite with you, pointing out risks and providing practical advice on how to correct problems and comply with the law. You will not be fined for any violations that the expert sees. You'll find a list of OSHA consultation agencies organized by state on the OSHA website, at www.osha.gov; select "Cooperative Programs," then "Find a Cooperative Program."

The Workers' Compensation System

Through the workers' compensation system, employers purchase insurance that provides benefits to employees who suffer work-related injuries and illnesses. The system strikes a compromise between the interests of employers and employees. Employees get benefits regardless of who was at fault; it could be the employee, the employer, a client, or a coworker. In return, the employer gets protection from lawsuits by injured employees seeking damages.

Workers' compensation is governed by state, not federal, law. Although each state's system differs slightly, the structure and operation of the overall system is similar from state to state. The main differences are the rates paid to injured employees and the procedures for making a claim, seeing a doctor, filing an appeal, and so on.

To find out the details of your state's law, contact your state department of industrial relations or workers' compensation. You can also find a state-by-state description of these laws at the U.S. Department of Labor's website at www.dol.gov. From the home page, click "Audiences: Employers," then "Workers' Compensation," then "State Workers' Compensation Laws."

Workers' Compensation Benefits

The workers' compensation system provides replacement income for days the employee cannot work, pays for medical expenses, and sometimes pays for vocational rehabilitation benefits such as on-the-job training, education, or job placement assistance.

An employee who is temporarily unable to work will usually receive two-thirds of his or her average wage up to a fixed ceiling. An employee who becomes permanently unable to do the work he or she was doing prior to the injury, or is unable to work at all, may be eligible for long-term or lump sum benefits. The system also pays death benefits to surviving dependents of workers who are fatally injured in work-related incidents.

HR's Role in the Claims Process

HR's main responsibilities with regard to workers' compensation will be to:

- designate someone at each site to be responsible for incident reporting there and provide that person with training and necessary forms to be kept at that location
- inform all staff about the importance of timely incident reporting, whether it's an on-the-job accident or an illness or condition that has developed, such as repetitive stress injury
- remind people that while their first instinct when injured may be to go to their regular doctor, for work injuries they'll probably need to file a claim right away, and possibly see a doctor who's preapproved by the workers' compensation system
- help staff understand how to file a claim and what documentation (such as medical certification) may be required
- file claims promptly with the insurance carrier and, in some states, the state workers' compensation agency
- follow up on claims, including investigating whether reasonable accommodations can allow an employee to return to work, and
- close claims as issues are resolved.

Workers' Comp Fraud and Abuse

In nonprofits, the possibility of actual injuries, from carpal tunnel to a strained back to an attack by a mentally unstable client, is very real. But every so often, an employee may realize that the workers' compensation system could allow them to ditch the day job and receive checks to stay at home. That's why workers' compensation fraud and abuse (two different ways of gaming the system) are a concern for both insurers and employers.

Fraud takes place when an employee fakes an injury, for instance, or makes false statements that result in a claim. Abuse, on the other hand, typically involves extending a claim beyond its legitimate period, such as when an employee keeps extending a claim for job-related stress so that he or she doesn't have to return to work.

It's good policy to make sure that HR monitors and oversees workers' compensation claims diligently and fairly. When employees abuse workers' compensation, employer insurance premiums can rise dramatically. In addition, other employees may feel tempted to abuse workers' comp, while those on the job become resentful toward others who are perceived as taking advantage of the system. Proper management of workers' compensation includes both supportive assistance to employees with claims and proper attention to managing and closing claims as appropriate.

> **TIP**
> **Why supporting your employees with genuine claims is important.**
> Because of a few bad apples, people with real injuries sometimes experience the workers' compensation system as stacked against them. Some doctors may be unsympathetic, insurance companies slow to respond, and employees may hear rumors of workers' comp investigators taking pictures of them lifting heavy groceries out of their cars at home. Be sympathetic and do what you can to make their situation tenable—especially if a doctor has insisted that the employee go back to work before he or she feels ready.

Ergonomics and Preventing Repetitive Strain Injury (RSI)

Most of us know someone who has suffered from carpal tunnel syndrome, thoracic outlet syndrome, or another type of repetitive strain injury ("RSI"). RSIs often involve pain and numbness in the fingers or arms, plus pain and weakness in other parts of the body. RSIs are commonly caused by many hours at the computer keyboard or laptop. But they can also be caused by driving, cradling a telephone between the neck and shoulder, sleeping with one's head forward (such as on a plane), and other activities. Many people can recover from an RSI with enough rest. However, some RSIs can last for months or years, and may even require surgery.

Clearly, your nonprofit's first responsibility is to prevent RSIs stemming from work. If you have employees putting in long hours on the computer or using a phone without a headset, you've got trouble waiting to happen. Or, ironically enough, if you've agreed to some employees' requests to work from home and they spend their work time bent over a laptop at the local coffee shop, you can expect more RSI trouble. For the sake of your workers' compensation insurance rates and your employees' health, invest in comfortable working equipment and train everyone in how and why to sit and type properly. More information on this can be found at www.osha.gov/SLTC/ergonomics. (You'll probably want to check out "eTools" and then "Computer Workstations.")

It's not always easy to tell whether elbow pain or neck pain originated from work activities or off-work activities—or a combination of both. (People use their hands in repetitive ways while cooking, gardening, and knitting, too, or on the computer for personal pursuits.) As part of the workers' compensation claims process, your insurance company will likely require a doctor's evaluation of whether the injury is job-related as well as recommendations for treatment.

If one of your employees must take leave due to an RSI, that person will hopefully be able to return to work within a matter of weeks or months, following treatment and rest. Improvements in technology allow employers to make reasonable accommodations to allow staff with RSI to return to their regular work. For example, purchasing a telephone headset can help someone who talks on the phone a lot. Ergonomic keyboards, voice recognition software, and frequent, brief rest breaks help people whose RSIs were caused by typing. Such supports are a good idea for any staff who may be at risk for a repetitive strain injury.

If RSIs are an issue for staff in your organization, look into investing in improved equipment. Training can also help employees understand better ways to use their hands and take breaks.

> ⓘ **TIP**
>
> **Have an expert make equipment recommendations.** A common scenario is for an employee to think a new mouse will help them with RSI issues. Then the mouse doesn't help, so the employee asks for a different mouse, then a different keyboard, then a different desk, and so on. The reality is that we nonexperts think we know what equipment we need, but we are often wrong. Before you spend money buying equipment or software that may not really address the problem, bring in an expert in ergonomics to talk to the employee and make a recommendation as to what is needed. Your insurance broker or carrier may be able to recommend experts near you.

If Jobs Involve Driving

With some nonprofit jobs, the primary responsibility involves driving organization-owned vehicles, such as paratransit vans or bookmobiles. There are other circumstances, such as a conference or special event, when employees may need to use a car for work-related reasons. Most likely employees will use their own cars, but some nonprofits also own or lease vehicles for employee use.

When Employees Drive Organization-Owned Vehicles

If your organization owns or leases vehicles for use by employees in performing their jobs, you will need a comprehensive and well-monitored set of policies. At a minimum, these should explain:

- the procedure for checking and periodically reviewing that anyone using a vehicle has a valid driver's license
- whether the vehicle can be used by the employee to commute to and from work or for any other personal reason

- who is responsible for regular service and maintenance
- who is responsible for damages to the vehicle that occur while the employee is driving it and whether that changes depending on circumstance
- how to report incidents and accidents related to the vehicle
- who is responsible for paying parking and other driving tickets, and
- if a vehicle is assigned full time to an employee, whether the employee can continue to use it while on leave (such as parental leave).

Also, be sure to coordinate with the supervisors of any employees who drive organization-owned vehicles to be sure that they've arranged for proper safety training for drivers.

RESOURCE

Check with your insurer for additional safety-related services. Your insurance carrier may have free safety guides, driver training, an "Am I Driving Safely?" monitoring service, and other resources for your organization. Ask your broker about what's available, or contact your carrier directly.

When Employees Drive Their Own Vehicles

Many nonprofits encourage or require employees to drive their own cars for work-related matters. Sometimes a condition of a job will be that an employee can use a personal car for work, such as for visiting student families or attending meetings in the state capitol. In other cases, employees may need to use their own cars only occasionally, such as for transport to an out-of-city staff retreat.

Before employees use their own cars for work, ask to see a valid driver's license and evidence of their personal insurance coverage. Check each of these every year and keep the documentation in their personnel files. Make it clear whether the employee or the organization will pay for parking and other tickets received while the employee is driving for work.

You can reimburse employees and volunteers for mileage costs at the rate established for mileage reimbursements to state government employees. (Confusingly, volunteers whom you don't reimburse for mileage have to use a different rate if they claim their costs of transportation while volunteering as a tax deduction.) Check with your state government for the current rate.

Employee Use of Cell Phones

Studies show that drivers who talk on cell phones— even hands-free ones—are more distracted and more likely to be involved in accidents than other drivers. To ensure your employees' safety and to avoid exposing your nonprofit to liability, add rules to your employee handbook clearly stating what is and is not allowed with cell phones while driving. You can create your own policies prohibiting all cell phone use while driving for work or requiring a hands-free device regardless of what is required by law.

In most nonprofits, employees can use their personal cell phones for occasional work-related calls and get reimbursed for the specific calls. If you decide to allow this, spell out how employees can request reimbursement for work-related phone calls.

If you require employees to have cell phones or rely on cell phone communication as an important organizational tool, you may want to purchase and pay for cell phones for employees (and for volunteers). If so, make it clear that the cell phones belong to the nonprofit, and what the rules are for making personal calls on nonprofit-owned cell phones.

RESOURCE
For sample cell phone policies and more information, see *Smart Policies for Workplace Technologies,* by Lisa Guerin (Nolo).

Sample Cell Phone Policies

For organizations that prohibit use of cell phones while driving:
- Use of cell phones is prohibited while driving an organization-owned vehicle or while driving on organizational business.
- If you receive or must make a call while driving: pull over safely and stop the car before taking or making a call. If you must read or send a text message while driving: pull over safely and stop the car first.

For organizations that allow the use of cell phones with hands-free devices:
- Talking on cell phones while driving is allowed only when using a hands-free device.
- If you must read or send a text message while driving, pull over safely and stop the car first.
- Employees must concentrate fully on the road while driving. If bad weather, traffic, or other conditions provide distractions, you must pull over and park safely before having a hands-free conversation.

Smoking in (or Near) the Workplace

Most states have laws that prohibit or restrict smoking in the workplace, and many cities have enacted similar legislation. For example, your state or city law may prohibit smoking in all workplaces, prohibit it only in certain kinds of workplaces such as hospitals or where food is served, or restrict it to designated areas. Most nonprofits choose to ban smoking in their workplaces—and within a certain radius of the exits, to avoid clusters of smokers by the doorways—even if not required to do so by law, because smoking is unhealthy and bothers most nonsmokers.

Be aware that some states prohibit discrimination against smokers. Employers in these states can limit on-site smoking but may not make job decisions based on an employee's or applicant's smoking outside of work.

For more information on state smoking laws, see *The Manager's Legal Handbook*, by Amy DelPo and Lisa Guerin (Nolo). You can contact your local government offices to learn about any applicable local ordinances.

Employee Abuse of Drugs or Alcohol

Employees who use or abuse alcohol or drugs (whether over-the-counter drugs, prescription drugs, or illegal drugs)—either at work or on their own time—can pose significant problems and risks for their coworkers and your nonprofit organization.

These problems can include weak job performance, behavioral problems, absenteeism, and health problems. And, when alcohol or drug use makes a workplace less stable and more dangerous, they can expose your nonprofit to legal liability, as well.

Alcohol Use at Work

Your employee handbook should make it clear that drinking on the job is not allowed. If you catch an employee drinking alcohol at work, follow the disciplinary procedures outlined in the handbook. If alcohol use has endangered the employee or others, the consequences should be more severe.

Many nonprofits hold dinners, receptions, and other fundraising events where alcohol is served. All participating staff should know your organization's rules about limiting one's drinking at such events.

Off-Hours Drinking

It is unlikely you would have any reason for concern about the occasional drink—or even the occasional overindulgence—by your employees when not at work as long as it doesn't affect work performance. But when off-site, off-hours drinking begins to take a toll on performance, there is reason to take action.

Handling an employee who has a drinking problem can be tricky. Particularly in nonprofits that fight alcohol or drug abuse, there may be a strong organizational culture against drinking at all—off or on the job. Alternatively, there may be great sympathy for those who struggle with—and occasionally fail to overcome—drinking problems. Also realize that the federal Americans with Disabilities Act (ADA) and many state disability laws protect alcoholics from workplace discrimination. You can discipline or fire an employee based on performance—even if the employee's problems result from alcohol abuse—but not simply because the employee is an alcoholic.

Besides, studies have shown that employers usually come out ahead financially by helping an employee obtain treatment rather than proceeding straight to termination, which would require you to recruit and train a new employee. Your best bet is usually to follow the disciplinary procedures described in Chapter 4, and also make the employee aware of treatment options available through your health plan or EAP, or of free local resources such as Alcoholics Anonymous. (Of course, you'll also want to preserve employee confidentiality in the course of such discussions.)

Can We Require an Employee to Take Meds?

"Our nonprofit employs many former clients of our social services, including people with mental disabilities. Can we require an employee/ former client to take his or her psychiatric medications that we know are prescribed?" Advisers Ellen Aldridge and Pamela Fyfe respond: "No, you can't require it. Once a client becomes an employee, your agency must take off its social service provider hat and wear only its employer hat.

"Remember, it's never appropriate to use any of the medical information you have about the employee from his or her client records. That person's privacy as a mental health client must remain protected."

Legal Drug Use

Things get complicated when legitimate drug use affects an employee's ability to do the job. If an employee is taking prescription medication or over-the-counter drugs (such as cold medicine or painkillers), you need not be concerned unless the drug use affects an employee's ability to do the job well. For example, allergy medicine might make an employee too sleepy to work accurately with numbers or operate equipment.

If you observe performance or behavior problems, you can use the "interactive process"—described in the Americans with Disabilities Act (ADA)—to ask the employee for medical certification of any disability, including limitations or needed reasonable accommodations. See *The Manager's Legal Handbook*, by Amy DelPo and Lisa Guerin (Nolo), for more information on accommodating staff with disabilities.

Illegal Drug Use

If an employee is under the influence of illegal drugs while at work, disability laws don't protect that person. If the employee hasn't created a safety concern or doesn't hold a highly sensitive position, a written reprimand might be appropriate for a first offense. You may need to take more serious action in other situations.

In some cases, an employee's job performance may be suffering due to drug use that is not occurring on the job or during working hours. The problem may be as minor as occasional tardiness or as major as disorientation or inability to focus. In these circumstances, address the performance issue, but unless you have evidence that the employee is using illegal drugs, it's best to leave drugs out of the performance conversation.

If an employee's use of illegal drugs endangers others—for example because the person is driving a paratransit van while under the influence of cocaine—something more drastic is called for. If you have a zero-tolerance policy, you can immediately suspend and then terminate an employee for such an action. Alternatively, your policies may allow you to suspend the employee until completion of a treatment program.

Whether to Test Employees for Drugs

While drug tests can be a valuable tool in preventing drug-related accidents or safety problems, they are also highly intrusive and subject to a wide range of laws. Avoid testing every employee for drugs. If you believe there is a reason to test a specific employee, or a group of employees whose work involves many safety risks, consult an attorney before proceeding.

Preventing Harassment and Bullying

Preventing harassment and bullying of any type is important to all nonprofits. Such actions are not only demeaning and damaging to productivity; they are against the law. Staff must be educated as to what constitutes harassment and bullying, and what steps to take if potential issues arise.

In this section, we'll first explain the various types of harassment and bullying, then suggest specific steps to prevent and deal with these issues.

Sexual Harassment

Sexual harassment is any unwelcome sexual advance or conduct on the job that creates an intimidating, hostile, or offensive working environment. Any conduct of a sexual nature that makes an employee uncomfortable has the potential to be sexual harassment. Sexual harassment can also include harassment that is not sexual in nature, but is based on one's gender—just as racial harassment would be based on one's race.

Because women are the majority of staff in most nonprofits, it can be easy to overlook the importance of educating everyone about sexual harassment. Sexual harassment can be committed by and against people of every gender. The following are all examples of sexual harassment:

- A supervisor implies to an employee that the employee must go on a date with him or her to receive a positive performance review.
- Employees regularly make sexually explicit humorous comments within earshot of the office manager, who finds the comments offensive.
- A volunteer manager at a food bank repeatedly puts his or her arm around the waist of a volunteer against the volunteer's will.
- An employee puts up a safe-sex education poster—which includes sexually explicit photos—on a cubicle wall where it can be seen by passersby.

- An employee sends emails to coworkers that contain joking, sarcastic remarks about men or women.
- An employee makes jokes about a coworker who is going through a transgender transition.
- A male choreographer makes demeaning comments about female audience members.

The harasser can be the victim's supervisor, manager, or coworker. The harasser can even be a nonemployee, if the person is on the premises with permission (for example, a client, volunteer, or vendor).

Sexual harassment is addressed in federal law by Title VII as a form of sex discrimination. In addition, each state has its own law prohibiting sexual harassment.

Sexual Orientation Harassment

Although some states prohibit harassment based on a person's sexual orientation, federal law does not. Regardless of the laws in your state, educate your staff about sexual orientation harassment the same way you do about sexual harassment. Just because the law may not protect an employee who is harassed for being gay, straight, bisexual, or transgender doesn't mean you should allow it.

Other Kinds of Harassment and Discrimination

Because harassment is a kind of discrimination, harassment can also be related to race, ethnicity, religion, nationality, age, and physical ability/disability. Although other characteristics may not be protected by law, it's still important to prevent all kinds of harassment, such as harassment based on immigration status, language ability, accents, hairstyle, and weight.

Your nonprofit's mission is best served by making all employees comfortable in the workplace. If some employees experience demeaning or derogatory remarks or behavior, even if they don't bring legal charges against the organization, they won't do their best work and may feel forced to leave.

EXAMPLE: A social services organization connected to the Catholic Church begins all meetings with a moment of silent prayer. Employees who do not wish to pray simply sit quietly during this time. One Catholic employee took a strong dislike to another employee, and continually "teased" him about what he was supposedly doing during silent prayer. Despite warnings from the supervisor and admonishments from coworkers, the harasser continued the behavior and was fired.

Bullying

Employers have only recently become more aware of the damage that bullying can cause. The Workplace Bullying Institute defines bullying as repeated mistreatment of a person that takes one or more of the following forms:

- verbal abuse
- offensive conduct and behaviors that are threatening, humiliating, or intimidating, or
- work interference.

Bullying behavior usually occurs frequently and over an extended period of time. The person being bullied is either unable to stop the bullying or doesn't feel able to do so. Bullying affects not only the person being bullied directly, but everyone who witnesses it. Other employees may become afraid of becoming the bully's next target, and may even feel required to defend a bully who is their supervisor.

A workplace bully is not the same as a tough, demanding boss. A tough boss is fair in giving sharp criticism, but a bully boss unfairly singles out some individuals for unwarranted criticism. A tough boss addresses conflicts directly and in private, while a bully often humiliates people in front of coworkers and spreads rumors secretly. Bullies are subject to emotional outbursts, while tough bosses are in control of how they communicate.

Bullying is not the same as harassment, although they are connected. A controller who is a workplace bully may single out staff of a particular ethnic background to bully about timesheet submission, although many staff may be delinquent in submitting their timesheets.

The law is just beginning to address workplace bullying, but some experts see bullying as "the new sexual harassment." Just as you let staff know what steps to take if they experience harassment, let them know how to report bullying, whether of themselves or coworkers. Assertive action against bullying is important in creating a culture of mutual respect, cooperation, inclusiveness, and fairness.

Steps Toward Combatting Harassment and Bullying

If your nonprofit allows harassment and bullying to occur, you will pay a high price in terms of employee morale, low productivity, compromise of organizational values, and lawsuits. If you are a manager, you are on the front lines concerning this issue. You have the legal authority to act on behalf of the nonprofit, which means that if you fail to act appropriately, the nonprofit can get into a lot of trouble. If you harass employees yourself, your nonprofit will be legally responsible for your actions. And if employees report harassment to you or you otherwise become aware that harassment is taking place, the nonprofit will be on the hook. This is why it's so important to be sure you learn what harassment and bullying are, and what to do about any situation if it occurs.

There are a number of steps your nonprofit can take to reduce harassment and bullying (and the associated legal risks)

- **Adopt a clear harassment and bullying policy.** In the employee handbook, include a policy prohibiting sexual harassment, harassment based on race, ethnicity, and other characteristics. The policy should define what behaviors constitute harassment and bullying, and state firmly that they will not be tolerated. Set out a clear procedure for filing harassment and bullying complaints; state that complaints will be investigated fully, and assert that the nonprofit will not tolerate retaliation against anyone who makes such complaints.

- **Train staff.** Once a year, require employees to attend sexual harassment training, and incorporate information about all kinds of harassment and bullying. In the sessions, teach employees what harassment and bullying are, review the complaint procedure, and encourage staff to come forward with concerns. Many nonprofit staff assume that harassment doesn't occur in nonprofits, and they may not be alert to harassment that doesn't come in the traditional "male boss gropes female subordinate" package. Connecting the prevention of harassment and bullying to your organizational values can help employees appreciate the importance of training.

- **Protect your clients too.** If your nonprofit deals with vulnerable populations, you should include safeguards to make sure staff can't take advantage of the inherent power imbalance (or be accused of it). In many nonprofits that work with children, for example, they don't allow an adult and a single child to be alone together.

- **Train supervisors and managers.** At least once a year, hold a separate session to train supervisors and managers. In addition to material covered for all employees, train supervisors in how to handle complaints. You and other managers should also be alert to what you see in the work environment, and ask staff for their observations as well. Are there offensive posters or cartoons on the walls? Are offensive jokes making the rounds via email?

- **Take all complaints seriously.** If someone complains about harassment or bullying, immediately follow your nonprofit's reporting procedure. Prompt and thorough investigation can nip negative behaviors in the bud, and help you defend against lawsuits. If the complaint turns out to be valid, make sure your nonprofit responds swiftly and effectively.

Workplace Violence

Violence in the workplace is often thought of as something that happens to someone else. Surprisingly, the U.S. government estimates that about two million assaults and violent threats are made against employees each year, and nonprofits are not exempt. In addition to violence against staff, nonprofits must be alert to the possibility of violence against visitors, clients, audience members, and so forth.

Workplace violence occurs with many causes and circumstances, including:

- a drunk, belligerent person enters your organization at random and demands money from the receptionist
- a fight breaks out between two clients while they wait in your lobby
- the angry spouse of an employee comes to the office and harms the spouse and nearby coworkers
- an employee who was fired comes back with the intent to harm a supervisor
- a focus group is disrupted when a man with a gun enters in the belief that his girlfriend is there seeing another man
- an activist who is against what your organization stands for throws rocks through the windows while driving by
- feeling insulted, one employee shoves another employee hard in the bathroom, or
- an employee who was working late is mugged in your parking lot.

As a person with HR responsibilities, become educated on how to prevent workplace violence. Also make sure your staff knows how to act if an incident appears imminent, and how to spot signs of potential violence.

Here are some suggestions from the National Institute for Occupational Safety and Health (NIOSH).

Preventing violence by strangers and outsiders:

- use physical barriers, such as locks, doors, counters
- install silent alarm systems and panic buttons, and
- control or limit access to your facilities.

Preventing violence from people receiving services:

- where possible, avoid having employees work alone with clients in a closed room
- train workers so that they know what to do in a violent situation
- meet often with employees to air concerns about safety and to discuss prevention and response strategies, and
- train people who do home visits how to handle an emergency.

Preventing violence by employees or acquaintances:

- review any act of violence that has occurred in the workplace, even if it seems minor
- state clearly what workplace violence is, and what is and is not acceptable behavior
- train all staff about what to do if violence occurs, and
- train supervisors to look for warning signs of violent behavior or the possible intrusion of domestic violence into your workplace.

> **RESOURCE**
>
> **Get more information.** The National Institute for Occupational Safety and Health (NIOSH), a division of the federal Centers for Disease Control and Prevention (CDC), offers many resources on its website: www.cdc.gov/niosh.

Shaping Your Organizational Culture

The term "organizational culture" refers to the norms of attitudes and behaviors in an organization that collectively influence how employees feel and behave. Organizational culture is linked to organizational values, but is often informally understood rather than articulated or regulated.

For example, the frequent use of swear words in one organization may be an accepted norm, while in another, even mild profanities are rare. This cultural difference may be based in the culture of the organization's constituents, the stated organizational values about religious beliefs, or the backgrounds of people on the staff. The organization's leaders may signal that swearing is allowed or discouraged by their own use of language. Everyone tends to pick up on the nonprofit's unspoken rules even though no one has ever had an explicit discussion about them.

Organizational culture is often observed in areas such as:

- topics and opinions expressed at the lunch table
- whether office doors are typically open or shut
- the emphasis on recycling (or lack thereof)

- how holidays and birthdays are marked (or not)
- whether meetings start and end on time
- whether food is served at meetings
- the degree to which consensus is relied upon
- how racial and ethnic differences are discussed
- clothing, hairstyles, and body art of staff
- tolerance for disagreement, and
- whether dogs or other pets are allowed in the workplace.

As you can see, each of these aspects contributes to an organizational feeling or culture. Some are related to personal behavior (body art) while others are organizational (emphasis on consensus). The same nonprofit can have two different organizational cultures at different facilities, or even in different departments. Taken as a whole, organizational culture affects employee satisfaction, productivity, and effectiveness.

Through an HR lens, you will want to observe organizational cultures and reflect on how they support or hinder individual and overall effectiveness. Remember that sometimes, a common behavior that might indicate a strong, positive culture can have some negative consequences, such as making one person feel left out or inadvertently encouraging groupthink.

Adviser Sonia Pérez is Senior VP for Strategic Initiatives at the National Council for La Raza, a national organization with 150 staff in six locations; she also helps local affiliates with nonprofit management issues. "We used to have one long statement about values, ethics, and standards," she says. "But we found that we could distill it into three words: excellence, accountability, and *respeto*/respect. This is easy for everyone to remember, and we talk about it frequently in the context of how people should act, and what kind of culture we want to have."

Recognizing Good Work

How an organization recognizes employees for their contributions can be a reflection of your workplace culture. Taking notice of an employee's efforts and giving informal praise is an important part of effective supervision. But organizations often go further by incorporating personalized or extra recognition for employee's work. For example, a supervisor might give one of his or her employees a small, inexpensive gift: perhaps flowers on a birthday or a gift card for going the extra mile on a project.

In addition, many HR departments have developed structured employee recognition programs. Some examples include:

- five-year pins presented at staff meetings
- lunch for a work group celebrating an achievement
- a framed plaque with tailored wording to recognize an achievement, and
- a jar of trail mix and a handwritten note from the supervisor on anniversary-of-employment dates.

Your organization will need to develop an employee recognition program that is compatible with your culture and budget. Whatever you choose, make sure it involves recognition in front of peers and that you are consistent and fair in administering the program.

The Multicultural Workplace

Most of today's nonprofits place value on diversity in the workplace. Nonprofits typically have both mission and business reasons for wanting a staff that is diverse in race, ethnicity, economic backgrounds, age, and more. A mission reason for diversity might be based in a community empowerment mission; a business reason for diversity might focus on the ability to reach target populations.

With a staff that is rich in diversity, you can appreciate differences and actively use them to bring a broader perspective to your workplace. Instead of trying not to notice that people are, for example, of different races or different ages, everyone can learn from the different backgrounds and cultures in your workplace. "It's important to normalize the fact that there are differences as well as commonalities," says adviser Sarah Gort. "Comments such as, 'I'm glad we got some different perspectives out in this discussion,' can go a long way toward helping people take advantage a diverse workplace."

A common mistake when discussing diversity is to assume that the issue is about sensitivity to people of color in a mostly white workplace.

Even the most diverse organizations can benefit from being sensitive to a multicultural perspective—for example, handling the integration of younger managers who will be supervising staff older than themselves. Or managing different languages and immigration backgrounds in a pan-Asian organization.

One way to foster a multicultural environment is to engage employees to discussing the multicultural aspects of their constituencies, their staff, and their board of directors. "Cultural competence" is a term used to describe the ability to interact effectively with people of different cultures. Many nonprofits need staff who are culturally competent in order to work effectively with donors, clients, patrons, students, members, and others. Some organizations hold discussions about cultural competence with clients and constituents. The principles and practices that emerge from these discussions can help frame and inform a discussion about cultural competence and multiculturalism and how it can be used to more effectively serve constituencies and the mission.

> **EXAMPLE:** The Koreatown Day Care Center was founded as a Korean-American organization to serve Korean families, but now serves all families in Koreatown, many of whom are Latino. To do so effectively, they brought on staff who are Spanish-speaking and from a variety of racial and ethnic backgrounds. The Center was careful to nurture respect and appreciation for cultural differences among the Korean and Latino and other staff, while recognizing that they are a Korean-American organization. For example, Latino staff are not only there to work with Latino children; they help educate all kids and staff about the Latino community and culture.

RESOURCE

Check out other resources on the topic. "Multicultural Organizational Development in Nonprofit Organizations," by Steve Lew and Laurin Mayeno, is a brief document with links to other monographs on cultural competence. You can find it at www.compasspoint.org; type "multicultural organizational development" in the search box.

Managing Employee Expectations

Some people join nonprofits with unrealistic expectations about their role or the influence they will have on the organization. It's not unusual for staff or volunteers when first starting out—even in an entry-level position—to anticipate that their ideas about how the organization is run or what it is doing will be taken seriously by senior management. In the for-profit sector, on the other hand, you're much less likely to find someone hired as a waiter or waitress with expectations that they should be giving advice to the owners about the menu. Establishing and reinforcing realistic expectations for new staff about their role is something that needs to be handled with thought and care to avoid disappointment and anger.

> **EXAMPLE:** A new receptionist came to a staff meeting just three weeks after starting work. At the meeting, the finance director passed around the newly adopted budget and went over various aspects of it, explaining the implications for the year and the reasoning behind it. The receptionist raised an objection: "I don't feel that I had any input in this budget. It is just being done at the top and passed down to us." The finance director was speechless, but the receptionist's supervisor came to the rescue: "Let me talk to you after the meeting." Later, he explained that everyone on staff has input, as appropriate, on things, but it's done in the right way at the right time, and that people with seniority and more responsibility have more input.

Even long-term staff can have unrealistic expectations about their role, particularly when it comes to their ability to participate in decision making. This may be in part because people tend to think of nonprofits as a more democratic and less hierarchical work environment than other places.

The key to success in this area is to set realistic expectations and focus on performance of the individual and the team. Coach your supervisors and team leaders to be explicit about roles and how decisions are handled. For example, in each discussion with their team, leaders can identify whether a decision will be made through consensus, through input and then a management decision, or in some other way. Being clear will help overcome any tendency for people to assume everything is done democratically.

Another awkward cultural dynamic can arise when professional-level employees switch from the for-profit sector to a nonprofit organization. They may assume that the work pace in a nonprofit is slower, the performance standards lower, and the culture less competitive than the for-profit world. Be aware that these stereotypes exist, and watch for signs of people coming on board with expectations that don't match the reality of your workplace environment.

MYTH

Nonprofits Are Warm and Fuzzy

People tend to think that nonprofit workplaces are warmer and fuzzier than other work environments, with less competition or strict discipline. This may be because nonprofits often have a more team-oriented environment where a shared commitment to the work and mission reduces rivalries and cutthroat behavior. However, a more supportive, group-oriented environment doesn't necessarily mean that employees won't be criticized or held to a high standard. And just as for-profit companies vary widely in culture, so do nonprofits. At some places, people may work at a more leisurely pace, while in others everyone may work under tremendous time pressure and for very long hours. There's no one type of culture that describes the nonprofit work environment, and broad generalizations can be very misleading in any given instance.

Involve your staff in shaping your organization's culture whenever possible. Something as simple as the type of food served at events can be an important reflection of your organization's values or even its mission. In one case, a staff person at an animal shelter argued that because it was a no-kill animal shelter, they shouldn't allow meat at organizational events. Everyone was happy to go along with this suggestion. When employees have a say in shaping the workplace culture, the office becomes more than a place staff shows up at every day—it's an environment that workers helped create.

Policies for Email and Internet Usage

Not only are computers, email, and the Internet essential tools for most nonprofits, these technologies are changing so rapidly that it's impossible for policies and practices to keep up. For example, social networking sites such as Facebook and LinkedIn blur the line between communications that are business-oriented and those that are personal in nature.

There are many management issues related to technology; in some organizations, technology policies are developed by the IT department or by an operations manager. This chapter focuses on the areas that are most closely linked to HR.

Email

Be sure that employees know your policies about the use of any email addresses provided to them by your nonprofit and the consequences of violating the rules. For example, you might require that all nonprofit business be conducted through your nonprofit's email, rather than through the employee's personal email account—and vice versa. Remind employees that when they are on the organization's email or computers, their messages are the property of the nonprofit and could be reviewed (or subpoenaed) at any time.

In addition, give staff some guidelines for email signatures, etiquette, and response time to email inquiries. Remind them that in their emails, they are representing your organization as much as if they were speaking at a public event; consequently, they always should express themselves with courtesy, circumspection, and respect for the law.

> **EXAMPLE:** The development director of the Dandelion School of Community Music often exchanged fast emails with volunteers on the gala committee about possible sponsors and donors to the event. A couple of emails went around joking about a donor's stutter. The exchange went on to other matters and another board member was added to the "cc" list; this person scrolled all the way through the messages and came upon the jokes. The Dandelion School now has a vacancy in the development director position.

Instant Messaging

The use of instant messaging by nonprofits varies widely. Some organizations rely on instant messages (IMs) for fast, convenient exchanges among employees. At these places, staff may leave their IM windows open on their computer desktops and communicate among each other—whether across cubicles or across the ocean—instantly throughout the day. At other nonprofits, people may not even know what IM stands for.

If you use IMs (or want to), develop a user policy and make sure everyone understands it. For instance, you might want to restrict IMs to a particular provider (such as Axium or Yahoo! Messenger), require that personal messaging be kept to a minimum (as you do phone calls), and remind staff not to divulge personal or confidential information through IMs.

> **EXAMPLE:** Even though José and Jasmine work only 30 feet away from each other at Porcupine Family Service Center, they communicate fastest and most conveniently through instant messaging. As the executive director and development director respectively, they frequently have quick questions that need quick answers and find that IMs are much easier than email, phone, or intercom. José is also using IMs now with the other three executive directors in their collaborative lobbying effort at City Hall. They find it a less intrusive and fast way to set up meetings and let each other know the latest in legislative developments.

Facebook Pages, Blogs, Tweets, Diggs, and More

Many nonprofits have their own websites, Facebook pages, blogs, and Twitter accounts with staff assigned to create and post content through these vehicles. In today's networked world, the line between organizational and personal posting is getting harder to distinguish. For instance, if your nonprofit wants to reach African Americans with information about osteoporosis, you might ask an African American staff member to post something on his or her BlackPlanet page or on a local African American site. And you may want to encourage your employees to tell their online friends about your upcoming special event, or invite sponsorship of their participation in your walkathon.

Like issues of employee dating and email use, however, it's important to have policies, and also to recognize that you will have to rely on employees to honor those policies online. Policies can support common sense and good judgment, but are not a substitute for those things. For issues involving technology, it's always a good idea to explain why the policy is important. Many people believe their online posts should be personal, and view any attempt at regulation by an employer as inappropriate. Once they understand, for example, how easy it is for clients and donors to read employee posts or how items the employee might intend as "humorous" or "edgy" could easily create the wrong impression, they will be more likely to understand and abide by reasonable rules. However, as an employer, you have to be careful not to cross over into protected areas of speech when dealing with employee tweets and Internet posts. This is an evolving area of law; some courts view employee tweets about their workplace as legally protected speech, unless they contain discriminatory or harassing content about other employees.

EXAMPLE: A board member of the Nuts & Bolts Learning Center googled the name of the organization and came upon an employee's tweets containing unflattering and extremely negative comments about the Center. The board member brought the issue to the attention of the executive director. Their first instinct was to fire the employee, but they decided to consult an employment lawyer before taking any action. The lawyer noted that courts have said that employees have the right to engage in "protected concerted activities" aimed at improving the terms and conditions of their employment. In the end, no action was taken against the employee. The board member and the executive director are still grinding their teeth when they think about it.

Here are some Internet use policies related to social networking by employees and other staff you can consider adopting for your workplace.

- Any employees or staff who post about the organization's services or attributes on a public site (such as Yelp, Facebook, or GreatNonprofits) must identify themselves as an employee of the organization.
- No one may use organizational logos or materials without the organization's permission.
- Photos of staff, volunteers, clients, actors, dancers, or donors may not be uploaded without the written permission of those pictured.
- Staff should use discretion and good judgment when posting any material anywhere on the Internet, as it reflects on the organization as well as the person doing the posting.
- Supervisors should not "friend" on Facebook or connect on MySpace or LinkedIn (or other social networking sites) with individuals that they supervise.

EXAMPLE: After one nonprofit internally announced the layoff of five employees, an employee took a photo of one of the to-be-laid-off women standing at the copy machine and posted it to his personal Facebook page with the caption, "I'm going to miss that Hispanic booty!" In one swoop, he divulged confidential information and committed both racial and sexual harassment. In the absence of a written policy on the use of personal social networking sites, he could still be reprimanded, but the seriousness of the infraction might be confused by the issue of whether he was required to be responsible for off-hours activities on a personal site.

In cases where you do hope that employees will post information about your nonprofit, it can be helpful to provide them with suggested text and links, such as, "Check out where you can buy tickets to the Saturday, April 11, 20xx performance of the International Women's Chorale (where I work)!"

For a comprehensive set of sample social networking policies, see *Smart Policies for Workplace Technology*, by Lisa Guerin (Nolo).

Workplace Romances

"It's one thing when two employees are dating," said one HR director. "It's another thing altogether when they break up." The same couple that's giggling together one day could be glowering at each other the next.

Nonprofits often have unwritten rules about romance between employees and coworkers or others whom they meet at work (such as clients, volunteers, or board members), but few explicit policies. For example, there may be an unspoken policy against public displays of affection, but not a written policy about employee-client or employee-employee dating.

Employee-client relationships. It's usually a good idea to prohibit relationships between employees and clients in human service and other organizations. If such a relationship begins to develop, require that the employee report the relationship, and have the client transferred to another staffer.

Employee-supervisor relationships. Require employees to disclose intimate or familial relationships with coworkers, so that a determination can be made as to whether potential problems and conflicts could arise and what actions will be taken to change supervisor lines.

In general, it's a good idea to prohibit managers from dating employees whom they supervise. These relationships pose increased risk of sexual harassment charges, and often cause other employees to suspect favoritism in the manager's actions. Have a policy that requires employees who begin dating other employees to let the responsible HR person know about it. A process can then determine whether no action is required, or whether one of the individuals should, if possible, be transferred to another department.

In small organizations (and even in large ones), transferring is often not possible. For example, the artistic director and the managing director may be dating in an arts organization, or the medical director and the head nurse in a clinic. In other cases, the nonprofit will have been founded by a married couple who continue to run it. In some instances, it may be possible to change supervisors, but in others, you may have to figure out what type of checks or other controls, if any, are necessary. For example, if the executive director and operations director of a nonprofit are married, neither should sign reimbursement checks for the other, and the salaries of both should be established by the board.

Employee–board member relationships. When these relationships develop, they often occur between a member of the senior management and a member of the board. Regardless of the level of employee involved, romances involving staff and board should be disclosed to the executive director and to the board chair. In most cases, the board will not mandate supervisorial changes, but putting the relationship in the open ensures that potential conflicts of interest will be managed appropriately.

Employee-coworker and employee-volunteer relationships. If there isn't a supervisory relationship between two individuals in a relationship, then you have more discretion in how you handle it. You may still choose to require that each person report the relationship to his or her respective supervisor.

Whether you decide to transfer an employee to another department or leave the situation alone, make sure other employees have a way to let their supervisors know if they are uncomfortable with a coworker romance. It may be because the person is directly affected or because he or she feels it puts the organization in a conflict of interest or at risk for a sexual harassment claim or another reason. In such a situation, a supervisor could initiate a process to determine whether any action is needed. With a relationship or the end of a relationship, the employees directly involved as well as others may need to discuss the matter with their supervisors and with HR. Moving desks, reassigning supervisors, or coaching the involved staff may be helpful.

Obviously, policies involving these matters will feel intrusive to some, and are more about management than they are about legality. If you decide to adopt policies about relationships, be sure that all employees and board members are aware of the policies and apply them consistently.

> **EXAMPLE.** In a small town, there was a good deal of dating among employees and between employees and volunteers at the LGBT (Lesbian Gay Bisexual Transgender) Center. In fact, at one point it was discovered that 14 of the 25 staff were involved in a relationship with a fellow staff member or volunteer. When a board-staff task force was created to develop policies, there was a lot of push-back from the staff. "This is the main place where we can meet each other!" was a frequent comment. Others remarked on the difficulty of defining when a relationship can be said to exist: after coffee? after three dates? And still others felt that the right to privacy about romantic relationships was an essential part of the organization's values. Ultimately, the following language was adopted: "Employees and volunteers should exercise good judgment in all relationships with others in the organization, especially those relationships that are economic, sexual, or romantic. If there is a supervisory relationship between individuals who are dating, the matter should be discussed with the administrative director, who can devise a plan for changing lines of reporting, or take other actions."

Dress and Grooming Codes

Codes outlining acceptable clothing and grooming are difficult to develop and enforce. Nonetheless, clothing and grooming are often important for staff working with the public, and help define the cultural climate of the organization.

When it comes to the law, there are no federal laws governing employee dress codes. Employers can implement dress guidelines to project the image of their choosing, as long as they do not discriminate on the basis of gender, race, and so forth. Dress codes get tricky when they collide with religious or gender issues. For example, legally you can have a policy that prohibits visible tattoos—except for employees whose religious beliefs or traditions include having them.

Some quick notes:

- You can require staff and volunteers to wear uniforms, but it's best if the organization pays for them. (Volunteers who are asked to buy their own uniforms can deduct the cost on their tax returns.) Make sure uniform choices are available for employees whose disabilities require accommodations (for example, an employee who uses a wheelchair may need a uniform that won't bunch up or otherwise create discomfort).

- You can require standard clothing, such as asking all employees in the cafeteria to wear black polo shirts. (A few states require employers to pay for required dress, even if it's "street wear.")

- You can impose different standards for different employees, as long as the standards are based on legitimate organizational purposes. For example, you can require business dress for instructors but not for others.

- Be careful not to discriminate inadvertently when developing your dress code. For example, don't require women—but not men—to wear uniforms. Even if you have a no-beard policy, allow exceptions, such as for men who have a skin disorder that makes it painful for them to shave, or those who have religious reasons for a beard.

- Identify a process for how questionable attire and grooming will be addressed. For example, a first step may be a private discussion between a supervisor and employee to discuss the issue.

RESOURCE

Need ideas for dress codes? See the Sample Dress Code for Nonprofits on the Blue Avocado website at www.blueavocado.org/content/model-dress-code-nonprofits.

Off-Hours Conduct

Employers have the right to control an employee's activities while at work, but what about when employees are on their own time? You need to know the basics of the law, but you'll also need to exercise judgment as various situations arise. Ideally, you should think about the areas where issues are most likely to occur and develop guidelines for when and how these matters should be handled. It's not something where you'll want to have an overly detailed set of rules.

There are some activities that are protected by law—in particular, whistleblowing and union organizing. If an employer punishes or terminates an employee for either of these activities, the employer will be subject to severe fines and penalties. If the employees' actions don't involve either of those, then you generally are allowed to discipline or terminate an employee under the following circumstances:

- if the off-hours conduct affects the employee's performance. For example, an employee who frequently drinks heavily after work may be too hung over to perform his or her work adequately the next day.
- if the off-hours conduct reduces the credibility of the employee or the nonprofit. For example, if a nonprofit employee who is running for city council makes public statements about rezoning directly in opposition to the nonprofit's stance on the issue, the nonprofit's credibility is damaged.

Before you take action against an employee for off-duty conduct, you should speak to a lawyer. State laws protect employees from discipline based on certain activities outside of work, and these situations can lead to questions about whether your organization has intruded too far into the personal realm.

Community and Political Activity

While nonprofit organizations are prohibited from endorsing or opposing candidates for electoral office, nonprofit employees can exercise their rights as individuals to do so. On their own time, employees can work on political campaigns, endorse candidates and ballot measures, sign petitions, and engage in other political activities, as long as they make it clear that they are doing so as individuals and not as employees of your nonprofit.

"National Council of La Raza is nonpartisan and we need to be able to work with all members of Congress," says Sonia Pérez. "If you're going to be campaigning for someone, it has to be on your own time and expense and not at NCLR's. You have to make it clear you are not campaigning as an NCLR representative. We send out the guidelines twice a year, and ask people to let us know if they will be spending significant time on any campaign."

There are some employees who are so high-level that they can't help but represent the organization at all times. For example, if the public policy director of a bicycle coalition makes a speech at a rally against increased taxes, the speech will be taken as representing the bicycle coalition's position on taxes, even if the person claims to be expressing personal views. Similarly, if the executive director of a nonprofit endorses a candidate for mayor, the public will view it as an organizational endorsement. Even if the person never mentions his or her affiliation with the nonprofit, or includes a statement that "organizational affiliation is for informational purposes only," people will make the connection with your high-level employees and staff.

In some cases, this assumption is exactly what your organization is trying to imply. In other cases, the executive-level person should refrain from public endorsements. From an HR standpoint, let all employees know that they are free (or even encouraged) to engage in political activities as long as they make it clear that they are acting as individuals.

Encourage executive staff to be intentional (rather than accidental) if they choose to act differently.

> EXAMPLE: The activities director at a Windy Pine Senior Center was also an active volunteer in an organization that fights fiercely for animal rights. She wisely sought out the executive director when she was preparing to participate in a planned confrontation with a local pet store. While the executive director supported the employee's right to free speech, they both acknowledged that many of the senior center's clients disagreed with her stand on pet stores and would be upset by seeing their well-liked activities director arrested. They ended up agreeing that the activities director would attend the event, but would take a lower profile by not acting as the animal rights' organization's spokesperson to the media.

You will need to find a balance between encouraging free speech and community activities by your staff on one hand and protecting your organization's credibility and avoiding political activity problems on the other. Instead of drawing up rules for this area, a better approach might be to hold regular discussions using case studies so that a group sense of judgment and responsibility can develop.

Moonlighting

It is legal to prohibit full-time employees from accepting other employment. Whether or not you want to do this will depend on circumstances. In some cases, you may not care if someone works after-hours at a recreation center or the family restaurant. On the other hand, in some situations you may want to prohibit an employee from working somewhere else.

One place this can become complicated is when employees earn money for work that is related to the work they do as employees. For example, suppose a teacher at your organization—an after-school tutoring program—starts to tutor students privately on weekends, including children that are in your program. Or imagine that the program director of your HIV testing program is asked to speak at a conference on cultural competency in HIV testing. Should the teacher be allowed to see clients for pay outside of the organization? Should the program director be allowed to keep the honorarium for the speech, or should those funds go back to the organization?

These circumstances are not governed by law. Your organization will need to develop its own policies that will cover these situations.

> EXAMPLE: The Par Center for Environmental Construction developed a well-received manual on green practices and technologies in housing design and construction. Then Todd, one of the staff who worked on the manual, started to contract on his own as a consultant to architects and builders. He argued that he was doing this work on his own time, that the Center did not offer consulting, and that it helped the Center's cause for him to be working with people in the industry. The executive director disagreed. She said that his moonlighting compromised the organization's carefully protected reputation for neutrality and that the extra hours he was working reduced the quality of his work at the Center. When faced with a choice, Todd opted to leave and establish his own consulting firm.

Gaining Insights From Employee Climate Surveys

An annual employee survey is one way for top management to "take the temperature" of the organization and get feedback about how employees are feeling about various matters. These surveys are also called employee engagement surveys and employee feedback surveys.

A climate survey gives management an objective way to assess morale and job satisfaction, rather than relying on what it seems that "everyone" is saying. A survey is also a way to draw employee attention to areas they might be taking for granted, such as workplace safety or paycheck processing. The results of the climate survey are useful to management and HR in planning for benefits, facilities improvement, and organizational practices.

If your organization conducts such a survey, it's important for its goals and the potential follow-up actions to be clear to all employees. One way to do this is to create a small committee of staff to work with HR to develop and administer the survey, which will then analyze the results and make a report to the staff and to the management team. This committee will ideally be composed of people from a diagonal cross-section of the organization, and from different levels, locations, and program areas.

If you conduct a climate survey, be sure to do the following:

- Let all staff members know that an anonymous climate survey is coming, and that they will be asked to complete the survey. Let them know whether they will see the full results of the survey, or whether a staff committee will review the full results and choose which ones to publish to the whole staff.

- Use an electronic survey tool such as Survey Monkey or Zoomerang. This makes it easy for employees to complete and for management to tabulate. In addition, you can let employees know that you are using settings that do not allow you to link answers with the person who gave those answers.

- Review the results and choose actions or next steps to take in response to the survey. For example, the survey may reveal that many employees feel unsafe leaving the building after dark; if so you can decide to purchase additional parking lot lights or develop an employee escort program.

- Decide which results to give to the full staff, and which results to give to the board of directors. If this is at least the second time you've done the survey, comparing the results to prior years will be useful. When presenting data, give context to the survey as well. For example, you might remind staff that last year's survey was taken just two weeks after layoffs.

- When presenting results, let people know what steps are being taken in response to the data. It may not be possible to address every issue identified, but it's important for the survey to be seen as initiating change.

- Don't ignore areas where the organization scores well. If, for example, many employees report that they are reasonably satisfied with their compensation, celebrate the success of raising salaries over the past two years. If employees report that the organization is demonstrably committed to quality science, remind people of this shared commitment.

The key to any employee engagement survey is plenty of communication. Let your employees know what you are doing as a result of the survey. Also, don't ask a question on the survey that you have no intention of reacting or responding too. For example, if you can't do anything about salaries because of your financial situation, don't ask if employees feel that they are being paid fairly. Also, keep in mind that the worst thing you can do with a survey is "nothing." By doing nothing, you are guaranteed that your employees will be skeptical in the future and will never complete another survey. You will lose their trust.

Here are some examples of questions for an employee climate survey. For most of the questions, you'll want to provide boxes indicating levels of agreement or disagreement with the statements being made. And, you may want to add space for comments in each area.

Climate Survey—Sample Questions

Employee status
Are you full time or part time?

Which of the following categories best represents your position:
❏ program   ❏ administrative/support   ❏ management?

Scale: 1 – 6 with 1 = Strongly Disagree and 6 = Strongly Agree

Mission & Vision Questions
_____ I understand the strategic vision for our organization.
_____ Our organizational culture reflects our shared values.
_____ I am satisfied with the direction in which the organization is going.
_____ Our organization has a positive image among the people we serve.
_____ I am proud of the quality of work we do here.
_____ Senior leaders behave ethically.

Working Conditions Questions
_____ I have enough physical space to do my work.
_____ I get enough support with the technology I use.
_____ I have enough time to complete my work responsibilities.
_____ I feel less regularly overwhelmed than I did a year ago.
_____ I feel I work in an environment free of harassment.
_____ Our organization is comfortable for people with diverse backgrounds.

Supervision and People-Management Questions
_____ This organization attracts qualified, competent employees.
_____ I get enough feedback about how I am doing my job.

The performance review system provides me with useful information on how to do my job.
_____ I have confidence and trust in my supervisor.
_____ Volunteers are treated with respect in our organization.

Communications and Decision-Making Questions
_____ My supervisor involves me in decisions that affect my work.
_____ Conflicts are resolved constructively here.
_____ I understand our organizational structure.

Climate Survey—Sample Questions (cont'd)

Management listens to employees.

_____ Good communication exists between departments.

_____ I trust the management team to make the right decisions for the organization.

_____ The role of the board of directors in this organization is clear to me.

Compensation and Opportunities Questions

_____ I feel valued and respected by management.

_____ I feel I am paid fairly.

_____ I am happy with the health benefits offered.

_____ I feel I am recognized for the value of my work.

_____ I have good opportunities for professional development.

_____ Overall, I am happy with my job.

Open-ended Questions

What aspects of the organization make you want to remain here?

_____

_____

_____

What most gets in the way of your doing your job?

_____

_____

If you could change one thing about our organization, what would it be?

_____

_____

_____

One of the important ways to analyze the data is to compare responses from different departments, different genders, and so forth. For example, you may find that your staff in one department is much happier with communications than your staff in another. Or, you may find that there are noticeable differences between how people of color feel about supervision and how white/European people feel about it. These differences provide opportunities to explore the reasons for the differences, to celebrate and reinforce practices that are working, and to correct problems where needed.

Look closely at changes from the past year, which may be more important than an absolute score. For instance, in addition to looking at satisfaction with communication, see if there has been improvement or decline since last year.

Don't feel obligated to report all the results from your survey. Instead, choose key themes to report while reminding staff that the full results are being reviewed by the management team. Make sure that actions are taken based on the survey results, and that at least some of these actions are reported to staff. In addition, where there are improvements, note what changes were instituted that may have contributed to those improvements. ●

11

Organizing HR Functions

Staffing the HR Office 326

HR Attorneys and Consultants 330

Outsourcing HR Functions 331

Who Does HR Report To? 333

Providing Feedback to HR About HR Functions 334

Professional Development for HR Staff 335

Personnel Files 337

    Employee Change Form 338

    What Not to Put Into a Personnel File 340

    Managing Personnel Files 341

Employee Handbooks 341

    What to Include in the Handbook 342

    Don't Create Obligations That Will Haunt You Later 346

HR's Role in Change Management 347

HR Audits 349

Meet Your Adviser

Joanne Krueger, PHR
Title: Vice President, Human Resources, Security
& Facilities
Organization: Planned Parenthood of Wisconsin,
Inc. (PPWI)
Location: Milwaukee, Wisconsin

What she does: Joanne provides overall strategic leadership,
vision, and direction to the agency and partners with managers and
employees to achieve business results. She leads the development and
implementation of human resources policies, programs, and services,
including recruitment, selection, retention, legal compliance, employee
benefits, employee relations, employment practices and procedures,
and employee communications. She provides strategic counsel to the
CEO and other senior leaders and serves as an internal consultant
to the agency's management team, supervisors, and employees on
personnel issues that affect performance and business relationships.

Formerly she worked for a major brewing company as a Corporate
Recruiter/HR Manager.

What her organization does: PPWI is the state's leading
reproductive health care provider committed to keeping all people
safe, healthy, and strong via affordable health care, comprehensive and
medically accurate education, and fearless advocacy.

Best tip for HR managers including the Accidental HR manager:
Join and get involved in an association, whether it's an HR association
like a local SHRM Chapter or a nonprofit association. Build a network of
peers you can call.

HR lesson learned the hard way: Don't start an employee
recognition program if you can't follow through with it during hard
times. If you've always given people a $100 gift certificate on their five-
year anniversary, you can't stop for a year or two even if times are tough.

Song title that speaks to you about HR: "Changes." By David Bowie. If there is one thing that you can always count on in HR, it is change! Like Forrest Gump said, "Life is like a box of chocolates, you never know what you're going to get." Whether through change management, staff changes, policies changes, employment law changes, etc., there will always be change. If you have a hard time dealing with change, then HR is not the role for you!

"HR isn't just a part of the organization," comments adviser Joanne Krueger, VP for HR at Planned Parenthood of Wisconsin. "HR goes through the entire organization." With HR matters touching every employee in the organization and covering so many different aspects of workplace life, making sure you have placed someone in charge of every HR responsibility—from posting job announcements to organizing exit interviews—is crucial. And, it can be very challenging.

In this chapter, we look at staffing HR in both small and large nonprofits, outsourcing HR, working with HR attorneys and consultants, and professional development for HR staff. We also cover some specific HR functions, including personnel files, employee handbooks, and workplace climate surveys. Finally, we'll address how to get feedback on how HR is performing its critical roles through HR audits and other checks and balances.

Staffing the HR Office

A long-time rule of thumb in industry has been to have one HR staff person for every 100 employees, while in service and knowledge businesses one HR person for every 50 employees is more commonly heard. These guidelines may or may not be relevant for your nonprofit, given your mix of staff and volunteers, funding availability, and your ability to distribute HR responsibilities among staff with other responsibilities.

A nonprofit with a small staff—let's say ten employees—probably won't have a full-time, dedicated HR staff person. Someone should, however, be designated as in charge of HR functions, even if it that person is the executive director. Doing so will help everyone remember that HR is an essential management responsibility.

For the ED Who Is Also the Head of HR

We interviewed several executive directors at small organizations who double as the HR person. Here are some of their comments and tips.

- "In a big organization they have human resources. We just have *people!*"
- "You can offload some of it, but never all of it. You can give the files to the bookkeeper, the posters to the office manager, and the performance reviews to a committee to manage. But you still have to be a leader in it, drive it, figure out what to do when the wild cards show up."
- "In a small organization you tend not to pay attention to professional development. Everyone's job is their professional development. But if you don't pay attention to it and everyone's jobs keep expanding, you'll run into real performance problems and have to play catch-up."
- "I knew I was responsible for personnel functions, but it took me a while to realize I was actually the HR Director. Thinking of it that way helped me take the job more seriously."
- "I keep forgetting that HR is going to be messy, no matter what you do. People are messy. Relationships are messy. HR is messy."
- "Develop good, strong policies before they're needed. Then as problems arise they can be relied upon like a bedrock. You'll be so glad they're there."
- "If you've given HR responsibilities to other people, be sure you also put those into their job descriptions and get them some training or professional development in HR."
- "An intangible leadership quality is to set a tone that says, 'We want a healthy, safe environment where we hold ourselves accountable to each other.' Repeat. Repeat."

Many nonprofits can assign most responsibilities to non-HR staff, but still need the skills and perspective of an HR professional. At the same time, they may not need or be able to afford a full-time HR manager. Working with HR consultants and outsourced HR staff are two ways to supplement the HR skills on staff.

If you have a small staff, you may decide to split up core HR responsibilities and assign them to different people on your staff. Here's one way you could divvy up HR responsibilities among staff in a small organization:

Bookkeeper
- Maintaining personnel files
- Payroll-related matters
- Handling paperwork related to hiring, job changes, and termination
- Tracking paid time off (PTO)
- Administering benefits.

Supervisor
- Hiring staff and performing reference checks
- Conducting performance reviews and strengthening performance.

Management team, either as a whole or areas assigned to various members
- Developing job descriptions
- Establishing salary ranges and salaries
- Designing performance reviews
- Establishing hiring practices
- Integrating new staff
- Defining benefits packages
- Drafting or overseeing drafting of employee handbook.

Executive director
- Final approval of all salaries
- Making sure performance reviews are completed and reviewing them
- Final approval of all hiring and terminations
- Ensuring that HR functions are taken care of appropriately
- Reporting on HR matters to the board of directors.

Board of directors

- With respect to the executive director: hiring, setting compensation, doing performance reviews, and, if need be, terminating
- Reviewing and approving salary ranges; reviewing to see that all salaries are in appropriate ranges
- Approving benefits package
- Approving employee handbook
- Instituting diversity goals and practices
- As part of budget approval, approving total staff and independent contractor expenses
- Conducting exit interviews for departing management team members.

MYTH

Not Every Organization Needs an HR Person

"We don't really need someone in charge of HR" is a commonly heard sentiment. Even if it's not expressed out loud, many nonprofit executives quietly think this is true. HR is often treated as something of an afterthought, with the responsibilities handed to someone who has little or no training or even inclination or interest in HR.

In every organization, responsibility for HR must be in someone's job description. And that person needs and deserves training, ongoing access to information, and time to do the job right.

Even if you don't have someone exclusively devoted to HR, make sure that the responsibility is clearly placed, and work toward giving that person the necessary support . . . so that they can support everyone in the organization with HR functions.

HR Attorneys and Consultants

An HR attorney or consultant can be a valuable partner to HR managers. Sooner or later, a question will come up that you can't answer, or a situation will arise that requires a fresh perspective.

In particular, there are some areas where it's important to work with an HR attorney:

- reviewing the employee handbook and various employee-related policies
- reviewing certain termination documents, such as a severance agreement
- responding to employment-related lawsuits and complaints, and
- reviewing employment contracts.

Not everything needs legal review. "There are many resources besides attorneys," notes adviser Joanne Krueger. "Sometimes you can find what you need online, such as on the Department of Labor website. There are management associations with good resources. There are good consultants and they're less expensive than lawyers."

In situations that present substantial risk to your organization, however, you will probably want to work with an attorney. Be sure to find an attorney who specializes in employment matters, just as you would see an orthopedist for a broken leg, not an allergy specialist. Talk with other nonprofits in your area to find appropriate legal help. Another resource is Nolo's lawyer directory at www.nolo.com for lawyers who specialize in employment law.

TIP

Look for free or low-cost legal help. In a few cases, your insurance carrier may offer free, expert legal help with employment matters, as the Nonprofits Insurance Alliance Group does for the 10,000 nonprofits it insures. In many cities, the local or state bar associations can match your nonprofit with a pro bono attorney, and some law schools welcome nonprofits at their pro bono legal clinics. Some communities have Lawyers for the Arts organizations that place pro bono attorneys with arts nonprofits. As with any attorney, make sure a pro bono attorney has the right background, and that you have a clear agreement about what services will be provided within the agreed-upon period of time.

Working with an HR consultant on an ongoing basis is a good way for many nonprofits to supplement on-staff expertise. A consultant can review your documents and forms, and advise you as questions arise, including on when an attorney should be involved. Look for a consultant with whom you can have an ongoing relationship, and budget for use of the consultant's time as a regular expense.

Many nonprofits also seek an HR attorney for membership on the board of directors. In the best cases, an expert HR attorney on the board knows the organization and its values well, and can advise staff informally on any number of employment matters. In a worst-case scenario, an attorney on the board may insist on giving inexpert legal advice on HR affairs, and either gets the organization in more trouble or restricts the organization too narrowly on what can be done.

Outsourcing HR Functions

A good solution for some small and midsized nonprofits is to outsource part of the HR function. For example, contracting with an HR firm or an HR consultant to provide a staff person for one day per week may give you a higher level of expertise than you can afford to hire as full-time staff. Although some outsourcing companies do all their work online and through 800 numbers, most nonprofits will feel more confident with an HR firm that places a particular associate in your organization face-to-face on a regular basis.

HR functions that can readily be placed with an outsourcing firm include:

- recruiting and background checks
- benefits administration
- performance review design and supervisor training
- salary schedule development and analysis
- drafting and updating the employee handbook, and
- sexual harassment training and other compliance training.

There are certain disadvantages to outsourcing HR. Employees may feel uncomfortable discussing sensitive matters with an "outsider." It becomes harder to integrate organizational values, strategies, and culture into HR policies and practices. And an HR perspective may get left out of your organization's countless formal and informal discussions about its management and goals.

Unfortunately, many nonprofits who want to work with an outsourcing firm have difficulty finding one with which they are satisfied. Such firms are usually unfamiliar with nonprofits and try to bring in practices and policies that your staff may find alienating and inappropriate. In other cases, the fees may be so high that outsourcing isn't cost-effective. Ask around to see if there are well-regarded firms in your area that specialize in working with nonprofit organizations with the same size staff as yours.

> EXAMPLE: Centro Santiago is a community-based nonprofit that works with families of children with disabilities in the Latino community, many of whom are Spanish-speaking. With 35 staff, they didn't need a full-time HR manager, but they needed more than their capable administrative director could provide. They worked with an HR consulting firm, but could never get a good fit. They tried working with solo-practice HR consultants as well before they "gave up." "In the end," said director Carmen Delgado, "It's easier to teach HR to someone who understands our community and client base than it is to teach an HR person about our community and disabilities." They promoted a talented employee and are paying for her to take HR classes at the state university—and she gets advice from an HR consultant. "It's not just about the law for us," adds Carmen. "Spanish, the Latino community, and our philosophy about disabilities need to be everywhere in our organization, especially in HR."

Who Does HR Report To?

In organizations with one or more dedicated HR staff, to whom should they report? Given the strategic role of HR in managing an organization's key asset—its staff—you might expect the HR director to report to the top executive. However, this form of recognition is rare.

Unfortunately, in some organizations HR is seen primarily as transactional work, focusing on compensation, benefits management, compliance, and shepherding performance reviews. And because many of the technical HR functions overlap with finance and payroll, the HR manager often reports to the finance director or to an administrative director or COO.

In other organizations, HR is understood more comprehensively and takes responsibility and leadership in the acquisition of organizational talent, retention of a diverse workforce, staff development, and training. The technical work may be done in finance while the HR staff looks closely at performance reviews, coaching, workplace climate, and other "soft HR" arenas. In these organizations, the HR manager is somewhat more likely to report to the COO or the executive director. Regardless of where HR reports, it's crucial for the executive director to be aware of HR goals and constraints, to appreciate the role of HR within the organization, and to set an example by completing performance reviews on time, respecting classification procedures, and so forth.

If the HR manager is not a member of the management team, the CEO or COO must be sure that an HR perspective is adequately represented in discussions. Adviser Sarah Gon notes that if the COO is someone with an HR background, it might not be necessary for the HR manager to be on the management team. But if the COO has a finance background and lacks experience in HR, the HR manager might be crucial to bring an employee-oriented outlook to decision making.

"The HR director is both an employee advocate and a business consultant," notes adviser Joanne Krueger. Whoever the HR staff reports to, it's crucial that both roles are brought appropriately into organizational decision making.

Providing Feedback to HR About HR Functions

HR directors are often stereotyped as heartless bureaucrats who make life miserable for employees by throwing the book at everything. In contrast, HR people often see themselves as the misunderstood, heroic guardians of the organization's legal wellbeing. Which is correct? (If you're reading this book, we think you might agree with the second statement.)

Here are some ways for the HR staff—and senior management—to get feedback on the performance of HR in an organization:

- **Exit interviews.** Include a question about the interactions an employee has had with HR.
- **Survey of new employees.** Send a quick ten-question survey to employees who've been on board for a month or so, asking how their hiring and integration process has gone so far, and what questions they have and assistance they'd appreciate.
- **Workplace climate survey.** If you conduct such surveys, include a question or two about an area of HR, such as handling of workers compensation claims, open enrollment, or HR involvement in conflict resolution.
- **Internal customer survey.** Every year or so, send a brief survey to employees and ask about their "customer satisfaction" with HR functions.

Feedback mechanisms not only help identify areas for improvement, they also serve to raise the profile of the HR function within the organization. Be sure to use the completion of the survey as an occasion to congratulate the HR staff and to remind everyone of the low-profile, crucial role of HR.

TIP

Being the HR director or manager can be isolating and frustrating. On one hand, you have to defend management decisions about HR to staff even when you disagree with them. On the other hand, you have to advocate for staff even when you are frustrated with them. It's hard to maintain confidentiality when, for instance, you know that the person who is always obnoxiously bragging about his involvement with his children is having his wages garnished for delinquent child support payments. And sometimes when you explain an HR process or benefits eligibility rule to an employee, they get mad at you as if you are persecuting them personally.

Take a deep breath and check your calendar for your next HR networking opportunity. Spending time with peers will help keep you sane without having to violate confidentiality. Others can make suggestions about what to do when you are feeling discouraged or resentful. Keep in mind that such feelings come with the job, and that acknowledging your internal conflicts will make you even better at the HR balancing act.

Professional Development for HR Staff

Whether you are a credentialed HR director with many years of experience or a new "accidental HR person," your ongoing professional development is important for your organization to invest in.

The most valuable resource for you may be networking with people in other nonprofits who have responsibilities for HR. Look for a structured network sponsored by a technical service provider or a nonprofit association. But you may just find that having coffee occasionally with other nonprofit HR folks works the best for you. Nonprofits are typically more than willing to share templates, samples, and information; such networks are places where you can give back as well as learn.

For many nonprofit staff with HR responsibilities, it's important to get nontechnical support as well.

Other professional development opportunities include the following:

Society for Human Resource Management (SHRM). SHRM has extensive online resources as well as dozens of local chapters. Participating in local events can keep you up to date with changing laws as well as emerging practices. Some SHRM chapters also have informal groups of nonprofit HR professionals that hold regular meetings. To find your lo-cal chapter, go to www.shrm.org and click on "Find a Chapter" in the membership section.

In addition to SHRM, many communities have other associations for HR professionals, as well as business associations that include HR groups. Nonprofit technical assistance centers often convene networks of nonprofit HR staff.

Professional certifications. Widely recognized are certifications from the Human Resources Certification Institute (HRCI), which grants two certifications, the Professional in Human Resources (PHR) and the Senior Professional in Human Resources (SPHR). Both require passing an exam as well as work experience. See www.hrci.org for complete information. Some SHRM chapters offer certification training at reduced costs.

Universities and colleges. Colleges and universities offer a wide variety of HR-related degrees at both the undergraduate and graduate levels, including HR emphasis programs within MBA and MPA degrees. SHRM maintains a directory of programs online along with some limited information about scholarship opportunities. Many extension programs have a good selection of nondegree courses as well.

Chambers of Commerce (www.chamberofcommerce.com/chambers). Many local chambers offer seminars on employment and HR matters for small businesses, and some state-level chambers have comprehensive resources, such as state-specific employee handbook templates.

Small Business Administration (www.sba.gov). In employment legal matters, nonprofits and small businesses have much in common. Depending on the location, you may be able to attend SBA-sponsored seminars or connect with volunteer, retired small business owners who advise nonprofits along with other small businesses.

Nonprofit associations. Some nonprofit technical assistance centers and nonprofit associations convene networks of HR managers. For example, adviser Sarah Gort of CompassPoint Nonprofit Services leads a Nonprofit HR Network that meets six times a year and offers outside speakers as well as peer case studies. A few publish state-specific nonprofit employee handbooks. State nonprofit associations can be found at www.councilofnonprofits.org/salocator.

> **TIP**
>
> **Join an HR association.** Adviser Joanne Krueger suggests that all new HR staff, especially the accidental HR manager, join and get involved in a local HR association like SHRM. "It's the quickest way of getting up to speed," she says. "You can build a base of peers so that there's always someone you can call when a question comes up."

And for a last word on professional development in HR, adviser Ashwin Jayaram has both a masters in HR from Cornell University and maintains his SPHR certification, but values his years of hands-on HR management: "I value education. By the same token, experience has taught me more than education."

Personnel Files

There's not much that's glamorous about well-kept personnel files, but maintaining them is essential task of HR. In a worst-case scenario, a personnel file can turn into evidence in a lawsuit brought by a disgruntled former employee. Make sure that you include all periodic evaluations, raises, commendations, and disciplinary actions in employees' personnel files to protect your organization in case of a lawsuit.

In addition, indiscreet entries that do not directly relate to an employee's job performance and qualifications—like references to an employee's private life or political beliefs, or comments about an employee's race, sexual orientation, gender, age, disability, health, or religion—may come back to haunt you. Many states give employees the right to see their personnel files, or at least certain documents in those files. Whether or not that's the case in your state, here's a good rule of thumb: Don't put anything in a personnel file that you would not want a jury to see.

On the date of hire, start a file for each employee. A personnel file should contain:

- a job description for the position (and previous positions held, if any)

- a job application and/or resume
- an offer of employment
- IRS Form W-4 (*Employee's Withholding Allowance Certificate*)
- a signed acknowledgment from the employee of having received the employee handbook, and separate acknowledgements for any updates or changes
- all performance reviews and, if applicable, employee responses
- all warnings and disciplinary actions
- any commendations or complaints from clients, constituents, coworkers, or others
- emergency contact form including next of kin information
- any notes related to tardiness or absences
- any contract or written agreement with the employee, such as an employment contract, an agreement related to an organization-owned computer, and so forth
- a copy of a currently valid driver's license and insurance certificate if the employee drives for work
- a photo of the employee
- all Employee Change Forms, showing changes in compensation, title, promotions, supervisor, home address, benefits, and so forth.

Employee Change Form

An Employee Change Form makes it easier for supervisors and employees to make sure that employment and personal changes are on file. Use it to document any changes in employee status, such as a salary change, a change in reporting, and so forth. Having one form for these many functions makes it easy for supervisors to remember which one to use. You can also put reminders right into the form that help supervisors make sure to include relevant back-up materials. This may be the most important form you'll use in HR.

Sample Employee Change Form

Employee Change Form

Use this form to report employment changes (such as new hire, salary, title, full time/part time, termination of employment) as well as personal changes (such as address, emergency contact). Give one copy to payroll and one to HR for the employee's personnel file.

Name: _____ Social Security #: _____

EFFECTIVE DATE FOR CHANGE(S) BELOW: _____

❑ New employee   ❑ Change to existing employee   ❑ Termination

Employment changes

❑ Salary/wages (note per hour, per year) _____

❑ Exempt/nonexempt: _____

❑ Work hours (such as full time/part time/hours per week): _____

❑ Work location: _____

❑ Title: _____

❑ Reports to: _____

❑ Job Description (attach): _____

❑ Other: _____

Personal changes

❑ Name change: _____

❑ Address: _____

❑ Marital status (may require new W-4): _____

❑ Home telephone: _____

❑ Cell phone: _____

❑ Emergency contact: _____

❑ Other: _____

Sample Employee Change Form (cont'd)

Note: this form does not automatically make changes in benefits. Please contact HR for forms related to benefits.

Employee signature (required for all changes):

_____

Date: _____

Authorizing signature (required for employment changes):

_____

Authorizer's printed name: _____

Date: _____

What Not to Put Into a Personnel File

Your personnel files should not be a catch-all for every document, note, or thought about the employee. Here are some things to pay attention to:

Medical records. For various reasons, medical information and documents may come into your organization; do not put these into personnel files. Instead, keep all medical records in a separate file, including medical information related to a workers' compensation claim or benefits—and limit access to only a few people.

Form I-9. Do not put Form I-9 into an employee's personnel file. (Form I-9 is a form called *"Employment Eligibility Verification,"* which comes from U.S. Citizenship and Immigration Services (USCIS), formerly the INS (Immigration and Naturalization Services). You must complete an I-9 for each new employee upon hiring, verifying that you have checked to see that the employee is legally authorized to work in the United States.)

You should put all Forms I-9 into one folder for USCIS to inspect if it comes to visit. The government is entitled to inspect these forms, and if it does, you don't want the agents viewing the rest of the employee's personnel—and personal—information at the same time. Not only would this compromise your employees' privacy, but it might also open your organization up to additional questions and investigation.

Unnecessary material. Although an employee's personnel file may contain any other job-related documents, don't go overboard. There's no need, for example, to toss in photos from the company picnic or a copy of the ED's clever roast of the employee at his or her anniversary lunch. Always remember that, in many states, employees have the right to view their personnel files.

Managing Personnel Files

Personnel files should be kept in locked drawers or cabinets, with access to keys sharply limited. If written performance reviews are in electronic form, make sure that access to them is restricted by passwords, with different levels of staff having access to different levels of information. For example, an employee may be allowed to see only his or her own performance review, while a supervisor may be allowed to see the performance reviews of all direct reports.

When employees leave your nonprofit, move their personnel files to storage. Your auditor can give you guidelines for retention of different kinds of records; a rule of thumb is to retain employee-related documents for seven years.

Employee Handbooks

No law requires employers to have an employee handbook, but it's a good idea to do so. Although compiling personnel policies will take some effort, you will save time, headaches, and possible legal fees in the long run. This is another essential HR function.

A handbook tells employees about workplace rules and expectations in an efficient way. Employees will know what's expected of them and what they can expect in return. An employee handbook can spell out the personnel policies that your organization has developed and put into practice. The handbook can also let employees know a bit about the history of the organization and its structure, values, and plans.

Written policies—and a practice of having employees sign acknowledgments that they were given the policies—can help show that someone fired for misconduct knew the rules and the consequences of violating them.

Be sure to have an employment attorney review your employee handbook before it goes to the board for final review and approval.

What to Include in the Handbook

Effective employee handbooks vary widely in size, style, and content. Some organizations produce extensive handbooks in multiple volumes that attempt to cover every possible aspect of the organization, right down to available parking spots and how to operate the coffee maker. More likely, you'll want to develop a limited handbook that covers the basics, has a user-friendly in size and style, and doesn't over-commit your organization.

Of course, the substance of employee handbooks tends to change fairly regularly, so you'll want to think through the practicalities of making those changes without having to reissue entire hardbound volumes. Some organizations use binders for employee handbooks, which allow for revised sections to be substituted for old sections. In other organizations, the employee handbook is kept on a server to which all employees have access, ensuring that everyone can be sure they are using up-to-date materials.

Here are some topics to consider covering in a handbook. If you are responsible for creating, updating, or troubleshooting your organization's handbook, you can use this list as a starting point.

- **Dates.** Be sure to have the effective date and the dates for any revisions on the cover page and at the bottom of each page.

- **Legal review.** If appropriate, include a note on the cover page: "This Employee Handbook has been reviewed by legal counsel on _____ date _____."

- **Purpose of the handbook.** Why the handbook was created, how to use the handbook, when the acknowledgement and receipt of reading the handbook is due for new employees. This sets the tone, explains that the handbook is either a general guideline or as a reference to specific policies, and tells employees where they can ask questions or seek additional information.

- **Basic information about the nonprofit.** Include the mission and vision statements, an organizational chart, a brief history (if relevant), and statements about organizational values, multiculturalism, clients' rights, or other matters.

- **At-will statement.** If your organization is an "at-will" employer, be absolutely sure to include a statement to that effect in the handbook.

- **Definitions.** Explain employment classifications such as full time and part time, the workweek, exempt and nonexempt classifications, and so forth.

- **Hiring rules.** Explain any rules or policies used when hiring staff, including job posting procedures, antidiscrimination or affirmative action policies, and so forth.

- **Pay.** Set out the rules on overtime, wage garnishments, expense reimbursements, pay advances, and other matters. State whether paychecks are weekly or semimonthly, and whether payroll advances and direct deposit of paychecks are available.

- **Hours.** Set out the rules on rest breaks and meal breaks, attendance, work schedules, timesheets, and eligibility for flexible scheduling arrangements, if applicable. Be clear about when rules differ for exempt and nonexempt employees.

- **Leave.** If you offer sick leave, vacation time, paid time off, parental leave, or other time off, explain the policies.

- **Performance reviews.** Explain the process and timing for performance reviews.

- **Benefits.** Explain the benefits available to employees, including health insurance, dental and vision coverage, life insurance, disability insurance, retirement plans, and the like.

- **Discrimination and harassment.** Include a statement that discrimination, harassment, and bullying violate organizational policies and values and will not be tolerated. State clearly that immediate action will be taken against wrongdoers.

- **Equal opportunity and nondiscrimination statements.** Include both of these policy statements.

- **Complaints and whistle-blowing.** Describe how employees can make complaints or report harassment and other misconduct. Describe what steps will be taken to investigate, and remind staff that retaliation is not allowed against an employee who complains in good faith. In particular, include a whistle-blower policy that has been approved by the board of directors. Encourage employees to report any concerns immediately.

- **Health and safety.** List all safety-related rules (for example, that latex gloves must be worn when handling food). Provide information on emergency exits, the location of fire extinguishers and first aid kids, and any procedures established for evacuating the building. Some organizations are required by a local government agency or funding institution to have a separate health and safety policy.

- **Disaster preparedness.** Include information on how to reach designated individuals or any other procedures in the event of a disaster such as a hurricane, earthquake, gas explosion, or epidemic. If your organization will be providing emergency services (for example, helping non-English speaking clients with relocation), explain what responsibilities staff have in a disaster.

- **Violence.** State clearly that violence and threats—whether internal or external—will be taken seriously. Explain how employees can report threats and violent incidents.

- **Privacy.** If your organization monitors employee phone calls, email messages, Internet use, or vehicle driving, or if you conduct any workplace searches or surveillance, let employees know.

- **Confidentiality.** State clearly your confidentiality policy.
- **Computer, Internet, and email policies.** Remind employees that computer records, including email and Internet logs, are the property of the organization and can be reviewed at any time. Let them know that such records can also be subpoenaed by people outside the organization in the case of a lawsuit: more reason to be careful about what gets written. Include any policies you have developed related to technology.
- **Workplace conduct.** Include policies on uniforms, dress codes, policies on grooming, bringing children (or pets) to work, and so forth.
- **Conflict of interest.** If your organization has a conflict of interest policy that employees are required to sign, include it in the handbook.
- **Discipline.** If your organization has a progressive discipline policy, describe it here. You can also note which infractions constitute grounds for termination, but be sure not to be overly detailed, to keep management's options open.
- **Terminations and layoffs.** If your organization has developed policies related to severance policies, termination procedures, references, or other matters, include them here.
- **Moonlighting.** State your policy on whether and how employees can hold other jobs or do other paid work.
- **Nepotism and relationships.** State your policy on how your organization handles employees who are related to one another, or in romantic and/or economic relationships with one another.
- **Travel.** State your policy for business mileage reimbursement, travel time for exempt or nonexempt staff during work or outside normal commute, training, travel advances (if applicable), meals, gratuity, and so on.
- **Solicitation.** State your policy on the distribution of literature or solicitation of any kind in work areas.
- **Right to change the handbook.** You cannot be sure that the employment policies you develop today will be adequate in the future. You might decide to change a policy, or new or amended

laws may dictate a change. The handbook should state that the organization reserves the right to change its policies at any time, for any reason.

- **Conduct not covered by the handbook.** Of course, no handbook can cover every possible workplace situation. Make this clear to employees by saying so in the handbook, and that the handbook does not represent a complete and comprehensive set of rules.

Don't Create Obligations That Will Haunt You Later

Some courts—and employees—interpret the language in employee handbooks as contracts that create binding obligations on employers. If you include or imply any promises in the employee handbook, there's a very real possibility that employees or former employees might try to enforce those promises in court. Here are some of the most common trouble spots:

- **Promises of continued employment.** Don't include language in the handbook that promises employees a job as long as they follow organizational rules. A court might interpret this to be an employment contract, guaranteeing that employees will not be fired without documented good cause. State in the handbook that your company reserves the right to terminate employees for reasons not stated in the handbook or for no reason at all. Even though the company may never have to rely on this language to provide a legal defense to a wrongful termination claim, at least employees will know where they stand.
- **Progressive discipline.** Many employers follow some form of "progressive discipline" for performance problems or less serious forms of misconduct such as difficulties getting along with coworkers or a habit of missing deadlines. Often, discipline starts with informal coaching, then a verbal warning in a counseling session, followed by a written warning, then termination. Whatever system your nonprofit uses, don't obligate managers to follow a particular disciplinary pattern for every employee in every circumstance. It's better to leave the organization's options

open, to make sure it can fire employees, if necessary, without facing a legal challenge.

Once you've created a comprehensive employee handbook, review and update it regularly as your policies and procedures change. An outdated handbook doesn't do anyone any good—and could create confusion or unwanted legal obligations. And a periodic handbook review will help you identify changes you want—or need—to make to policies.

CAUTION

If it's in your employee handbook, you have to do it. Be careful not to include too much detail or too many procedures in your employee handbook. If the handbook says you will do something—such as conduct quarterly performance reviews—you are obligated to do so. If you haven't, an employee can legitimately complain, perhaps as a defense to disciplinary action, that procedures weren't followed.

RESOURCE

Don't start from scratch when creating your employee handbook. Many state Chambers of Commerce publish templates that are updated annually with changes to state law. Nolo publishes a book with companion CD as well: *Create Your Own Employee Handbook*, by Lisa Guerin and Amy DelPo. Reach out to nonprofits in your field and of your group's size to see if they'll share theirs. The best handbooks often come from evaluating and combining several samples.

HR's Role in Change Management

Nonprofits are always changing. Sometimes the change comes after deliberate consideration, such as a decision to merge with another nonprofit, start a new program, move to another location, or restructure the management team. Sometimes an organization is thrust suddenly and unexpectedly into change, perhaps triggered by the departure of a key staff member, the loss of funding, or the emergence of a new competitor. Some changes may seem small to some and huge to others, such as instituting timesheets if they have not been required previously. And other times change happens gradually, until at some point everyone realizes, "Things are different!"

Organizational changes mean that people will have to change, too. Some people will simply have to accept change; some will have to drive change; most will need to work through what a change means to their jobs and to themselves. The people with HR responsibilities can act as a bridge between top management and organizational staff, understanding both the goals of intentional change and the way that change affects individuals. Some ways that an HR lens can support a change initiative include:

- help management explain change and engage employees in implementing change
- listen everywhere for employee concerns and adaptations
- identify obstacles and "bumps" and work to create solutions
- help with developing benchmarks and timelines
- advocate for appropriate resources and processes
- design and provide training and learning opportunities that support the initiative,
- in some cases, help employees decide for themselves whether they can support the changes or whether they need to leave, and
- provide support during staff changes such as layoffs, new hires, training, changes in reporting structure.

Of course, managing change is not the sole responsibility of HR. But too often, the executive director and other senior staff can neglect to bring an HR perspective to organizational change.

> EXAMPLE: When two small railroad museums decided to merge, no one expected there would be many problems. After all, the museums had shared the same railroad yard for years; the staff and volunteers at both museums had worked on many joint projects, and they shared

many of the same demographic characteristics. But after the merger it seemed as if everything turned into an argument. Accusations flew about proper care of the locomotives, which "side" was raising more money, and whether modern materials should be used to repair historic cars.

After a big blow-up at a board meeting, two board members with HR backgrounds (one from each of the original museums) sat down with the executive director and preservation director. The group discussed the conflicts that were arising and realized that not enough effort had been made to understand the great changes that the merger was requiring of staff, board members, and volunteers. They established a set of small work groups involving people from each of the former museums to work out new procedures and guidelines, and framed some talking points for explaining the reasons behind the merger. The board members spoke to some of the staff individually to engage their support for the new, merged organization. Although not everything was immediately rosy, bringing an HR perspective to a strategic change was crucial in helping the individuals—who are, after all, the organization—move forward.

HR Audits

An HR audit is simply a periodic review of your organization's HR policies and practices. It's usually performed by an HR expert, though some organizations also conduct self-audits of HR. The expert or designated staff person reviews documents, interviews staff, and may conduct a survey of some or all employees. The result is a report to senior management and the board on HR functions. You can get the sense of what an HR audit entails by knowing the types of questions that an auditor may ask:

- Is the employee handbook up to date, reflecting any new laws and regulations or concerns that are especially important at your organization?

- Are performance reviews regularly completed for all employees, in line with the process established in the handbook?
- Do personnel files have all the necessary documents and no inappropriate documents in them?
- Are sound hiring practices in place?
- Do employees understand how to make a complaint if they have one?
- Is there an emergency response plan?
- Are open enrollment meetings held?

An HR audit can reassure senior management and the board that HR functions are being managed adequately. The audit can also point out places for improvement and reinforce recommendations from HR.

If your nonprofit will conduct its own HR audits rather than hiring an outside professional, use an HR audit checklist. That lets you work through the items on the checklist and make a report on areas for commendation and areas for improvement.

> **TIP**
>
> **Ongoing self-auditing creates checks and balances.** In charge of managing the paperwork for more than 200 employees at 27 sites, Joanne Krueger of Planned Parenthood of Wisconsin knows that, invariably, something will fall between the cracks. "We have a checklist and we work through it," she says. For example, one month someone in the HR department will look through all the personnel files to be sure that key items are in every one. Or they'll make sure that the required posters are up at all sites. They'll double-check to be sure that the benefit selections match the payroll records. This way they touch all areas over time, ensuring that the wide breadth of HR activities is monitored.

Your CPA auditor may be able to provide you with an HR audit checklist, or another nonprofit may have one it can share with you. Some checklists are much too abstract ("Are all employees treated equitably?") while others focus on bureaucratic detail ("Was the employee handbook approved by a meeting of the board at which a quorum was present?"). You'll want to develop your own checklist after looking at several samples

Rather than seeing an HR audit as a test, think of it as a walk-through of your house looking for leaks, broken locks, and areas where perhaps weather stripping could result in energy savings. Whether you work with an outside expert or conduct your own HR audit, working through a checklist that's appropriate to your organization is a simple way to get an overview of how strong your HR systems are and where a little maintenance or repair work would be useful. ●

Index

A

Absenteeism, by executive directors, 261–262

Administrative support staff
   compensation analyses for, 68–71
   exempt/nonexempt status, 78
   job titles, 159

Advertising, job postings, 20–21

Age Discrimination in Employment Act, 59

Alcohol and drug testing
   for employees, 293
   for job candidates, 35

Alcohol use or dependence
   drinking problems, 291–292
   EAPs and, 93, 292
   of executive directors, 261–262
   firing employees for, 282
   use at work, 291
   workplace violence and, 299

Aldridge, Ellen, 168

Alternative work weeks, 103

Americans with Disabilities Act (ADA)
   alcohol dependency and, 291–292
   certification for prescription drugs, 293
   discrimination issues, 59

AmeriCorps volunteers, 213

Apprenticeships, 155

Attorneys. *See* Legal advice and lawyers

At-will employment
   basics, 43–45
   performance reviews and, 132
   probationary periods and, 43, 46, 51–52
   statements in handbooks, 44, 52, 343
   terminations and, 170, 176

B

Background checks
   for job candidates, 33–35
   outsourcing, 331
   personnel file information, 338
   for volunteers, 216, 217–218

Ballotpedia.org, 75

Bargaining units, 267–268, 270, 274, 275

Behavior problems
   attempts to improve, 171–173
   terminating employees for, 170, 179

Benchmarking
   in compensation analyses, 69–72
   for individual bonuses, 73

Blog postings, employee use of, 308–310

Blue Avocado, 21

Board of directors, 252–262
as anti-union, 265, 270–272
basics, 253
bonus review role, 74
complaints/grievances response by, 261
diversity monitoring role, 260
employee benefits role, 260
employee/executive compensation role, 61, 258–259
exit interview role, 190, 262
hiring role, 253, 260
HR attorneys on, 331
HR responsibilities, 256–262, 329
interview/hiring role, 25
layoff roles, 185, 261
myths about, 256
new-member orientation role, 223–224
nonprofit role, 4
oversight of executive director, 253–256, 261–262
performance review role, 127–128
personnel policies/handbook review by, 258
as recruiters, 20
reference checks for, 224
romantic relationships with employees, 311
volunteer roles, 209, 223–224

Bonuses. *See* Commissions and bonuses

Bookkeepers, HR responsibilities, 328

Brown Morton, Lisa, 109

Budgeting issues
layoffs and furloughs, 184–188, 191
money for education and training, 153
performance reviews and, 133

Bullying. *See* Harassment, bullying, or teasing

Burnout, staff, 149–150

Business agents, for unions, 274–275

Busse, Meg, 9

C

Cafeteria plans, 94–95

Career path development, 157

Cell phones
driving and use of, 282, 289–290
privacy issues, 344
reimbursing employees for, 289

CEOs. *See* Executive directors

Chambers of commerce
handbook templates, 347
HR seminars, 336

Change management, HR role, 347–349

Charity offices, state, 62

Checklist performance reviews
agreeing/disagreeing with, 118–119
based on rating performance standard, 117–118
basics, 115, 117
completed by employee, 135
measuring performance against goals, 119–120

Chief financial officers, search consultants for, 21–22

Child care, cafeteria plans and, 94–95

Churches/religious organizations, as volunteer source, 214

Civil Rights Act, 59

Clients
feedback by, 127, 162–165
romantic relationships with employees, 310

Climate surveys
basics, 317–319
data analysis and reporting, 321–322
feedback on HR functions, 334
sample questions, 320–321

Coaching employees, 147–149

COBRA (Consolidated Omnibus Budget Reconciliation Act) benefits, 186, 193

Collective bargaining, 268–269

Colleges and universities, for HR-related degrees, 336

Commissions and bonuses
employment contract provisions, 45
ethical issues, 76
funder/constituent attitudes on, 76
for fundraising, 75–76
for individuals, 73–74
spot bonuses, 74

Community activities, of employees, 315–316

Commuting
expenses related to, 85–86
in organization-owned vehicles, 287–288

telecommuting, 103–104

Compensation, 55–106
analysis of, 67–72, 254–255, 258–259
basics, 56–57
board roles, 254, 258–259
cost of living adjustments, 77
excess benefits and compensation, 62
for exempt vs. nonexempt employees, 77–81
housing and meals as, 84–85
laws governing, 58–62
overtime, 59, 77–81
rest breaks, 85
for top executives, 60–62
See also Commissions and bonuses;
Employee benefits; Payroll taxes and deductions; Salaries and wages; Unions

Compensation consultants, 61–62

Compensatory time, 104–105

Complaints and grievances
about harassment and bullying, 297–298
board role in handling, 261
legal advice, 330
policies in handbook, 344
policy audits, 350
union role in handling, 269, 272–273, 274–275

Computers
email policies, 306–307, 344, 345
employee training, 49
Facebook pages, blogs, and tweets, 308–310

instant messaging policies, 307

policies in handbook, 344, 345

terminated employees and, 182, 186

Conferences, sending staff to, 154–155

Confidentiality policies, in handbook, 345

Conflict of interest policies, in handbook, 345

Consultants, HR, 331

Continuing education opportunities, 153–154

See also Education and training

Corporations

employee classification for, 233

employees of as volunteers, 213

Cost of living adjustments (COLA), 77

Council for Certification in Volunteer Administration, 226

Court-ordered community service, "volunteers", 214–215

Criminal record checks, 34–35, 216–219

Customer satisfaction surveys, 163

D

Death of employee, workers' compensation benefits, 284

Defamation claims, by fired employees, 198

Defined benefit retirement plans, 98

Dental benefits, 95

Directors and officers (D&O) liability insurance, 196

Directors of volunteers (volunteer coordinators), 201–202

information resources for, 227

professional development for, 226

thank-you programs organized by, 224–226

Disability insurance, 89, 219

Disabled persons

alcoholics as, 291–292

Americans with Disabilities Act, 59, 291–293

discrimination favoring, 3

minimum wage exception for, 83

state disability insurance for, 89

Disaster preparedness plans, 344, 350

Discounts and perks, as employee benefits, 105

Discrimination

against alcoholics, 291–292

antidiscrimination laws, 26–28, 58–60

diversity monitored by board, 260

dress codes as, 313

by executive directors, 261–262

information resources, 28

job descriptions as, 13

layoffs viewed as, 184–185

mission-related context of nonprofits, 3

performance reviews and, 132

policies in handbook, 344

union role, 265

wrongful termination complaints, 177, 194–195

See also Harassment, bullying, or teasing

Diversity, supporting and monitoring, 260, 302–303

Donors
    attitudes about commissions, 76
    as volunteer source, 210–211

Dress and grooming codes, 312–314, 345

Driving on the job, 287–289
    cell phone use by employees, 282, 289–290, 344
    employee-owned vehicles, 288–289
    illegal drug use and, 293
    liability insurance, 220, 287–288
    mileage reimbursement, 289
    organization-owned vehicles, 287–288
    RSIs and, 286

Driving records
    of job candidates, 35
    for jobs that involve driving, 287, 288
    in personnel files, 338

Drug and alcohol testing
    for employees, 293
    for job candidates, 35

Drug use or dependence
    EAPs and, 93
    of executive directors, 261–262
    illegal drug use, 293
    prescription drugs, 292–293
    requiring employees to take meds, 292

E

EAPs (Employee Assistance Programs), 93–94, 106, 292

Education
    background checks of job candidates, 33–34
    HR-related degrees, 336

Education and training
    anti-harassment training, 297–298, 331
    basics, 150–151
    budgeting for, 153
    career path development, 157
    colleges and universities, 336
    computer training, 49
    conferences, 154–155
    continuing education opportunities, 153 154
    as employee benefit, 100
    external, 153
    in-house training, 152
    KASA, 151
    leadership development, 145, 160–161, 222–223, 226, 335–337
    for managers, 44
    myth about, 151
    neglecting, 140
    OJT/apprenticeships, 155
    outsourcing, 331
    professional development, 226, 335–337
    for team leaders, 145
    for volunteer managers, 226
    for volunteers, 222–223

on workplace injury response, 284

on workplace violence prevention, 299–300

See also Organizational culture

Email policies, 306–307, 344, 345

Employee Assistance Programs (EAPs), 93–94, 106, 292

Employee benefits

    administering benefit plans, 106

    alternative work weeks, 103

    basics, 86–88

    board roles, 258, 260

    cafeteria plans, 94–95

    comp time, 104–105

    cost of, 101

    discounts and perks, 105

    education and training benefits, 100

    for employees vs. independent contractors, 81–82, 231–232, 234–235

    flexible time, 86, 102–103, 154

    furloughs and, 191

    health benefits, 86, 91–92

    housing and meals, 84–85

    job sharing, 105

    for laid-off employees, 186

    life insurance, 86, 96

    noneconomic benefits, 102–105

    policies in handbook, 344

    retirement benefits, 86, 98–100

    sick pay or paid time off, 96–97

    telecommuting, 103–104

    See also Payroll taxes; Unions; Vacation or holidays, time off for

Employee Change Forms, 181, 338–340

Employee evaluations. *See* Performance reviews

Employees

    alternative perceptions of, 2

    at-will employment, 43–46, 51–52, 132, 170, 343

    burnout, 149–150

    citizenship verification, 340–341

    climate surveys, 317–322, 334

    coaching/mentoring, 147–149

    compensation for government contracts, 59

    contact information, 338

    distinguished from independent contractors, 81–82, 231, 236–240, 247

    executives as, 4

    exempt vs. nonexempt, 77–81

    HR office staff, 326–329

    idealism of, 4

    internal recruiting/hiring, 18, 19, 39–40, 158

    job expansion, 156–157

    managing expectations of, 304–306

    misclassified as independent contractors, 235, 238–240

    nonprofit role, 4

    nonunion, 268, 273–274

    off-hours conduct, 314–317

    orienting new, 46–52

    performance review value to, 111–112

promotions, 143, 156–157, 159

recognizing good work of, 301–302

as recruiters, 20

reporting to board, 254

romantic relationships within
organization, 310–312, 345

sexual harassment by, 294–295

surveys of new, 334

as team leaders, 144–147

360-degree feedback by, 162–165

union representation, 267–268

verifying citizenship of, 42–43

volunteerism by, 161

working abroad, 58, 86

Employment contracts

basics, 43, 45

firing for breach of, 178

handbook promises as, 346

in personnel files, 338

Employment law

antidiscrimination laws, 26–28

basics, 5–6

on compensation, 58

discriminatory job descriptions, 13

for employees vs. independent
contractors, 81–82

employees working abroad, 58, 86

for exempt vs. nonexempt
employees, 77–81

FEPA, 194

illegal reasons for firing, 176–178

living wages, 82–83

minimum wage laws, 59, 82,
83–85

OSHA, 280–281

for overtime, 59, 77–81

for performance reviews, 131–132

supervisor actions and, 142–144

for unions, 266–267

See also Federal laws; Lawsuits;
State laws; Wrongful termination
complaints/lawsuits

Equal Employment Opportunity
Commission (EOC), 58–59,
194–195

Equal Pay Act, 59

Ergonomics

OSHA requirements, 280–281

repetitive stress injury prevention,
285–287

Executive directors

board oversight of, 253–256,
261–262

change management role, 348–349

compensation analyses for, 68–71,
254–255

compensation limits for, 60–62

as employees, 4

employment contracts for, 45

exempt/nonexempt status, 78–79

exit interviews for, 190

hired by board, 253

hiring role, 31

HR responsibilities, 327, 328

layoff role, 185

myth about salaries, 65

performance review role, 127–128

performance reviews for, 134,
254–255

political endorsements by, 315–316

search consultants to recruit, 21–22
support for volunteers, 223
Exempt employees
classification rules, 77–81
compensatory time and, 104–105
job sharing and, 105
temporary layoffs and, 192
Exit interviews
basics, 188–189
board role, 262
feedback on HR functions, 334
for laid-off employees, 186–187
for management team members, 190
for nonmanagerial employees, 189–190

F

Facebook pages, policies on employee use of, 308–310
Fair Employment Practices Agencies (FEPA), 194
Fair Labor Standards Act (FLSA), 58, 77–78
Federal laws
ADA, 59, 291–292, 293
antidiscrimination laws, 26–28, 58–59
COBRA, 186, 193
on compensation, 58, 60–62
compensatory time, 104–105
drug testing, 293
Fair Labor Standards Act, 58, 77–78
government contracts and, 59

IRCA, 177
minimum wages, 82
reporting on new hires, 43
rest breaks, 85
See also Employment law
Federal unemployment taxes (FUTA), 3
FICA taxes (Social Security), 88–89
Fingerprinting, volunteer candidates, 216–217
Firing employees. *See* Layoffs; Terminating employees
501(c)(3) organizations, 4
501(c)(5) organizations, unions as, 265
501(c) plans, 99
Flexible time, 86, 102–103, 154
FLSA (Fair Labor Standards Act), 58, 77–78
For-cause terminations, 178–179
For-profit organizations, distinguished from nonprofits, 3–5
401(k) plans, 98, 99
403(b) plans, 98, 99
457 plans, 98
Fraud, workers' compensation, 284–285
Free speech vs. organizational credibility, 316
Funders, 360-degree feedback by, 162–165
Fundraising
commissions for, 75–76
by professionals, 75–76
volunteer roles, 209, 222
Furloughs, to avoid layoffs, 191
Fyfe, Pamela, 169

G

Gon, Sarah, 138–139

Gort, Sarah, 230

Government contracts
federal compensation laws, 59, 76
stipended volunteers, 83

Grooming and dress codes, 312–314, 345

Guidestar.org, 60, 64

H

Harassment, bullying, or teasing
basics, 294
bullying, 296–297
combating, 297–298
by executive directors, 261–262
harassment as discrimination, 295–296
policies in handbook, 344
sexual harassment, 294–295, 297–298, 331
sexual-orientation based, 295
by supervisors, 143
unemployment insurance and, 196–198
wrongful termination complaints, 194–195
See also Discrimination

Health benefits
basics, 86
cafeteria plans and, 94–95
COBRA, 186, 193
dental benefits, 95
health insurance, 91–92, 220

health savings accounts, 95
for job-sharing employees, 105
postemployment, 180, 186, 192–193
vision care, 95
See also Workers' compensation insurance

HealthCare.gov, 88

Health care reform legislation of 2010, 91–92

Health Maintenance Organizations (HMOs), 91–92

Health Savings Accounts (HSAs), 95

Hiring, 156–157
antidiscrimination laws, 26–28
at-will employment, 43–45, 46, 51–52, 343
audits of practices, 350
background checks, 33–35, 216, 217–218
board roles, 253, 254, 258, 260
Civil Rights Act, 59
Equal Pay Act, 59
first-day paperwork, 42–43
Form I-9 and, 340–341
HR office staff, 326–329
internal, 18, 19, 39–40, 158
interns, 40
job descriptions, 11–17
job offers, 41–45
job promises by supervisors, 143
orienting new staff members, 46–52
reference checks, 36–38
responsibility for, 9–10
rules in handbook, 343

screening and selection, 23–40

skill testing, 31–33

union issues, 275

volunteers, 40

See also Interviews; Recruiting; Screening job applicants

HR director for volunteer human resources. *See* Directors of volunteers

Human resources associations, 335–337

Human Resources Certification Institute (HRCI), 335–336

Human Resources (HR)

  attorneys and consultants for, 330–331

  audits of, 349–351

  board HR committee/task force, 257–268

  board's role, 252–262

  change management role, 347–349

  employee handbook role, 342–346

  feedback on HR functions, 334–335

  hiring role, 9–10

  HR office staffing, 326–329

  myth about, 329

  nonprofit vs. for-profit, 3–5

  organizational culture role, 300–322

  organizing HR functions, 324–351

  outsourcing HR functions, 331–332

  personnel records management, 337–341

  reporting issues, 333

  staff development for, 335–337

Human resources managers

  challenges, 334–335

  executive directors as, 327

  on management team, 333

  roles, 333

I

Idealism, as nonprofit characteristic, 4

Illegal actions, by executive directors, 261–262

Immigration Reform and Control Act (IRCA), 177

Immigration status

  Form I-9, 340–341

  H1-B visas and furloughs, 191

  illegal termination and, 177

  verification of citizenship, 42–43

Incentive pay, 73

Income taxes

  for employees vs. independent contractors, 231, 232, 234, 239

  federal, withholding for, 90

  state, withholding for, 90

  union exemptions, 265

Independent contractor agreements

  benefits of, 233

  creating, 243

  recordkeeping, 249

  sample, 244–246

Independent Contractor Determination Form, 240–243, 247, 249

Independent contractors, 230–249

  basics, 231

  benefits of hiring, 233, 234–235

  distinguished from employees, 81–82, 231, 236–240, 247

drawbacks of hiring, 235–-236
frequently asked questions, 232–233
information resources, 238, 249
intellectual property rights, 233
managing, 247–248
misclassified as employees, 235, 238–240
myth about, 247
overtime rule exemption, 78
paperwork required for, 233, 249
Individual retirement accounts (IRAs), 98
Instant messaging (IM) policies, 307
Insurance
    D&O, 196
    disability, 89, 219–220
    health, 91–92, 220
    liability, 196, 220, 287–288, 338
    life, 86, 96
    requirements, 5
    for volunteer activities, 219–220
    See also Unemployment insurance/taxes; Workers' compensation insurance
Intellectual property rights, for independent contractors, 233
Internal equity, 64, 67, 72
Internal Revenue Service (IRS)
    employee vs. independent contractor classification, 231, 235, 236–240, 247
    website, 62, 90
Internet resources
    background checks, 34, 217
    Ballotpedia.org, 75

chambers of commerce, 336
Department of Labor, 82, 85, 185, 283, 330
Facebook pages, blogs, and tweets, 308–310
Guidestar.org, 60, 64
HealthCare.gov, 88
HRCI, 336
IRS, 62, 90
NLRB, 266
OSHA, 281, 286
posting job announcements, 21
Small Business Administration, 336
state charity offices, 62
state nonprofit associations, 336
state unemployment offices, 90
telecommuting, 104
to track performance reviews, 116
for volunteer job openings, 211
Interns and internships, 3, 40, 83–84
Interviews
    antidiscrimination laws, 26–28
    exit, 186–190, 262, 334
    in-person, 25–26
    internships as, 40
    job description role, 12
    post-interview discussions, 30–31
    questions to ask, 28–30
    telephone screenings, 24–25
IRS audits, independent contractor classification, 235, 238–240
IRS Form I-9, Employment Eligibility Verification, 340–341
IRS Form W-4, Withholding

Allowance Certificate, 42

IRS Form W-9, 249, 338

IRS Form 990 (990-EZ), 60–61, 62

IRS Form 1099, 249

IRS Publication 15, Employer's Tax Guide, 90

J

Jayaram, Ashwin, 108

Job applicants or candidates
  acknowledging all applications, 24
  interns or volunteers as, 40
  rejection protocols, 41–42
  See also Hiring; Recruiting; Screening job applicants

Job descriptions
  assessing job candidates against, 30–31
  basics, 11–13
  discriminatory, 13
  information resources, 17
  input from workgroup, 16
  interview questions from, 12
  job expansion and, 157
  performance review role, 12, 114, 126
  in personnel files, 337
  as recruiting tool, 12
  rewriting, 178
  short version, 16–17
  for volunteers, 205–206, 207
  as wish lists, 16

Job description worksheets, 13–15

Job expansion, 156–157

Job offers, 41–42, 338

Job Safety and Health Protection posters, 281

Job sharing, 105

Job titles, 157, 159

Jones, Terrence, 252

K

Krueger, Joanne, 324–325

L

Language problems, 106

Language problems and interpreters, 173

Lawsuits
  HR attorneys for, 330
  impact on nonprofits, 5
  independent contractors and, 234–235
  for safety violations, 282
  See also Employment law; Wrongful termination complaints/lawsuits

Layoff interviews, 186–187

Layoffs
  basics, 184–185
  board role, 261
  distinguished from firings, 170, 175
  furloughs to avoid, 191
  pay cuts to avoid, 188
  preparing for, 185–188
  temporary, 192
  unemployment insurance and, 196–198
  WARN Act, 185–186
  See also Terminating employees

Leadership development
    basics, 160–161
    for HR staff, 335–337
    for team leaders, 145
    for volunteer managers, 226
    for volunteers, 222–223
    See also Education and training
Legal advice and lawyers
    on board of directors, 331
    free or low-cost help, 330–331
    HR attorneys, 330–331
    off-hours employee conduct issues,
        314–315
    review of handbook, 330, 343
    termination issues, 195, 330
    union-related issues, 273
Letters of recommendation,
    limitations, 37
Liability insurance
    for jobs that involve driving, 288,
        338
    for volunteers, 220
Life insurance, as employee benefit,
    86, 96
Living wage laws, 82–83
Local antidiscrimination laws, 59–60
Logan, Daphne, 55

M

Management-by-Objective
    performance reviews, 119–120
Management teams
    anti-union attitudes/actions, 265,
        270–272
    change management role, 348–349

collective bargaining role, 268–269
exit interviews for members of, 190,
    262
HR roles, 328, 333
leadership opportunities for, 161
team leader role, 144–147
Managers and supervisors
    anti-harassment training, 297–298
    anti-union attitudes/actions, 265,
        270–272
    bonuses reviewed by, 74
    collective bargaining role, 268–269
    compensation analyses by, 67–72
    exit interview role, 189
    exit interviews for, 190, 262
    Facebook "friend" policies, 309
    hiring role, 9
    HR responsibilities, 328
    of independent contractors,
        247–248
    integrating new employees, 48
    layoffs and, 184, 186–187
    leadership development for, 160–161
    as nonunion employees, 273–274
    outsourcing training of, 331
    performance counseling session
        role, 171–173
    performance review training for,
        134–135
    romantic relationships with
        employees, 310–311
    sexual harassment by, 294–295
    team leaders and, 144–147
    termination role, 179
    360-degree feedback by, 162–165

training, 44

union issues, 275

volunteer coordinators, 201–202, 222, 224–226, 227

See also Supervising employees

Masaoka, Mark, 264

Medical records, excluded from personnel files, 340

Medicare tax, 89

Mental disabilities

of executive directors, 261–262

requiring employees to take meds, 292

Mentoring employees, 149

Mileage, reimbursing employees for, 289

Minimum wage laws

exceptions to, 83–85

federal/state laws, 82

government contracts and, 59

Minors, minimum wage exception for, 83

Mission

employee commitment to, 4

as recruiting tool, 18

training to convey, 152

Montana, employee probationary periods, 43

Moonlighting by employees, 316–317, 345

Multicultural environment, supporting and monitoring, 260, 302–303

Multisource or multi-rater (360-degree) feedback, 162–165

N

Narrative essay performance reviews, 115, 121–124, 135

National Institute for Occupational Safety and Health, 299–300

National Labor Relations Act (NLRA), 266

National Labor Relations Board (NLRB), 266, 270–271

New America Media, 21

Newsletters, as recruiting tools, 19

Nonexempt employees

classification rules, 77–81

compensatory time and, 104

job sharing and, 105

travel expenses for, 85–86

Nonprofit organizations

characteristics of, 3–4

distinguished from for-profits, 3–5

501(c)(3) organizations, 4

Notice of Right to Sue, 194

O

Occupational Safety and Health Act (OSHA), 280–282

Occupational Safety and Health Administration (OSHA), 283, 286

Off-hours employee conduct, 314–317

community and political activity, 315–316

drinking problems, 291–292

illegal drug use, 293

moonlighting, 316–317, 345

On-the-job training (OJT), 155

Organizational charts, 12

Organizational culture

    basics, 300–301

    change management, 347–349

    dress/grooming codes, 312–314

    email policies, 306–307

    employee climate surveys, 317–322, 334

    employee expectation management, 304–306

    employee recognition programs, 301–302

    Facebook pages, blogs, and tweets, 308–310

    instant messaging, 307

    multicultural workplace, 260, 302–303

    myth about, 305

    off-hours conduct, 314–317

    workplace romances, 310–312, 345

    See also Personnel handbooks; Personnel policies; Safety in workplace

Orienting new employees

    basics, 46

    checklist, 47

    computer training, 49

    integration into organization, 48–50

    orientation sessions, 49, 50–51

    probationary periods, 43, 46, 51–52

Overtime

    calculating pay for, 81

    for exempt vs. nonexempt employees, 77–81

    government contracts and, 59

P

Paid time off (PTO), 96–97, 343

"Pay-per-signature" laws, 75

Payroll taxes and deductions

    basics, 86

    disability insurance, 89, 219

    for employees vs. independent contractors, 231, 232, 234, 238–239

    FICA and Medicare taxes, 88–89

    information resources, 90

    paperwork for new hires, 42

    sample worksheet, 90

    union dues, 267

    withholding for, 88–91

    See also Unemployment insurance/taxes; Workers' compensation insurance

Pérez, Sonia M., 279

Performance counseling sessions, 171–173, 174

Performance improvement plans (PIPs), 172–173, 174

Performance problems

    attempts to improve, 171–173

    documenting, 174

    terminating employees for, 170, 179

Performance reviews, 108–136

    alcohol/drug dependence issues, 282

    alternative terms for, 110

annual salary adjustments and, 66–67

audits of, 350

basics, 110–111

benefits of, 111–113

board role, 254

budget issues, 133

checklist for, 131

checklist reviews, 115, 117–120, 135

components of, 115

customer feedback, 127

danger of skipping, 114

defining expectations, 124–125

for executive directors, 134, 254–255

forms, 134

gathering information for, 126–128

illegal drug use and, 293

internal feedback, 127–128

job description role, 12, 114, 126

judgment role, 128–130

layoffs and, 184–185

legal issues, 131–132

myth about, 129

narrative essays, 115, 121–124, 135

online systems to track, 116

outsourcing design of, 331

personnel records and, 126–127, 338

policies in handbook, 343

procedures, 134–136

progressive discipline and, 346–347

setting up process, 130–131

for small organizations, 114

tracking employee performance, 125

types of, 115–124

union issues, 272, 275

when to conduct, 132–133

Personality/aptitude tests, 32–33

Personnel handbooks, 341–346

acknowledging receipt of, 338

alcohol use policies, 291

at-will employment policies, 44, 52, 343

basics, 341–342

binding obligations implied in, 346–347

board review of, 258

failure to follow policies in, 195

information resources, 347

legal review of, 330, 343

outsourcing drafting/updating of, 331

pre-firing policies, 174, 175

right to change, 345–346

updating, 331, 349

what to include in, 342–346

Personnel policies

anti-harassment policies, 297

board review of, 258

on diversity, 260, 302–303

terms for union/nonunion employees, 274

See also Organizational culture

Personnel records, 337–341

audits of, 350

contents, 337–338

Employee Change Forms, 338–340
for independent contractors, 249
managing files, 341
performance review role, 126–127
poor performance documented in, 174
what not to put into, 340–341
Phonemail, terminated employees and, 182
Political activities
of employees, 315–316
"pay-per-signature" laws, 75
volunteer roles, 209
Preferred Provider Organizations (PPOs), 91–92
Privacy policies, in handbook, 344
Probationary or trial periods, for new hires, 43, 46, 51–52
Professional certificates and licenses
background checks for job candidates, 34
for HR staff, 336
Professional employees, exempt/ nonexempt status and, 79–80
Professional in Human Resources (PHR), 336
Progressive discipline, 346–347
Project managers, compensation analyses for, 68–71
Promotions, 143, 156–157, 159
PTO (paid time off), 96–97, 343
Public policy violations, illegal firing for, 178, 195

R

"Reasonable compensation," defined, 60
"Recognized hazards," OSHA definition, 280–281
Recruiting, 41–45
announcements to constituents, 19–20
basics, 17–18
Civil Rights Act, 59
employee benefits role, 87
Equal Pay Act, 59
high-level volunteers, 222
information resources, 21
internal postings, 18, 19, 39–40, 158
job description role, 12
myths about, 23, 65
online/newspaper advertising, 20–21
outsourcing, 331
salary role, 64, 69–70, 258
scope of search, 18–19
search consultants, 21–22
for volunteers, 210–212
See also Hiring; Screening job applicants
Reference check letters, 38
Reference checks
for board members, 224
for job candidates, 36–38
for volunteers, 218–219
References, for terminated employees, 180, 198
Rejection letters, 42

Repetitive stress injuries (RSIs), preventing, 285–287
Research assistants, compensation analyses for, 68–72
Rest breaks, 85
Retaliation, terminations as, 177
Retired Senior Volunteer Program (RSVP), 213
Retirement benefits, 86, 98–100

S

Safety committees, 281
Safety in workplace, 279–300
    basics, 280–282
    cell phone use, 282, 289–290
    ergonomics and RSI prevention, 285–287
    frequently asked questions, 282–283
    harassment and bullying, 294–298
    jobs involving driving, 287–289
    OSHA, 280–281
    penalties for violating laws, 282
    policies in handbook, 344
    smoking in workplace, 290
    telecommuting and, 104
    union role, 265
    unsafe conditions, employee leaves job due to, 196–197
    workplace violence, 298–300, 344
    See also Alcohol use or dependence; Drug use or dependence; Workers' compensation insurance
Salaries and wages
    annual adjustments/raises, 65, 66–67, 73

benchmarking, 69–72
benefit cost and, 101
board roles, 254, 257, 258–259
cost of living adjustments, 77
for employees vs. independent contractors, 232, 235–236, 237, 238
ensuring salary scale compliance, 259
Equal Pay Act, 59
for exempt vs. nonexempt employees, 77–81, 192
final paychecks for terminated employees, 180, 181
incentive pay, 73
internal equity issues, 67, 72
for interns, 40
minimum wage laws, 59, 82, 83–85
myths about, 23, 65
for overtime, 59, 77–81
pay cuts instead of layoffs, 188
performance review role, 133
policies in handbook, 343
rate schedules, 258–259
setting individual, 62
setting ranges, 62–65, 258–259
severance pay, 181, 186
wage garnishment, 191
    See also Compensation; Employee benefits; Payroll taxes
Salary surveys, 60–61
Sarbanes-Oxley Act, 62
Scientists, compensation analyses for, 68–71

Screening job applicants
    antidiscrimination laws, 26–28
    background checks, 33–35, 216,
      217–218
    basics, 23–24
    fingerprinting, 216–217
    information resources, 35
    in-person interviews, 25–26
    reference checks, 36–38
    skills tests, 31–33
    telephone screenings, 24–25
    volunteers, 216–219
Screening service databases, 217
Search consultants, 21–22
Service clubs, as volunteer source, 214
Severance pay, for terminated
  employees, 181, 186
Sexual harassment
    basics, 294–295
    training staff to prevent, 297–298,
    331
Sexual orientation, harassment based
  on, 295
Shop stewards, for unions, 274–275
Sick leave/pay, 96–97, 343
Skills tests, for job candidates, 31–33
Small Business Administration, 336
Smith, Amy, 200
Smoking in or near workplace, 290
Social networking sites
    policies on employee use of,
    308–310
    posting job announcements on, 20
Society for Human Resource
  Management (SHRM), 87–88,
  335–336

Solicitation policies, in handbook, 345
Sororities and fraternities, as volunteer
  source, 214
Spot bonuses, 74
Staff development. See Career path
  development; Education and
  training; Leadership development
Staff meetings, for training, 152
State disability insurance (SDI), 89
State laws
    antidiscrimination laws, 26–28,
    59–60
    compensation, 58, 62
    drug testing, 293
    employee termination, 178,
    179–180, 181, 186, 192
    FEPA, 194
    fingerprinting job applicants, 216
    living wages, 82–83
    minimum wages, 82
    overtime, 77
    "pay-per-signature" laws, 75
    postemployment health benefits,
    193
    reporting on new hires, 43
    smoking in workplace, 290
    See also Employment law
State unemployment insurance (SUI),
  3, 196–197
Students, minimum wage exception
  for, 83
Supervising employees
    basics, 140
    burnout problems, 149–150
    career path development, 157

coaching, 147–149
internal hiring benefits, 158
job expansion issues, 156–157
leadership development, 160–161
legal issues, 142–144
mentoring, 149
one-on-one, 140–142
performance/behavior problems, 142, 143, 150
team leader role, 144–147
360-degree feedback, 162–165
See also Education and training; Managers and supervisors; Performance reviews

T

Tax exemptions
for retirement plans, 100
for unions, 265
Team leaders, 144–147
See also Management teams; Managers and supervisors
Teasing. *See* Harassment, bullying, or teasing
Telecommuting or teleworking, 103–104
Terminating employees, 168–198
for alcoholism, 282
at-will employment and, 43–46, 51–52, 132, 170, 176
basics, 170
for behavior problems, 170
board role, 254
for cause, 178–179
communicating to staff, 183–184
employee change forms, 181
exit interviews, 188–190
final paycheck, 180, 181
firings vs. layoffs, 170, 175
"firing" volunteers, 201
furloughs to avoid layoffs, 191
for illegal drug use, 293
illegal reasons for, 176–178, 195
vs. independent contractors, 237
IT issues, 181
layoffs, 184–188
legal advice, 330
"on-the-spot" firing, 179–180
for performance problems, 170
performance review role, 132
policies in handbook, 345
postemployment health benefits, 180, 186, 192–193
probationary periods and, 51–52
references, 180, 198
severance pay, 181, 186
steps to prevent firing, 174–175
timing of departure, 180
warnings before firing, 175
wrongful termination complaints, 44, 170, 174, 189, 193–196, 346
See also Unemployment insurance/ taxes
Termination letters, 181
Termination meetings, 182–183
360-degree (multisource or multi-rater) feedback, 162–165
Training. *See* Education and training

Travel time and expenses, 85–86, 345

Trial or probationary periods, 43, 46, 51–52

Twitter accounts, policies on employee use of, 308–310

U

Unemployment insurance/taxes
 claims process, 197–198
 eligibility for, 196–197
 for employees vs. independent contractors, 81–82, 231–232, 234–235, 238
 federal (FUTA), 3, 89
 for laid-off employees, 186
 state (SUI/SUTA), 3, 89, 90, 196–197

Uniforms, requiring staff and volunteers to wear, 313, 345

Union contracts, 269–270
 collective bargaining and, 268–269
 HR functions under, 272–273
 key points, 275

Union drives, 270–272

Union dues, deductions for, 265, 267

Unions, 264–275
 anti-union attitudes, 265
 bargaining units, 267–268, 270, 274, 275
 basics, 265–266
 benefits of, 268
 business agents/shop stewards, 274–275
 elections, 268
 employees not joining, 268
 for employees vs. independent contractors, 234, 236
 employees who are not part of, 273–274
 information resources, 275
 laws governing, 266–267
 legal advice for issues related to, 273
 as nonprofits, 265

United Way, 61

USCIS Form I-9, Employment Eligibility Verification, 42–43

U.S. Citizenship and Immigration Services (USCIS), 340–341

U.S. Department of Labor
 independent contractor classification, 236
 layoffs, 185
 minimum wages, 82
 rest breaks, 85
 website, 82, 85, 185, 283, 330

V

Vacation or holidays, time off for
 furloughs and, 191
 paid time off, 96–97
 payment for accrued, 181, 186, 192
 policies in handbook, 343
 union role, 269

Violence in workplace, 298–300, 344
 See also Harassment, bullying, or teasing

Vision care, 95

Vocational rehabilitation, 283–284

Volunteer advisory councils, 204–205

Volunteer centers, 212
Volunteer coordinators. *See* Directors
  of volunteers
Volunteer Protection Act, 219
Volunteers, 200–227
    administrative volunteers, 208
    attitudes about commissions, 76
    basics, 201
    as board members, 209, 223–224
    common positions, 206–209
    court-ordered community service,
      214–215
    defining jobs, 205
    departmental management of,
      202–204
    directors of, 201–202, 224–226,
      227
    direct service volunteers, 206–208
    encouraging staff volunteerism, 161
    "firing", 201
    fundraising by, 209, 222
    hiring onto staff, 40
    information resources, 227
    insurance for volunteer activities,
      219–220
    integrating new, 203
    interns, 3, 40, 83–84
    job descriptions, 205–206, 207
    leadership positions for, 222–223
    myth about, 225
    nonprofit role, 4
    orienting new volunteers, 220–221
    overtime rule exemption, 78
    policy volunteers, 209

    political action volunteers, 209
    recruiting, 210–212
    reference checks, 218–219
    romantic relationships with
      employees, 311
    screening, 216–219
    sexual harassment by, 294–295
    stipended, 3, 83
    thanking, 224–226
    360-degree feedback by, 162–165
    "work-study", 216

W

Wage garnishment, furloughs and, 191
Whistle blowing, 177, 195, 344
Worker Adjustment and Retraining
  Notification (WARN) Act, 185–186
Workers' compensation insurance
    basics, 89–90, 283
    benefits, 283–284
    for employees vs. independent
      contractors, 231, 234, 235
    for employees working from home,
      104
    fraud and abuse, 284–285
    HR's role in claims process, 284
    RSI prevention and, 286
    safety committees and, 281
    for volunteers, 219
Work hours
    alternative work weeks, 103
    compensatory time, 104–105
    flexible time, 86, 102–103, 154
    furloughs and, 191

job sharing, 105

moonlighting by employees, 316–317, 345

overtime, 59, 77–81

paid time off, 96–97, 343

rules in handbook, 343

sick leave, 96–97, 343

See also Vacation or holidays, time off for

Work-related injuries. *See* Safety in workplace; Workers' compensation insurance

"Work-study" volunteers, 216

Wrongful termination complaints/ lawsuits

   at-will policies and, 44, 170, 176

D&O insurance for, 196

discrimination complaints, 194–195

exit interviews and, 189

firings referred to as layoffs, 175

legal advice, 195, 196

negative references and, 198

tips for handling, 193–196

tips for preventing, 174–175

unemployment insurance and, 197–198

unrealistic promises in handbook, 346

NOLO *Keep Up to Date*

1 Go to Nolo.com/newsletters to sign up for free newsletters and discounts on Nolo products.

- **Nolo's Special Offer.** A monthly newsletter with the biggest Nolo discounts around.

- **Landlord's Quarterly.** Deals and free tips for landlords and property managers.

2 Don't forget to check for updates. Find this book at **Nolo.com** and click "Legal Updates."

Let Us Hear From You

3 Register your Nolo product and give us your feedback at Nolo.com/book-registration.

- Once you've registered, you qualify for technical support if you have any trouble with a download or CD (though most folks don't).

- We'll send you a coupon for 15% off your next Nolo.com order!

HRNON1